CAKE DREAMS

A Memoir of Survival

Hoyt J. Phillips, III

ISBN: 1540356396
ISBN 13: 9781540356390

For
My parents, Beth & Hoyt
Your guidance, love and thirst for knowledge inspire me everyday.

⚘

"Even after all this time, the sun never says to the earth, 'You owe me.' Look what happens with a love like that. It lights up the whole sky." - Hafiz

NOTE TO THE READER

Most of the names in this memoir, except for those of my immediate family, have been changed to respect privacy.

As with most stories, not every event that I experienced during the year described in this book has been included nor every person I encountered. The events described in this book are from my perspective and memory, and as such others might have slightly different recollections. However, this memoir taken in its entirety captures the essence of a challenging year from my life.

1

J ournal Entry:

Wednesday, February 20, 2002

Been a while, kid! I don't know why I haven't written before or why it has taken something bad to happen before I would write. Maybe it's because I was scared to sit down and actually think about what I was feeling. Lord knows I am good at masking how I feel and putting on a happy face, so much so that half the time, I don't even know how the hell I truly feel. Maybe it was sheer laziness or maybe I was stuck on that day in September and my life has felt defined by that moment.

By all important measures, I have not dealt well since September 11. The drinking has increased and my obsession with weight and food has become almost all-consuming. I think September 11 just magnified my problems. It didn't make any new ones. It just seems to have sped everything up. So instead of hitting rock bottom in, say, two years, I might have hit it now! Imagine that – welcome to rock bottom!

I have to admit I am very scared and really don't know where to turn. This past weekend, I go out Saturday night to a party with intentions to drink light, and of course, you guessed it, I got piss drunk. Somehow I made it home okay and proceeded to drink months-old OJ with months-old Cointreau while sitting on the kitchen floor and cutting my right arm and wrist with a serrated kitchen knife (twelve slashes in all). I proceeded to get more drunk and upset. I puked and somehow put myself to bed. I woke up to my alarm for church, covered head to toe in my bed in my own vomit! I had to bag up all my sheets, good pillows, and comforter. They were all ruined. I spent the whole day trying not to puke or pass out from the pain my body and ego were experiencing. I had ransacked my place and my body. Now over the past two days I have bought a whole new down comforter, sheets, pillow, and feather bed topper. They are great and hopefully a sign of a new start.

My first reaction, like so many other times before, is to say no more drinking! This time, somehow, has been more of a sobering reality (pun intended). I think this is the sign I asked God for. I have been struggling with, how do you know if you are an alcoholic? This couldn't be any more clear. I'm afraid I use booze to self-medicate in hopes of freeing myself from the torture my emotions put me through, but in the long run, I make it worse for myself. So tonight I write this so I won't forget. Things can't go on this way. I have to deal with myself, sex, food, & booze, and my past. This is a plea – please do not forget and GET HELP!

I go back to being scared. It's hard, but somehow I just have to take it one day at a time.

Other than my life being out of control, not much else going on here. That should keep me busy. So the next entry better be talking about how therapy is going and how getting control of my life was the best thing I could have ever done. So until next time ...

PART I

Five Months Earlier

2

Seven thirty. *Ugh, time to get up.* Another day at a job I really don't like.

Brush my teeth. Shower. Get dressed. My hair is driving me nuts. *Why can't it ever do what I want it to do? Maybe I should just shave my head again. Okay, I guess I look the best I'm going to look today.* Leaning out the bathroom door, I notice the clock. Yeah, I need to be getting up five minutes earlier if I'm going to keep obsessing about my hair.

Grab my black messenger bag, keys, and money clip. Down the flight of stairs and onto the noisy Hoboken street. *Ahh, it's a beautiful morning.* Sunny, warm, and not humid. A perfect Tuesday in September. It would be nice to call in sick and bum around the city.

Turn right and follow my usual route down Washington Street on my way to the PATH station. Just before I turn down a side street, I pass the bakery with the beautiful wedding cakes in the window—the bakery that will have its own reality show in eight years.

I make it down to the platform and find a World Trade Center train already waiting. I love these mornings when I don't have to wait on the train.

Once I'm inside, the train car is more crowded than usual. I stand holding onto the rail above. I don't sit anymore. One morning a year earlier, I sat down without looking at the seat and suddenly realized I was sitting in a large pool of liquid. I had to run home and change my suit. Of course, I comforted myself by thinking that it was only water. It didn't smell like anything else.

The train pulls into the basement of the World Trade Center complex. Again, I follow my usual route moving as quickly as I can up the escalators on the left-hand side. For a job that I don't like, I sure do hustle getting there. Walking through the mall area, I pass the GAP, Banana Republic, and the coffee stand. I notice a new travel store that will be opening soon. I make a mental note that I should stop in there and check it out.

I make my way through the first set of revolving doors and I'm now in the lobby of 1 WTC, with its grand ceilings, marble walls, and beautiful crystal chandeliers. I hurry through the lobby like a man on a mission, up the escalator and through the second set of revolving doors. Now I'm in the non-air-conditioned, covered walkway over the West Side Highway. I enjoy gazing out the wall of windows at all the cars passing underneath. This is one of those days when I would love to be in one of those cars, speeding off to somewhere more exciting than the job I am heading to.

It's such a beautiful day out. Not a cloud in the sky. Yet I'm going to an office in the middle of a huge tower in lower Manhattan.

As I push my way through the third and final set of revolving doors on my route, I enjoy the sight that greets me on the other side. Standing at the top of the stairs of the Winter Garden always makes me smile. This area connects the World Financial Centers. I love this view. It's all glass—floor to ceiling—and full of massive palm trees. They cover the palms in white lights during the winter holiday season.

Just beyond the glass outside is the water, where people with more money than they know what to do with park their obscenely large yachts. I like to stroll by those yachts on my lunch break, imagining what it must feel like to be out in the middle of the Mediterranean with not a care in the world.

I remind myself that I don't have time to stop to enjoy the view. I turn right and head down the hall and turn right again. I pull out my ID card and swipe it at the turnstiles. Now I'm in the lobby of

Three World Financial Center. I make my way to the last elevator bank on the right and wait with everyone else. These elevators will take me to the part of the building that Lehman Brothers, my employer, occupies.

The elevator doors open and I'm able to squeeze in. Thankfully, my stop—Floor 26—is the first one. I get off into the hallway, then enter the stairwell, and quickly walk down two flights of stairs and out into the lobby of the twenty-fourth floor. I hate taking the elevator that stops on this floor because it takes forever, making a stop at almost every floor before twenty-four.

I make it to my cubicle without running into anyone. I like that, since I'm not much of a talker in the morning. I boot up my computer, unlock my cabinet drawer, and—in the blink of an eye—I feel the entire building shake violently. The windows sound like they are going to implode and there is a deafening BOOM!

I stand up, speechless. I feel like one of those meerkats on Animal Planet that pops its head up out of a hole when it's looking for something as I turn around and see my boss standing at her office doorway. I walk into her office and we just look out her window in horror.

Staring us in the face is 1 WTC, engulfed in fire coming from the largest black hole I have ever seen. Flames are shooting out in all directions as thick black smoke snakes its way up the exterior of the tower. Pain and fear radiate from the scene. Debris is flying everywhere.

I'm shocked. I don't know what to do. Fear takes over. *This is not good. A bomb has gone off—and we need to get out, NOW!*

Our senior vice-president starts running through the hallway yelling at everyone to get away from the windows and into the hall. We do as we are told. At this point, I'm doing everything I can to keep from crying and shaking.

I hear someone in the distance screaming something about a plane. *That's nuts!* I don't believe it. It was a bomb.

At that moment, a man's voice comes over the intercom system. He tells us to stay calm and says that the tower we are in was not affected. He doesn't explain what it was that just happened, but we are to stay put. For some reason, this calms me—somewhat.

I need a few minutes alone. Sprinting to the bathroom, I slam open a stall door and collapse onto the toilet. I just stare at the back of the stall door, thankful that I'm the only one in here. *Those people. All those poor people inside that building.* No, no, I can't go there. There is nothing I can do.

My legs begin to twitch. The energy slowly moves up from my legs and engulfs my entire body until I'm shaking. This is just too much. *Damn it!* Grabbing some toilet paper, I blow my nose. Deep breaths, deep breaths. It's going to be okay. Everything is going to be okay. After a while, I'm able to pull myself together and leave the bathroom. I go back to my desk, knowing that I need to make some calls.

"Dad, it's me, Jeff."

"Hey, what's up?" he casually asks.

"I just wanted to let you know, before you see it on CNN, that I'm okay. It looks like a bomb just went off at One World Trade Center. But we are okay."

"What? You sure you're okay?" he stammers as his mood changes instantly.

"Yeah, I'm fine. Listen, I gotta go, but I will call you back soon."

"Okay, be safe."

Hang up. Next call. *Ugh, of course it's the answering machine.* Trying to get my mom on the phone sometimes takes an act of God.

"Mom, it's Jeff. I just wanted to let you know that I'm okay. Something has happened at the World Trade Center, but I'm okay. I just talked to Dad. I'll call you back later."

The phone goes dead before I can hang up. The lights flicker. I shudder. My computer beeps. I look down and see that I've just gotten an email. I click it open; it's from a colleague in our Tokyo office asking if everything is okay.

Tokyo already knows about this? Damn, news travels fast. I don't know if this makes me feel better or worse. Is there something more going on that I don't know about? Are things worse out there than they are telling us? I ignore the email. *Deep breaths. Deep breaths. You have got to hold it together.* But at this moment, all I can think about is those poor people in the burning building.

Another BOOM! This one less intense than the previous one. Again, in the distance, someone yells something about another plane. At this point, I turn around and see my coworker, Melanie, who is looking at me with tears welling up in her eyes.

"I don't want to be here anymore," she stammers as several tears streak down her left cheek.

"It's okay. Grab your bag. Let's go," I manage to say authoritatively. I feel somewhat protective of her, almost as if she is my little sister.

We head for the lobby with the elevators. People are milling around, jabbering like chickens with their heads cut off. Out of the corner of my eye, I see someone push the elevator DOWN button. *They've got to be crazy! There is no way in hell I'm getting on an elevator right now.* My heart is pounding, my mind blank, my body numb. All I can think about it is that someone is trying to kill us! Instinct takes control. *We have to get out now!* I usher Melanie around the corner and into the stairwell.

We start our descent. The stairwell, all metal, has never felt so small and so long. I've been using this stairwell for more than two years, and it's almost always empty. Now it is wall-to-wall people. A sea of people, as far as you look up and as far as you look down. And with every door we pass, more and more people flood into the space.

The amazing thing is, you can hear a pin drop. There is total silence except for the drone of shoes clanging on the metal steps. It creates an eerie musical background for this surreal scene we all find ourselves in.

We just keep moving. Moving. One foot in front of the other. My mind is screaming, *they are trying to kill us!* They are trying to kill us. At any moment, that BOOM I heard at 1 WTC could happen *here*, and we could be gone. In an instant. *Just keep moving.*

I look down, trying not to notice what floor we just passed. I don't want to know how much further we have to go. When I do look up, I catch someone's eyes, and they are full of tears. *Look down.* I keep my head down. Some time later, I look up again, and a door opens. I recognize the floor for a split second. It's the third floor, where I used to work. In that brief second that the door is open, I notice that paper is everywhere. It looks like a bomb has gone off in there, and it's empty. There is no one to be seen on that floor.

Finally, we make it to the bottom. We enter the lobby and I instinctively turn left, since that is the way I would go home. But that way is blocked off, and people are yelling at us to go the other way. We follow orders. I head down more stairs and out the Vesey Street entrance. Out into the street. Fresh air. *Thank God!*

Melanie and I turn left and walk along the building. Out of the corner of my eye, I notice people, bloody, sitting against the building. It looks like EMS is there with them. I can't look. I don't want to really see it. I know I can't help them.

My heart is still pounding. I'm like a rabid animal who has been let out of his captor's cage. *I've got to get out of here! My life depends on it.*

All I want to do is talk to my parents. I start dialing my cell phone, but the damn thing won't work. I cross the street and keep moving. I'm in a sea of people. It's like a huge rock concert just let out at Madison Square Garden and everyone is just milling around. Everyone just seems to be stopping and staring in a daze.

I look up a couple of times, and it's still there: the huge, gaping hole that seems to be swallowing 1 WTC. Debris is still flying everywhere, lightly floating above us. Every once in a while, a piece of paper will brush my shoulder. If I wasn't so scared, I might think this was a ticker tape parade. But instead of confetti strips, this is paper from people's desks, seventy-plus stories above us. What's showering down on us is work that people were doing just a few minutes ago. It's their life floating down upon us while we look up, witnessing their last moments.

I hear people gasp in horror as they point up at the people who are jumping. I look down. Keep my head down. I don't want to see the horror.

Melanie and I finally stop and look at each other. Tears are now flooding her face. We both turn to our cell phones, but to no avail.

"I'm walking home," she says clearly. "I need to leave."

"You sure? You want me to walk with you?" I offer, almost pleading not to be left alone.

"No, I'll be fine."

I nod and she leaves, almost instantly disappearing into the sea of people.

I just stand there, feeling like the Lone Ranger. Tonto has left, and now I'm alone. Fear kicks me in the ass suddenly, and I'm off like a frightened horse. *I've got to get out of here!*

Where do I go? *Just walk north.* As I make my way through the crowd, I want to yell, "Why are you still here? Get out of here! They are trying to kill us!"

I cross the West Side Highway and hear ambulances and sirens blaring past. I have to keep moving. I just keep walking north.

I keep moving like the freed animal I am. My mind and body are pretty much blank and numb. I'm just moving. Survival of the fittest. I'm not going to stay around here to see what will happen next.

I pass a line of people at a pay phone. I glance down at my cell again—still no service. I keep walking.

Up ahead on the left, I see a black van parked. Several men are huddled around it. The doors are open. As I approach, I hear our President speaking. I get closer. He is talking about what happened. Here I am with perfect strangers, listening to the President talk about this catastrophe. To my left, just a couple blocks away, are the two most prominent buildings in the U.S.—on fire, with smoke billowing out of them. *It doesn't seem real.* Where are the movie cameras? This is a movie scene. It's time for Spielberg to yell "Cut!" *Please.*

The President is done talking. My fight-or-flight instinct takes over again. I have to keep moving north.

I now realize I'm making my way to John's place. I just have to make it to Washington Square Park. I keep passing more people lined up at pay phones. Good for them, they are getting to talk to their loved ones. My cell is still useless.

I walk. I walk, fighting back tears of agony, thinking of all those poor people. I feel this overwhelming sadness and pain. It's palpable—you can feel it, smell it, taste it. All the suffering. I can hear the screams, sirens. This is what war is like. God, please watch over my friends. I can't give in, can't stop to feel, so I just keep moving.

Finally, I make it to Christopher Street. I turn right, and head down the street I've been on countless times before. I keep walking for what seems like forever. With a thousand-mile stare frozen on my face, I don't see anything, or anyone now. I keep moving.

At Fifth Avenue, I look to my right—and yes, it's still there. The towers are on fire.

I make it to the lobby of John's building on Fifth. I stand there, frozen. I don't know what to do. This is the first time I have felt sheltered since all this started happening. *What now?*

At that moment, like a lightening bolt, Luke—John's best friend—storms into the lobby. He must have gotten out of his building downtown at the same time I did. My mouth is open, but words aren't coming out. Silence. Luke just nods and I follow him. The doorman knows us and lets us go up.

A somber John opens the door. The TV is blaring in the background.

"You guys okay?" he asks wearily.

I nod and throw my bag down and make my way to the bathroom. Sitting down on the toilet, I sob. I shake. *Am I safe? What is happening? I'm okay. I'm okay.* I want to talk to my parents. I grab the phone that is over the toilet. I've always made fun of this feature, but I'm now in love with this phone being here.

I dial the number, and as soon as I hear my dad's voice on the other end, all at once I'm three years old again. I need to be protected. I almost break down again.

"Jeff! Where are you? Are you okay?" he demands.

"Dad, I'm fine. I'm at John's. I got out. What is going on?"

"They've hit the Pentagon. It was planes. There are supposedly more in the air." He continues, but I freeze.

Planes? The Pentagon? *What the fuck is happening?* I cut him off. "I can't believe this. Dad. I've got to go. I'm fine. I promise. I'll call you later."

As I slam down the phone, John starts yelling. I run into the family room. I can hear screaming coming from outside.

"They're falling!" John says, almost incoherently. I run over to the TV. CNN is showing a tower in what seems like a bad special effects scene, slowing falling. I run to the front window and look to the left and see it for myself.

Right behind the Washington Square Arch, one of the towers is falling to the ground. People are screaming, and I'm standing there with two friends in disbelief. I'm here, but I'm not, because I don't feel anything. On TV, it's one thing. Seeing it out the window in real time is incomprehensible. The energy coming off the street is too much. I step back and turn to the TV.

The three of us sit glued in front of the set. First they report there were six planes, then seven, then more, and then less. First there were more planes still in the air, then all of them were accounted for. We were in the center of the storm. We didn't know it, but we were at Ground Zero of what would soon be a war on terror.

We sit in silence, barely speaking except for the occasional expletive. I want to be anywhere but in this crazy city, this city that I couldn't wait to work in after college. Now New York was trying to kill me, and I wanted no part of it.

Seven hours passed. It felt more like thirty minutes. With the lack of hard facts, the news somehow kept us engrossed. We didn't want to move, in case something changed that we needed to act upon.

"We need to get some food. I'm starving," John says with a hint of anger in his voice. "Let's get out of here for a while." Luke and I agree.

Out onto the street, we're met with silence. *Where are the cars? The people?* It's like an empty movie set. I don't like it. John reminds us that everything from Fourteenth Street and below is now off-limits to traffic.

In a strange way, the traffic ban makes it convenient for us to maneuver. We can walk anywhere we want and cross any street at any point. Kind of cool—if not for the circumstances.

Heading left, we stop in Washington Square Park, which is usually alive with artists, street musicians, students, druggies, and freaks. It now feels like a vacuum of emotions. Walking through the arch and into the park, I feel this force sucking the life out of me. It is depressing, scary, and strangely familiar.

Looking around, I see a fair number of people, but no one really seems to be interacting or talking. Silence seems to rule. I notice this younger guy, probably about my age, in a suit, his jacket off, sitting on this ledge. He looks like hell. He looks lost. Lonely. Shell-shocked. I now have a newfound understanding for that term. I wonder where he lives. *Where is his family?*

It then strikes me as I look around. Almost all these people look lost. Some probably are. They probably can't get back home. Some are just feeling lost because of what has happened to their city. The life force in all of us has drained away.

I want to scream, "This shit shouldn't fucking be happening to us! We're Americans! We're the prosperous, safe ones."

John ushers us on, but I'm not exactly sure where we are going. We tread our usual routes to food places, hoping they are open. They aren't. So we keep walking.

It's a beautiful day out. Warm, but not that humid. We keep walking. Every once in a while, we pass some little grocery store that has the doors open and the owner blaring his TV or radio. We hear more of the same news, just talking heads on the airwaves trying to explain to Americans in the heartland what the scenes in N.Y. and D.C. are like. The commentary is starting to annoy me. I don't need to hear their long-winded drivel about the horrifying details. The more graphic, I guess, the better the ratings.

Finally, on some random side street, we find an open Chinese place. None of us has been here before. We go in, order some food, and sit down at the few chairs that are available. We're the only ones here. The guy behind the counter seems surprised to see us. He quietly makes our food.

"It doesn't seem real does it?" Luke asks, breaking the silence.

"You can say that again," I reply.

John is unusually quiet. Even though Luke and I were down there today, John has a connection to this city that neither of us can fully appreciate. This is his home. Born and raised here, he's grown up riding the trains at all hours of the day, just exploring the city. To him, what has happened is not only an attack on those two towers—it's the equivalent of his own home being blown apart.

After a standard, fast-food Chinese dinner, we head back to the apartment. Dusk is falling. We watch more TV without learning much. Exhausted, now that it's finally dark, we decide to get some sleep. John goes to his room, Luke gets the extra bedroom, and I get the sofa. The seven-foot, blue sofa that was in style in the 60's; now, having held its ground, it has finally come back into style. It's not comfortable, but at least my six-foot frame is not dangling off.

I position myself so that my head is facing the large window from which, earlier that day, I witnessed the towers falling. The darkness envelopes me like a sinister spirit and I shiver. Lights in the building across the street come on, some go off. There are noises from the street— popping sounds, barking dogs, the general street noise that I've grown accustomed to over the last two years—but those sounds now make me jump.

The aliveness of the city that people love now unnerves me. Do I need to be vigilant? Do I need to run to the window with every noise that I hear, to make sure it's not another attack? Thankfully, I'm still in my work clothes, ready at a moment's notice to jump up and run for my life. My heart still hasn't returned to its normal pattern. I'm exhausted, but I'm not sure I can calm down enough to fall into sleep. I toss and turn. Night slowly turns into day.

"I'm good but I think I'm going to just head home and crash. Maybe take a nap."

Peter and I are standing outside Marble Collegiate Church, the stately church made famous by Norman Vincent Peale.

"You sure? You don't wanna go get something to eat," Peter asks.

"No thanks," I assure him.

The church has provided Peter and I a much-needed refuge from the deluge of a broken city. It's the first Sunday service since the attacks.

As we descend the front steps, I glance to my right and see the metal statute of Rev. Peale with his hand extended to the sky. I look away quickly, knowing full well that I'm not thinking positively at the moment. Fear is still churning through my veins.

The service was wonderful and haunting at the same time. It felt somewhat healing to be around people who all had been affected—but I also feel alone.

Peter was not at Ground Zero. He works in mid-town. He doesn't have this new fear of being inside and not being able to get out. He doesn't shake at night in his bed when he's all alone with his thoughts and the sounds from the city flood his apartment. *Or does he?* We don't talk about what happened or how it has affected us.

"Thanks for coming today," I tell him. "I'm glad we did it."

"Yeah, me too. Call me when you get home?"

"Sure." I can't keep from smiling. It's sweet how concerned he is. He's the worrier and protective one of our little group.

We head in opposite directions, me toward the PATH at 33rd Street and him toward the nearest subway line to get back uptown.

For the past five days, I've done my best to ignore the flyers that are taped on every available post, bus shelter, wall, fence, or building. On my walk to the PATH station, it's getting harder and harder not to notice them. The faces seem to be staring back at me from everywhere, some in black and white and some in color. Some old, some young. All seem to have a longing in their eyes just to be found.

Their loved ones' pleas are written in large type across the flyers:

"Please call …"

"Have you seen …?"

"Last seen …"

Right after the attacks, the TV news broadcasts had highlighted the readiness of all the hospitals for receiving the injured. Everyone was preparing for the worst, or what they thought would be the worst— having to triage so many people at once. But the victims never came. Some injured people were found but not in the numbers that everyone was expecting. And now the staggering casualty count keeps climbing.

Now all I can do is try not to gaze at the flyers' eyes staring back at me. I know that if I do, I'm confronting death. I'm looking at someone who was taken too early, too violently, someone who didn't get a chance to say goodbye.

My mind briefly, vividly, flashes to the black hole that I saw in 1 WTC. I know that some of these faces staring at me on my walk belong to people who were dying while I was just staring at that black hole. I start going into shut-down mode. *Too much pain. Pick up the pace.* I keep my head down and just move forward. *They're dead, and there's nothing I can do about it.* Survivor's guilt. No you don't—you can go away, too.

Inside. Home—although, for the last few days, this hasn't really felt like a home. Do other people feel anxious in their own homes? Is it normal to feel both dread and relief to be home? I'm too wired to sleep or eat. I guess I will do some writing. My journal has always been a good outlet for venting and conveying my feelings.

I've already started my 9/11/01 journal entry, and I decide it's time to update it. Pulling the brown, leather-bound book out of my nightstand, I notice the embossed symbol on the front: a beautiful compass with a starburst behind it. I've never really looked at it before. Ironic. A compass is used to guide us, to prevent us from getting lost—and if we are lost, to aid us in getting back on course. I'm certainly lost, but I doubt that writing will do anything to guide me back to my path. *Whatever.*

I open the journal to where I left off and just write.

Sunday September 16, 2001

After waking up at John's on Wednesday, I make it home for the first time. I have twelve messages on my home phone. I shower and call my Dr and decide to keep my appointment. I go back into the city – still numb. Walk down 14th Street – pass the barricades, the armored trucks, soldiers, cops with guns and masks. Copters flying overhead. Everyone is quiet and I just keep walking.

Today is now Sunday and I don't know where the last five days went. Time stood still. I have no concept of time – I can't remember who I have talked to or when. It all runs together. I was finally able to sleep somewhat on Friday night – that's also when I started shaking again. I think the numbness is wearing off. I think it might be starting to sink in. Yesterday, Sabrina, Peter, Mike, and I ate at East LA and then hung out at my place. It was nice to sit down and talk and we laughed. It felt so good. I walked outside yesterday morning and saw the first commercial plane in the sky since Monday. It was weird – I guess things will never be the same.

I get waves of emotion – fine one moment and the next want to scream or cry or yell. Just kinda walk around and don't know what to do. Life is forever changed and work is up in the air. Guess I need to look for another job just in case.

I went to church today and it felt good to be around people. It was a good service and at the end we are all standing in silence and up in the balcony this woman sings "Amazing Grace." It was chilling and not a dry eye in the house. Here I am standing in this huge, beautiful church listening to this song that I have heard a thousand times. Just more surrealism.

I felt and tasted the pain, agony, and hate on Tuesday. Now I feel and taste the love and amazing resolve of the American people. We are rising from the ashes! We persevere. I hope to never forget this feeling. I have seen these last few days the worst of humanity, but also the best. We have shown our full potential. The way everyone has reacted after this is how we should have been all along – more loving, patient, kind, and supportive of everyone. I just hope I won't change back to the old way. I hope people will keep this love going!

Life is slowly going back to normal. More cars on the streets, more businesses opening up. Slowly we move forward.

The next day, Monday, I get out of bed earlier than I care to, but I have to get dressed and go to Sabrina's apartment. She's my best friend and she lives a good fifteen-minute walk from me in Hoboken.

Sabrina and I met at orientation for Lehman. We were both right out of college, dopey-eyed and eager to get our lives started in the big city! Boy, were we young and dumb. We've had some great times—sitting by the river with the Winter Garden at our backs and enjoying happy hour with all the other overworked banking stiffs, eating at our favorite Mexican spot, *East LA*, dancing till all hours to 80's pop music in alphabet city, going to the Bronx Zoo, shopping at Macy's. Yeah, it's been nice, but now I know we are in a new chapter of our lives, one that I'm afraid will see us parting ways.

Sabrina worked at 1 World Financial Center, which is several buildings down from where I worked. She had just come up to street level right after the first plane hit and didn't know what was going on. Making her way to her building, she had passed debris, dead bodies, and body parts. She knew something catastrophic had happened. But as a dedicated worker, her main focus had been just getting to work.

When she'd finally made it to her building, she had looked up in time to see the second plane fly overhead and into the second tower. Running for her life, she was able to make it to the waterfront, where she met up with some people she knew from work. After a ferry ride to Staten Island, she was safe at a coworker's family member's home. Sabrina had been outside during everything, so she was in no hurry to go outside again after she made it home that night.

Once I found out that she was expected back at work today, I offered to escort her to and from work. I still don't have to go back yet; Lehman hasn't found a place for my department to work. Our corporate headquarters at 3 World Financial Center is not open; the last I heard, they were using its lobby as the morgue.

I'm really in no hurry to go back. I'm just concerned that Sabrina is not up to this. She seems broken, in a way that makes me feel helpless. The more we talk, the more I hear her longing just to quiet this chaos we all now find ourselves in. She expresses a desire to move back to Texas. I don't blame her, really.

For some reason, I don't have a strong desire to move. I'm not happy and I don't feel all that safe, but I feel somewhat obstinate. Like, why the hell should I leave? I didn't do anything! If I leave or change my life in any way, then they win. Win what, I don't know. Of course, my mom would say I'm just being stubborn – something I know I'm good at.

Sabrina and I make our way from the 33rd Street PATH station to the 34th Street subway station. Thankfully, she doesn't have to go back to 1 World Financial. Lehman has relocated her department to another building, close to midtown. Sabrina is leading the way. Once above ground in the city, I can sense her body stiffen and I hear her step quickens.

One reason Sabrina and I get along so well is that neither of us are loiterers. When we walk, we mean business. This is one reason we both avoid Times Square, with its annoyingly slow walking tourists. But her walk today is even quicker than normal. She wants to be outside as little as possible.

I don't mind being outside. I like the fact I can see things and feel like I know what is going on. I let her lead the way. When we make it to the building, I notice the Waldorf Astoria Hotel across the street.

"Nice area," I comment.

"Yeah, it's okay," she says. "I've been here a few times." This is the longest conversation we've had up to this point, because neither of us quite knows what to say. Awkwardness is the tone of the day.

Inside her building, we stop at the elevators. She pushes UP and we wait. Seeming a bit more relaxed, Sabrina turns around to survey the area. Now it's my turn to stiffen. *Huh, I wasn't expecting this feeling.* Inside this generic office building, I don't feel comfortable. Then again, it's my first time back in an office building since the attacks.

Ding. The elevator opens and we walk in. We're alone. The doors close. My pulse increases. *Yeah, I don't really like this. This doesn't feel good.* First time in an elevator since … well, it's not fun. My mind flashes to Tuesday, explosions, fire, people being trapped inside elevators. *Time to get out of here.* Ding, the doors open. Just in time. We step out into the waiting area.

"I think I'm good now," she says, half smiling.

"You sure?" I ask. "I don't mind walking you to the offices and hanging around a bit. I have my employee ID so they can't kick me out." I get a small giggle out of her. That feels good.

"No, but you're sweet. Thank you so much."

"Okay, then. I'm going to come back this afternoon and we can go back to Hoboken together. What time do you think you will want to leave?" I ask, remembering her penchant for working long hours and hoping she doesn't plan to stay too late.

"Uhh, good question. I don't want to be here that long. How's four?"

"Perfect," I say, relieved. But suddenly, I'm not all that sure I want to leave her. I begin to feel over-protective, the way I imagine parents might feel dropping their child off for the first time at school. Though I would imagine most parents aren't afraid that school is a dangerous situation for their child.

I still have this nagging feeling that something else catastrophic could happen. *What if I can't get to her to pick her up?* She leans in to hug me. We embrace tightly.

"Okay, Miss, have a great day and I will see you at four sharp," I say with a smile. She smiles and walks down the hallway. I turn around and push the DOWN button. Where are the stairs? I don't know. I've never been in here before. *Damn, I guess I'll have to suck it up and take the elevator.* I have to get used to being inside buildings again.

Once back on the street, I breathe more deeply. Who knew New York air tasted so good?

What to do? I really don't want to go back home. I have nothing to do and I don't want to just sit around inside all day. Walk. Just walk. I love walking. Ever since I started working in the city, I walk everywhere. It's done wonders for my calves. They are so cut now. And I've lost some weight. Not that I needed to, but you can't help it when all you are doing is walking. People have noticed. I have to admit, I've enjoyed the attention.

So I head down Park Avenue. I love walking around this city. It's so alive, and people-watching can entertain me for hours. I like this area. Everyone around here acts like they have somewhere to go. They move. I can keep my pace up and not have to dodge too many people.

It's Monday and I'm not at work. I have no plans, nothing to do and nowhere to be. That's weird. It feels odd. Like I'm lost.

As I look around, I'm struck by how everything seems to be so normal. People are busy with their lives again, getting to work, darting in and out of Starbucks, talking on their cell phones. Bike messengers are weaving through traffic. By the looks of things, you would never know anything horrific had happened a few days ago. The world goes on, even if my world has fallen apart. I guess that's a good thing, although it feels cold.

Shouldn't everything just stop so people can mourn until I feel better and my world has been put back together again? Is this how a widow feels a week after her husband has been killed in a car accident, when she ventures out of the house for the first time and notices that nothing has changed around her? I know it's good for people to move forward with their lives, but at the same time, I want things to stop. Really, I want to go back eight days, to when I had just left church and met two friends at B Bar for brunch. That was a great afternoon. Life was good then. Life was safe.

Before I know it, I find myself close to the area I usually avoid at all costs. Subconsciously, I guess I know it won't be crowded with tourists—which really is a sad thing. The allure of Times Square is the energy created by all the people in awe of being in its presence. The bright lights don't hurt, either.

A movie. *Perfect idea!* That will kill some time.

I make my way over to the AMC on 42nd Street. This is my favorite movie theatre in the city. It's beautiful and large, and it shows pretty much everything. Though I'm still getting used to paying ten dollars for a movie.

I walk up and stand in front of the electronic billboard at street level that lists all the shows, scanning. Nothing really looks all that promising. *The Others.* That's the one with Nicole Kidman and I think it's some kind of supernatural thriller. Sounds interesting. Why not? Next show is in twenty minutes. *Nice timing.* I go in, swipe my card at the kiosk, and make my selection. These are useful time-savers when this place is packed—which it's not, at the present moment.

I wind my way up the numerous escalators. I like escalators now more than I could have imagined. They are open, you can see above and below you, and if need be, you can run up and down them. Works for me. Elevators, not so much.

On the floor, the guy takes my ticket and, without looking, points me in the correct direction. Bright lights in front of me blink on and off, announcing that I should be stopping to pay an obscene price for some refreshments. *No thanks, I just ate.*

Down the hall into the theatre. I stop. It's huge. Massive, really. High ceilings. A very wide theatre that must sit at least four hundred people. I don't think I've been in one this large before. Or if I have, I've never been in one this empty.

It's fairly dark. Scanning up the aisle, I don't see anyone else. This is creepy. The thought of being in an empty theatre is cool, but actually being in one this large, about five stories up in the middle of Manhattan—it's just bazaar.

I settle on a seat in the middle of a row about ten rows from the top. I have a great view overlooking the entire theatre. Ahh, there is someone else further down, sitting by themselves. *I guess I'm not alone.* Breathing more easily, I stare at the screen at the endless advertisements.

This is just too strange. Here I am on a late Monday morning, sitting in a movie theatre almost alone. Just killing time. I've never done this. I would feel somewhat rebellious if not for the fact that I have no job to go to right now. So there is nothing I'm really rebelling against—unless you count the desire to curl up in a fetal position and not leave my apartment. Yeah, maybe I am rebelling from feeling despair—or more accurately, from feeling anything.

The movie starts. I'm entertained. Enthralled, actually. It's beautiful with its scenery and period setting. Escape has always been easy for me. Movies, television, books, music have always provided me with wonderful new worlds to experience, new worlds that I often longed to be part of.

I'm very engaged, and the movie is progressing well. I think I'm starting to figure out the plot line and what is really going on. What's that? That's strange. A man with a duffle bag has just come in and sat down in the first row, near the exit ramp. Why would anyone come into a movie that is more than half over? I turn my attention back to the screen. More clues are revealed. Yeah, I think I know what is going on now.

That man with the duffle bag has just gotten up and left. He left his duffle bag next to where he was sitting. Okay. That is very strange. I get chills. I don't like this. Why would you come into a movie very late, sit for maybe twenty minutes and then leave? And leave a bag behind? This is New York. People don't just leave their stuff lying around. They know it might get stolen.

Deep breaths. He's not a terrorist who's going to blow up this theatre. Just calm down. It's okay. Why would he blow up this theatre? It's practically empty. Just watch the movie.

About two minutes later in the movie, they do the big reveal in a scene that has a psychic opening a closet door, and it flashes back and forth from her to these dead kids. It scares the hell out of me! I jump out of my seat and let out a small yell. Damn, that was crazy! Falling back into my seat, I immediately feel like a total idiot. Luckily, the other movie-goer doesn't seem to have noticed my over reaction.

Then again, did that person even notice that other guy, the one who got up and left his bag? Thankfully, the movie ends and I get up and get the hell out of there. Having to pee, I go to the theatre's bathroom. I do my business and leave. I haven't seen that guy with the duffle bag again, and I'm more than happy to get back outside into the sun and fresh air.

For the rest of the day, I just wander around the city. I get some enjoyment out of not having a plan. Window shopping seems to take my mind off obsessing about what's going to happen next in my life.

Before long, it is time to go back and pick up Sabrina. My second time back in that office building is less stressful, and our trip back to Hoboken is filled with more conversation. Sabrina seemed to do fairly well at work. She mentions that it felt odd to be at work when she knew so many of us were not. Both feeling drained from the day, we part at her apartment, deciding not to do dinner.

That was to be the last day I escorted Sabrina. She said she was fine after that first day and said she didn't want to burden me. It didn't burden me at all. In fact, it gave me something to do. It made me feel useful, like I had a purpose. But I understood where she was coming from and offered to be around if she needed anything.

Less than three weeks later, Sabrina was packing and moving back to Texas. I knew this was coming. I go over to say good-bye. I meet her parents for the first time—they have driven up to help her move—though I wish I didn't have to meet them this way. The mood in the apartment is a hurried but controlled chaos. Movers are carrying things out, and Sabrina is just standing there. I think she is still somewhat in shock.

"Well, I guess this is it," I say, mustering the most positive tone I can. What the hell can I say? She's leaving, I'm not. End of story.

"Yeah. It's hard to believe," she says, eyeing her apartment. "You'll have to come visit me in Austin," she adds hopefully.

"Of course. I loved my first visit there with you. I'm so there," I say honestly. It's a great town and I would really like to go back.

We stand around making small talk. Nothing earth-shattering. Neither of us really knows what to say. We can be with each other and say nothing at all now, and we know what the other is feeling. Like it or not, we both have this horrible experience in common, and it will bind us together forever. We've been through hell, and now we have the shared memories to which only we can relate.

I should be feeling a lot right now, but I'm not. Some of it is because I'm on overload. I'm a little bit jealous that she has the courage to leave and that she is going to a town that she loves so much. I wish I had that—but I don't. There is nowhere that I really want to go.

I never thought past working in New York, never thought about what would be next. To me, there was no next—New York was the end all and be all. I'm also mad that she is leaving. Part of me wants to yell at her to stick it out. I want to insist that we can get back what we had before this all happened, that it's not always going to be this rough. But I can't promise that, because I don't know.

I don't know how powerful these memories are going to be. I do know that I don't want my best friend to leave. But she is leaving, so I just suck it up, hug her good-bye, and walk away. It's that simple. Walk. Just keep walking.

3

S eat 3A, seat 3A, there it is. Yes, on the right, all by itself. I love these seats. Now I don't have to worry about anyone trying to make small talk with me. It's the best of both worlds, an aisle *and* a window seat.

I maneuver into the tiny seat, trying to be graceful and not to hit my head on the overhead bin. These planes are nice in that they are fast, but I wouldn't mind a bit more room and thicker padding on the seat cushions. *Damn, these seats are hard!* I shift my weight to my left butt cheek and stare out the window. Thankfully, the weather is nice out today. I hate flying in bad weather. My mind flashes to a flight into Nashville in a thunderstorm, when I was in high school. I've been on roller coasters that were tamer than that landing.

The ground crew is scurrying around, loading the bags into the underbelly of the plane. It seems like any other normal day at Newark. I can't help but wonder how the jobs of the guys down there have changed since the attacks.

It's been five weeks and three days—but who's counting?

As a passenger, I can definitely tell a difference. The security is much tighter than is used to be. Now they don't allow non-passengers past the security line; it feels somewhat odd, but in a weird way, I kind of like that. I'm not a crowd person, so fewer people at the gate area is fine by me. Anyway, when I travel alone, the sight of people with their loved ones makes me feel more alone.

Five weeks and three days. It feels more like five years and three days. So much has happened. Work finally started back for me. They put me in the Jersey City office at 101 Hudson Street, on the twenty-fourth floor overlooking lower Manhattan. So now, every day when I go into the office, I have a bird's eye view of Ground Zero—not exactly my idea of a room with a view.

I've actually been reassigned to a new department. I am now in the department that oversees corporate services, so my office is right off the mail room. Actually, calling it an office is too generous. It's really an oversized closet that has two walls of floor-to-ceiling windows—hence the view—and I have to share it with five other people. The other day, it was so crowded in there I had to sit on top of a small filing cabinet. Yeah, this is what I thought I would be doing with my college degree. I know I should be happy I have a job, but most days, I would love to be anywhere but there.

The atmosphere at work is tense. It's what I would imagine it would be like in the trauma unit of a hospital treating war victims: management/doctors projecting a reserved air of optimism and compassion while the underlings/patients do their best to hold it together and project inner strength they aren't sure is even there.

Not a day goes by without coworkers standing around rehashing where they were or what they saw. Everyone seems to have a friend, cousin, aunt, mother, or father who is out of work or couldn't go back to work because of the trauma they experienced. Some days, it is comforting to be around other survivors, because we have a common bond through a shared experience. But most days, I feel trapped in some insane hamster wheel where I can't escape, being reminded over and over again of what I've been through and what I have lost.

Controlled chaos seems to be the theme of the day, everyday. I go to work and it's chaotic; I go home, and it's so quiet that all I'm left with is my internal chaos, the feelings that I don't know what to do with.

The concept of resilience has been thrown around a lot lately. The media loves to mention it in reference to how, as a people, New Yorkers will get through this. Everyone seems to be talking about external signs, such as people going back to work, businesses reopening, and commercial planes flying again. So in that sense, I guess I'm resilient, since I'm back at work.

But what about internally? I don't feel resilient. I don't feel normal, settled, or even safe. Hell, half the time I don't even feel anything. What about that aspect of resilience? No one seems to be willing to talk about that. I guess as long as things on the outside look "normal," it's easier to pretend everything is normal.

Lord knows I'm good at pretending. Just how good will be put to the test in about ninety minutes, when I touch down in Greensboro.

I'm looking forward to going home, but not looking forward to the emotional roller coaster I'm afraid awaits me. I know mom is thrilled I'm getting out of the city, but I don't know how she is going to react when she sees me. I don't feel all that comfortable around overly emotive people—I never have. But part of me is excited, too.

Dare I hope that, for the first time, I can escape the 9/11 cloud that has hung over me daily? Is it possible that several hundred miles away, life will actually be normal, in a town that wasn't directly affected by the attacks? That I can just hang out without being reminded every minute of what happened five weeks earlier? Damn, that would be nice. But I'd better not get my hopes up.

"Flight attendants, please prepare for take-off," the captain robotically announces over the intercom. Like a good little boy who follows the rules, I've already fastened my seat belt and made sure my seat is in its upright position and my tray table is stowed, so the attendants don't have to instruct me to do anything. Look out the window? Don't look out the window? I don't know what I want to do. My mind is not cooperating.

All it wants to do is imagine that this is what it was like for those people on the planes that day. They had an early morning flight. They were just sitting in their seats, totally unaware that their lives were about to change. Most of them probably ignored the pre-flight safety script they had heard many times before and settled in for what they thought would be a routine trip.

Visions of planes crashing and flames shooting in all directions begin flashing through my mind. *Stop it!* The more I fight it, the more power I seem to give the intrusive images. Sweat is slowly beading along my hairline. I've never been afraid to fly before. I love to fly. I have glorious flying dreams—or I used to. I can do this. Just take a deep breath.

"Please be seated. We're Number Two for take-off," the pilot informs us. *Good, I can handle this.* We will be up in the air in just a few minutes, and then everything will be alright. Yeah, that is what those passengers thought that day as well. Everything was okay for them at take-off and several minutes after take-off. It wasn't until they were well into their flights that things went horribly wrong. *Okay, this is going to stop now!* I can't keep thinking about all of this and keep my sanity.

I notice my tailbone is hurting, and I'm grateful that the pain has drawn my attention. I don't have enough padding to sit straight up in this chair. I shift all my weight back to my left cheek and look out the window. Looking up, the sky is beautiful. Ahh, I like that sound, the engines roaring to life. *Here we go.* Big exhale. One Mississippi, two Mississippi, three Mississippi … fourteen Mississippi, and we lift off.

Another reason I like these small planes is that they get off the ground in a hurry. *Okay, I'm good.* This is smooth. It's fun looking down and seeing how the perspective changes so quickly. Buildings, roads, cars, and people suddenly become ants just scurrying around. I smile. At least I still get some enjoyment out of this. Maybe the attacks didn't take away everything.

One hour and five minutes later, we have touched down in the exciting town of Greensboro, N.C. I did it. My first flight since 9/11. I have a feeling I will be ending a lot of thoughts with "since 9/11." I've already noticed how that has become my reference point.

As I exit the plane, I'm struck by just how quiet and empty it is in the gate area. I liked it on the way out, but now that I have people waiting for me, I'm not sure I like being met with silence. Then again, it gives me a chance to go the bathroom and more time to work up the resolve to put on a happy face.

While washing my hands, I gaze into the mirror. Is this what twenty-four looks like? When I was in college, mid-twenties always seemed somewhat old, or at least mature. It's funny now, because I feel anything but mature. I don't look old enough to have been through college, let alone a terrorist attack.

I finish washing my hands and then stick them under the automatic dryer. These things annoy the hell out of me. I don't like waiting for them to dry my hands. It takes too long. *That's good enough. Okay, I know everyone is waiting for me, so I'd better get moving.* Deep breath. They are family and I can do this. It will be fun. We are going to have a nice weekend. Nothing too emotional.

Out the bathroom door, turn right, and down the aisle. It's wide open. No one blocking me from keeping my fast pace. Walking fast allows me to enter this zone to where I can just numb out, move toward my destination and not think about what's up ahead. Just move and let life throw at me whatever it may.

A bit further up, I see the security rope, and people are standing just beyond that. The excitement and joy radiating from those family members waiting for their loved ones is startling.

I do a quick scan left, scan right. I don't see anyone. Wait, left again, there they are. *Wow, there they are!* They are all smiling. Damn, I feel my tears welling up. *Hold it together, don't start crying now.* Twelve feet, ten feet, past the security guard sitting in his chair, six feet, my mom makes it to me first. Huge smile across her face.

"It's so good to see you Jeff," she exhales as she's hugging me tightly. I make a mental note that I'm Jeff now. Sine I'm the third Hoyt, my family doesn't like to call me by my first name. Ironically enough my friends don't like to call me Jeff.

"You too," I say as I look up and notice both of my sisters standing behind her. I can't help but smile.

"Amy, what are you doing here?" I ask my older sister who lives in Colorado with her husband and two small boys. By this time, my mom has let go, and I quickly hug Amy.

"I wanted to see you. I'm your older sister, you know, and I had to make sure you're okay," she says, laughing. I love her laugh.

"It's great to see you," are the only words that I can manage. I'm feeling a bit overcome at this point.

"Hey, Jess." I lean in and do the one-arm hug around my younger sister, Jessica, who at sixteen looks too grown up for me. I still think of her as the obnoxious toddler who seemed to get too much enjoyment out of dropping her Fisher Price record player on top of my head after I had made her mad.

"Hey. How was your flight?" she asks.

"Good. Kinda strange, but everything was smooth." I'm trying to be reassuring now that I feel a bit more composed.

"Hey, Dad." My father seems to perk up as I acknowledge him.

"Hey. You check any bags?" he asks. Always the practical one.

"Nope," I reply. "Packed everything I need in my book bag. I love this thing. It holds everything." I swing my right arm around and loop it into the arm strap of the bag, signaling my readiness to get out of here. That's one thing my dad and I have in common: we don't like to just hang out. We like to move and get to where we are going.

"I'm ready if you all are," I add. Wow dare I say it? I feel happy, almost light-hearted. Maybe this trip home is what I needed. Maybe it won't be all that emotionally draining.

Once we get back to the house, I discover my mom has made more food than any of us could eat in a week. Fulfilling her role of the doting mother, she has made all of my favorite foods, which makes me smile and at the same time feel a bit anxious. For some reason, I'm not sure I want to be around that much food. But whatever.

We have fun catching up. I love hearing stories about my nephews, who are one and three. I'm so thankful I was able to visit them in Colorado last August, just before everything happened. That was a wonderful trip. Those boys have opened up something in me that I never knew was there, a love that seems to grow exponentially every time I'm around them. I can't imagine life without them.

Jessica always has news regarding her active love life. Gosh, where did the time go? She's in high school. I feel old.

My parents seem to just be reveling in the fact that they have their kids in one place. I like this feeling. It feels safe.

We talk about Halloween being close and I mention that we need to get pumpkins. My parents agree. So, in true Ozzie and Harriet fashion, our happy little family piles into the car and we drive out to the local pumpkin lot at the Methodist church my family attends.

I have always loved this time of year. The crisp but not too cold nip in the air, the fall colors starting to break through, and the rows and rows of beautiful orange pumpkins. We spilt off, with each kid going in a different direction and my parents hanging back. Jessica, the decisive one, finds her pumpkin in about three minutes flat. I find mine next. Amy, the comparison shopper, has to make sure she has walked every aisle before making her final selection.

When we get back home, we start the tradition of attempting to cut off the tops of each pumpkin. We get frustrated and my dad has to step in to finish the job. I don't necessarily love the carving process, but I do love baking the seeds. My mom has already pulled out her cookie sheet. There is nothing better than warm, baked pumpkin seeds, lightly salted.

During all of this, my mind struggles unsuccessfully to stay present in the moment. Instead, I remember when we lived in Pennsylvania. I loved it back then. We lived in a small town, Yardley, which seemed like something out of a Thomas Kincaid painting.

Every fall there was a festival downtown with arts, crafts, and booths that provided countless activities. I loved pouring colorful sand into antique soda bottles that had been stretched and distorted. But my favorite activity—the one that every parent hates—was tossing a ping pong ball into a fish bowl. I somehow managed to always win that one fish that defied the odds and lived much longer than anyone expected.

Life was less complicated back then. I was a kid and I didn't have any real responsibility. I was protected. I basically lived in a safe little bubble. Maybe that's why my mind lingers on those memories. I don't want to grow up—or at least, I don't want to be a grown-up in the world I've found myself in recently.

Back to the present—I'm done with my pumpkin creation. It's simple: triangle eyes and nose and a big, wide grin. One top tooth and one bottom tooth. I'm not putting too much effort into this. I know it's only going to sit outside for a few days and then get trashed.

"Your dad and I thought we would take everyone to Marisol's to-night for dinner," my mom announces unexpectedly.

"Ooooh, nice," Amy coos.

"I'm game," Jessica adds.

"Sounds good to me," I chime in.

Going to one of the nicest restaurants in town gives my sisters a reason to dress up—not that they need much of a reason. Amy is glad that she brought her cosmetics "caboodle" for such an occasion. The caboodle, to the best of my knowledge, weighs more than the entire contents of my book bag. She's the high maintenance one in the family.

The girls' routine of camping out in Jessica's spacious bathroom while they decide which make-up to apply and how to do their hair starts early that evening. After I shower and get dressed, I wander into Jessica's bathroom. I enjoy just marveling at their primping and gossiping. Jessica likes to entertain us with the latest "news" of who in Hollywood is doing what with whom. Where she gets all this informa-tion, I'll never know—but I have to admit, listening to it is a guilty pleasure. I need that right now. I need to escape into someone else's world.

My dad makes his rounds, nudging the girls and my mom to hurry so we won't be late for our reservation. The routine is complete once he has made this announcement for the third time and my mom has scolded him, saying that she will be ready in a minute and asking him to leave her alone.

We all meet in the kitchen. My mom wants a picture of us kids in front of our pumpkins, which have now been placed on the front stoop. I groan because I hate pictures, but the girls readily agree, since this will capture the fruits of their labor in front of the mirror. After taking the picture, we leave.

Dinner is pleasant and the food is wonderful. I enjoy it more than I expected, which makes me feel a bit awkward. Not sure why. When we get back home, we all change into more comfortable clothes. Despite all the primping and preparing they did, the girls can't wait to get changed. I change into a new, long-sleeve, red, fitted tee-shirt that I bought a few months earlier at the GAP. It's one of those tees that would show off my muscles beautifully, if I had muscles. But since I don't have any to show off, the shirt just hangs on me.

I walk out of my room and my mom is behind me, making her way down the hall toward the rec room.

"You look great in that shirt," she remarks.

Startled, I turn around. "Yeah I guess," I say, trying to laugh it off.

She hugs me, for the twentieth time today. "You're so thin!" she says. "It must be so nice to be able to wear anything you want." She says this almost longingly. It makes me feel uncomfortable, so I change the subject as we both head into the rec room.

That night in bed, I keep thinking about that brief exchange in the hallway. My mom isn't overweight at all. She's a former beauty queen and high school basketball star. As I was growing up, all my friends loved her. I view her as a cross between Donna Reed, Martha Stewart, and Carol Burnett: beautiful, charming, and a wonderful hostess with a mean funny streak.

For some reason, though, I can't help but think how nice it felt hearing those words. I'm thin. I can wear anything. I've never really thought about that. *Is she right? Am I all that thin?* I don't really feel that way—but then again, what does thin feel like? I'm not sure. I just know the attention feels nice.

Making no progress whatsoever with this train of thought, I drift off to sleep.

Sunday seems to come too early. It's time for me to go back to a life that I'm slowly realizing may not be the best place for me. But I'm committed. I wanted to work in New York City after graduation, and that is what I'm doing. Once I set my sights on something, I go after it and accomplish it. My parents have taught me to never quit, and I'm not going to give up now.

Everyone wants to accompany me to the airport, and I reluctantly agree. Saying good-bye is a numbing experience for me. I don't like the awkward feelings it evokes. The good-byes further remind me that life is always changing. I don't like change. I like routine. So I do what I do best. I just walk. Just trudge on through and keep moving until I get to my destination, hoping that I won't feel too much.

After I check-in at the ticket counter, I turn around and find everyone is just standing there, looking at me. I notice what appears to be pity in their eyes. It's as if I'm heading off to some horrible place with the possibility of never being seen or heard from again. It's possible that my parents do feel this way. I wouldn't be surprised if they were secretly wishing that I would say, forget New York, I want to move to Greensboro.

We make our way to the security line. I assure everyone that I'm fine.

"I promise I will call when I get home," I say.

My mother corrects me. "Your home is here."

I smile. She hasn't adjusted yet to the fact that I've moved away. I don't blame her, and actually, she is right. I don't feel like where I live right now is home. Then again, I don't feel like their house is home, either. I don't feel like I really belong anywhere at the moment.

I hug everyone and flash a reassuring smile, thinking that is what they need from me, as I enter the security line. Once through, I turn around and wave. They are all still standing there, waving back. I try hard not to really look at my mom's or sisters' faces, not wanting to see the sadness in their eyes. I don't worry about that with my dad, though. We're alike in that way: we can hide anything.

As I walk down the hallway, I relax somewhat in the emptiness of the area. I like the space, the personal and emotional space that I'm now feeling.

This weekend was a good idea. I'm glad I could get away. We all seemed to be in high spirits, and it wasn't too emotional. We all kept things fairly light and upbeat. As I look back on it now, I have the feeling I was handled with kid gloves. Nothing of importance was really asked of me.

That day that changed everyone's lives never came up in conversation. They asked me about work a little bit, but didn't want to know anything of substance. And I'm good with that. I don't need to rehash everything. Or at least, I don't want to.

The flight back goes smoothly and my anxiety is much more in check. Back at my apartment, I make my obligatory call to my folks. But when the call is over, I feel this terrible letdown. I'm back.

I feel trapped in this small apartment and trapped in this city. I start dreading the thoughts of going back to work, back to that view of Ground Zero.

I don't know what I really want to do or where I want to be. So I decide I'll just keep doing this, just keep moving. As long as I don't think too much, then I don't have to worry about feeling too much. It's worked for me so far.

I unpack, skip dinner and head to bed. I'm glad that I had a vacation to "normal." But now I drift off to sleep with the knowledge that I'm back to anything but.

4

I login to my account on my.yahoo.com. I love this site. It gives me the headlines from every major newswire. I could spend all day reading about news from around the world.

Hell, let's face it—I pretty much do.

Being tucked away in my new cubicle gives me a lot of privacy. It sure beats that cramped closet I was trying to work out of for so long. Now several of my coworkers and I are on this almost-empty floor in the Hudson building. I like it, as far as cubicles go. I can come and go as I please, and it's not noisy. And best of all, I don't have to look out a window at downtown Manhattan anymore.

If it weren't for my mind-numbing job, I probably wouldn't mind working here. I feel somewhat grateful for this job because I don't have much pressure on me and I can follow a routine that I like. But on the other hand, I hate what I do—or don't do, for that matter.

What I am *supposed* to be doing is ambiguous, and everything around here—even three months after the attacks—is still so much in flux. Employees are still working out of two different Sheraton hotels in the city, and we are over capacity in this building.

I get to see the bomb-sniffing dog every day. Under normal circumstances, it would be cool to see a cute yellow Lab every day, if it weren't for the fact that he's here sniffing for bombs. Bombs in New

Jersey! Who the hell cares about New Jersey? This isn't Manhattan! But this building has had two bomb scares, so I guess the dog is a reality we now have to live with.

It's wild that the dog's presence doesn't seem to bother anyone else. Everyone goes nuts over him, and some are now stocking dog treats at their desks. Then again, maybe that's their way of dealing with the awkwardness of the situation.

I'm cursed. I can't help but think of the reason that dog is here, every time I see him.

Ah, it's 9 a.m., time for breakfast. I do like the new routine I've been able to set up. In at 8:30, read some online news, go downstairs to the cafeteria for breakfast, bring it back up, eat, read some more news, and then get some work done. Pretty soon it's time for lunch, get some more work done, read some more news, and then it's time to go home. My day is low stress and very little brain functioning is required.

I take the stairs—as I do more often now—down to the cafeteria, which is starting to come to life. This is one of the perks of working for such a large corporation: they usually have good cafeterias. This one is pretty good, though not as good as the one in 3 World Financial— the building that Lehman has decided to vacate permanently.

I pass the entry door, turn right, and grab the small, cardboard box that I use to cart my food back up to my desk. Doing a 180, I cross to the other side of the room, where they keep the muffins. After scanning the rows of different selections, my body calms when I see my favorite: a large blueberry muffin. I'm thankful they have it today. I get so mad when they are out of them.

Next on my shopping list: yogurt. Scooting over to the other side of the room where the large fridge section is, I reach in and grab a no-fat raspberry yogurt. Luckily, they have this every day. And last but not least, a large hot tea. Gotta have something warm on these cold mornings—plus the caffeine helps get me through the morning. Can't forget the butter. I grab one pat of butter for the muffin.

While I wait in the checkout line, I gaze at the TV screens hanging from the wall. Don Imus is on railing about something, trying to be funny. Never really got into him.

I walk back out of the cafeteria and climb the stairs. I love taking the stairs. It's great exercise.

Back at my desk, I eat the yogurt first, since that's cold. Next, I carefully unfold a napkin and place the muffin on top. I slice off the top of the muffin and spread some butter on both halves. The best part of the muffin is the top, so I save that for last. I love these things. I can't help but smile, because the muffin instantly brings me back to being a kid. I loved waking up on Sunday mornings and rushing downstairs to see if mom had made her miniature blueberry muffins. They were so good, and you could eat so many of them. Sunday just seemed like more fun when she baked those muffins, and so dull when she didn't. Of course, now that I'm an adult, I appreciate that she had three kids, and I know it's a miracle any baking was done at all.

Now that my food is gone, I feel more relaxed. My breakfast is somewhat filling, but not so much that it brings too much attention to my gut. I've satisfied my body just enough so I can now ignore it again.

I grab my tea and slowly bring it to my lips, testing the temperature. *Ouch! Still too hot.* After carefully setting it back down, I return my attention to the computer.

I don't have any work emails to respond to. I love not having any emails, or voicemails, for that matter. I laugh to myself. *If I'm not careful, I'm going to turn into one of those reclusive office inhabitants that everyone talks about.* I'm friendly, but I just don't go out of my way to be social. I can put on a good smile and make small talk with people when needed.

Okay, I've read pretty much everything that I can on this site. Now it's time to turn to GOOGLE. Gosh, the things I've learned by Googling! It's amazing that all this information is out there just waiting to be read. *Hmmm, B.M.I., body mass index ... I wonder what mine*

is? Let's find out. This first site looks good. It says I can calculate my
B.M.I. Clicking on it takes me to the National Heart Lung and Blood
Institute website. Cool.

On the right side of the page is a nifty little box where I can input
my height and weight: 6 feet tall, and 145 pounds (I think, but since I
don't have a scale, I'm not sure. I do know I've lost some weight). My
answer is 19.7, which is within the normal range. *Huh, okay. Not bad.*

Let's see what 140 pounds does. That's a 19.0 B.M.I. Still normal.
Looks like the cut-off for normal is 18.5, and anything below that is
considered underweight. Playing around with the calculator, I discover I would have to be about 135 pounds to be underweight or "not
normal."

I like numbers. It's fun playing around to see what different out-
comes you can get. Life pretty much comes down to numbers anyway.
How long you live, how tall you are, how much you weigh, your I.Q.,
how much money you make, how many friends you have—all numbers. All of which can be manipulated.

I already know that 3,500 calories equals a pound, so to lose one
pound in a week, all I would have to do is cut out 500 calories each
day. That's pretty easy. I haven't been eating dinner during the week
for more than two years now; it's just too much trouble, and cooking
for one is depressing.

I wouldn't mind being thinner. My stomach area annoys me. I
would love to have that "V" shape that guys get; of course, to get really
ripped like that, I would have to work out, which is not fun. But I can
do the food thing. It just comes down to consuming less. When I eat
less, the weight comes off. Nothing else is needed. And I already walk
a ton anyway, so I'm getting lots of exercise.

After finishing some work, I leave for lunch. I decide to get out
of the office for a few minutes, so I head across the street to the
convenience-type store that has an expansive salad bar. While loading a plastic container with vegetables and salad, my mind keeps
interjecting that I need to "go easy." I don't want to fill up the whole

container. I also tell myself to drink a large diet soft drink so I'll feel full. I grab a large Diet Pepsi—they are out of Diet Coke—and check out.

As I head back to the office, I start feeling anxious. That's the way I tend to feel these days, right before I eat. The anxiety is a mixture of anticipation and fear that I seem all too ready to embrace. The anticipation is that this has to be the best-tasting food ever, and that it has to fill me up so I don't feel empty inside. That goal seems almost unobtainable. Maybe that's what the fear is about. I'm afraid that this food can't possibly do for me what I feel it needs to do. *Well, at least I didn't get that much to eat.*

The afternoon goes by in a blur, and five o'clock comes quickly. I get the hell out of Dodge as fast as I can. I don't get paid enough to hang around.

Since it's Thursday, I'm going to go into the city to meet friends for "happy hour" at our favorite bar, Splash. I don't feel like going home first to change, so I just take the PATH directly to the 14th Street station.

This bar has given me a lot of good times. It was the first gay bar I ever went into in the city, and it has lived up to everything I ever thought a gay bar in New York City would be like. The gauntlet you have to walk through, passing rows of men. If you're viewed as hot enough, they might reach out and grab your ass. The boi dancers who "shower" on top of the bar. The cavernous bathroom that has porn playing on small TV screens above each urinal. And my personal favorite, Show Tune Mondays. I love me some classic videos of old broads belting out Broadway favorites in a room full of queens who know every word.

Thursday night happy hour at Splash used to be something I cherished. It was a time to just hang out, cut loose and shoot the shit with friends. I'd spend my time trying too hard to look hot, aloof, and mysterious enough so that some gorgeous guy across the room would make the first move and come over to talk. I used to enjoy those games, but now I feel ambivalent. More often than not, I realize that I wouldn't mind being home alone.

As I get closer to the bar, I'm more anxious. That's the story of my life these days. But this anxiety is different from the emotion I felt earlier today.

I love being in this city and having places to go where I can be open, where I can just be myself without feeling like a freak. And it's wonderful to be in a place full of other gay guys and to see men being openly affectionate with one another. But the flip side of being in an area with so many gay guys is that I feel somewhat self-conscious—hell, a *lot* self-conscious. I feel like I have to look a certain way to be viewed as beautiful or even acceptable.

I had never seen so many beautiful men in my life than before I came to this city, and that hasn't helped my self-esteem any. It only adds fuel to the fire of wanting to look perfect in the hopes of finding the perfect guy who will come and sweep me off my feet. I really want to find "him" and settle down, and then everything will be perfect. And the only way I'm going to do that is by looking perfect.

I have a sinking feeling that this mindset keeps me stuck in a trap that doesn't have a happy ending. It's the trap of telling myself that I'm "less than," so I'd better do this or that. And the "doing" is always centered around how I look. *Huh. Maybe this anxiety isn't so much different from what I was feeling earlier.*

Could finding "the guy" really do all those things for me? Fuck it, who cares? I like hard work and a challenge. And if nothing else, I love the eye candy in this place.

Once inside, I walk down the narrow aisle that connects the front bar area to the back. Men crowd around both sides of this aisle to hang out. Since I prefer the back bar area, I have to walk through this area. On occasion, my ass has been pinched. Amusingly enough, it has never offended me when that happens. In fact, it makes me smile, almost in a sick way. It's validation that I'm desirable enough.

Of course, I've never seen who has pinched me, and I know I might be appalled at the sight of the guy. And sometimes, I have to admit, I feel a bit let down when I walk through all those guys and there's no pinch. I know I shouldn't care, but some part of me feels like I've been rejected.

Tonight, I just plow through. I want to get to the back and look for my friends. No pinch. Once in the back, I scan the area. I hate being the first one here and having to get a table. *Oh good, I'm not. Cool, everyone is here!* I spot Tony, Andy, Mike, and Peter, and they all nod in my direction. I snake my way through the crowd to the small, bar-height table they are huddled around.

"Hey, guys."

"Hey Hoyt," they all seem to say in unison. I make my rounds giving everyone a hug, all the while scanning the crowd. I've gotten adept at being able to carry on whole conversations while scoping an area for guys. Since I'm always on the hunt for "the guy," I can never let my guard down.

Everyone seems to be in a good mood, sipping on their first drinks of the evening. I put my bag down and head to the bar to order the obligatory Cosmo. Then I stand there just oogling the bartender. He's shirtless, showing off his rock-solid chest with abs that you could scrub your clothes on. When he turns around, my eyes are drawn lower, to his perfectly round ass. It looks hard enough to crack walnuts on.

I notice the bartender is wearing underwear so small and so tight it looks like they were sewn onto him. In fact, I think I have handkerchiefs that have more material in them than what this guy is wearing. *Damn, I love this city.*

He's gorgeous, but at the same time, it makes me sad. I'm staring at this beautiful specimen of a man, but I can't help but think that he is probably straight—and if not, then he is light-years out of my league. *Damn it, why can't I just enjoy the show?* I should be basking in the glow of this free, non-fat eye candy. But for some reason, I'm making myself miserable over the fact that I'm single.

The bartender hands me my drink with a bright smile. I pay and, of course, leave him a big tip. I'm a sucker for smiles attached to half-naked bodies. Yeah, I'm easy. I'm every friendly bartender's dream.

I stand at the table sipping my drink while the guys make small talk, raising their voices so they can be heard over the music and conversations around us. I add my two cents every once in a while, but I feel a bit off and somewhat removed from the group. I love these guys, but social events haven't been my thing these days. I find myself withdrawing more and more every time I'm out with anyone. I feel detached from what's happening around me.

It's almost like I'm watching everything play out on a TV screen, and I'm some kid with his nose pressed up against the screen, wanting to get into the action but not knowing how. All this makes me feel more self-conscious. I blow off these feelings, reassuring myself there is nothing I can do about it.

"Hoyt, have you lost weight?" Tony asks, leaning toward me so I can hear.

"Yeah, I think I have, some," I say nonchalantly as I adjust my belt and slowly tug up on my pants. The pants are too big for me in the waist now, a fact I love.

My heart starts racing. I feel excited and uncomfortable at the same time. I love the fact that he noticed my weight loss but I also feel awkward about the attention being placed on my appearance. *But wow, he did just notice that I'm thinner! Yeah, I look good, don't I?* I decide I'm doing something right and I should keep it up.

Of course, I never stop to realize that Tony actually says nothing after his first comment. He didn't say I looked good or bad. He didn't say anything. But my mind is telling me I look good and to keep going in this direction. His comment and the one my mom made two months ago become the fuel that keeps me going.

I will use these two innocent comments, made by people who care for me, to my worst advantage.

After several drinks and more mindless chatter, we all say our good-byes and scatter in our directions. Feeling strangely euphoric and buzzed, I head home with thoughts of beautiful men dancing through my head.

But then my obsessing turns to my weight and I remember what Tony said. The euphoria slowly fades into fear. Tony noticed that I lost weight, but now there is pressure to keep this up. I have to keep up this appearance that people have evidently started noticing about me. I'm thin, and I need to stay this way. *Great, now I feel pressure.*

I'm afraid that if I don't keep this up, then I'm not worthy of attention for anything. And without attention, who am I?

I can do this. It's okay. I tell myself there is nothing to be nervous about. *It's easy. Just keep doing what you're doing and it will be fine. You will get there.*

After skipping dinner, as usual, I get ready for bed. I feel more relaxed because of what I have worked out in my head. I know I can do this. Although I ignore what the actual steps are going to be toward achieving a goal I've yet to define, I'm able to soothe myself to sleep with some abstract thinking that I can do whatever it is I need to do. My disordered pep-talk does the trick. For now.

5

I hate the feeling of having to pick something perfect to wear to a party. I hope I can find something that will make me look so hot that no guy can resist me. *God, I need help.* No clothes can make me look perfect. I just need to pick something.

Black. Yeah, that's easy. Scanning my closet, I'm amazed at how many black clothes I own. It's pretty much a sea of black. My sister Amy had noticed, that first summer she visited me, that I wear a lot of black. I hadn't realized it until she made that comment.

There is something about living in this city that makes the color black slowly start to take over. At first, it's totally subconscious. I had no idea it was happening. But then, when I did realize it, I liked it.

Black is so versatile. It makes you look thin. Also, black doesn't show dirt. I can't remember how many times I have put on some khakis, only to notice when I get to my destination that I have a mysterious black spot on my pant leg or my ass. I've made fruitless attempts at wearing lighter colors, but I just gave up. Now I pretty much wear black.

Okay, these black pants will do. Pulling them off the hanger, I casually peek at the waist label to see what size they are, even though I know they have a thirty-one-inch waist. I slide them on, zip them up, and fasten the button. *Yeah, they're too big in the waist.* I find this both gratifying and annoying. I realize I will need to buy new pants soon, but these will do for tonight.

Now I just have to figure out what shirt to wear. I reach down to the shelves at the bottom of my closet and grab the luxuriously soft, black cashmere sweater I got for Christmas. This will be perfect. It hangs down right below my waist, so it will hide the fact that these pants are too big.

After the sweater is adjusted, I bend down to put on my standard black dress shoes, thus completing my Gay Johnny Cash look.

After several minutes of peering into the bathroom mirror, intently inspecting my face, I'm relieved that there are no noticeable blemishes. I'm almost twenty-five now. It would be so nice if I didn't have to worry about zits anymore. I never thought I would be dealing with acne at this age.

I know I'd better put on some powder before I do my hair. Yes, I'm gay and insecure enough to believe I need face powder to smooth out my complexion. I justify this by telling myself that my face does get shiny, and the powder really does tone everything down. I'm hoping that no one really notices it. At least, I've never had anyone say anything to me about it. The powder makes me feel more comfortable. Sabrina was kind enough to buy it for me at Macy's. But now Sabrina is gone, and I have no idea what I'm going to do when I need to buy more.

The last thing I tackle is my hair. I'm growing it out, which is driving me nuts, but I think it will look good longer. Every guy, gay or straight, in this city seems to be sporting that ultra-short cut with the flip in the front—the kind that reminds me of that scene with Cameron Diaz from the movie *There's Something About Mary*. So I'm more than willing to grow my hair out, to be somewhat different from the pack.

I grab the hair gel and squeeze a generous amount into my hand, then violently run my hands through my hair in different directions, trying to create texture. Several more minutes pass. I have to finally admit that my hair is as good as it's going to get, so I wash my hands.

My hair and I have an interesting relationship. I have some grand idea of how it should look, but it never seems to want to cooperate with me. I have obsessed about how my hair looks for my whole life, so much that I never wear hats of any kind, ever. I give my hair the power to totally ruin my day or, on those rare occasions when I think it looks great, to uplift my mood. Then I have to tell myself not to get too happy, because I know my hair won't always look that good.

I'm so fixated on my hair that I even style it before bed. It's crazy, I know, but I keep obsessing about it. I guess obsessing about my hair affords me little time to worry about other things that probably need more of my attention. Plus, this is a freakin' Valentine's Day party I'm getting ready for, and I'm nervous.

It's Saturday night, two days after Valentine's Day, and I'm heading to the depths of some random town in New Jersey to a party—a party with only gay men. Yeah, I'm nervous and somewhat sad. I'm single and would love not to be, so the prospect of meeting a guy tonight is a bit nerve-wracking. And the prospect of *not* meeting a guy a bit depressing. Plus, I'm just nervous in general in social settings where I don't know everyone. At least I'll be going with several friends.

Leaning out the bathroom door, I notice the clock on the wall. *Damn! I'd better get a move on.* I have to meet the guys at the Hoboken train station soon. I turn around in my tiny bathroom, pee, and turn back around to wash my hands one last time. This bathroom is so small that I can do all of this without changing my stance. In fact, it's so small that when I sit on the toilet, I have to sit up as straight as possible so my knees won't hit the sink. And forget about closing the door, which only makes the bathroom seem smaller. I think airplanes have bigger bathrooms than mine.

Checking myself in the mirror again, I smile to reassure myself that I'm going to have a good time tonight. Then I grab my coat and walk down the hall to the front door. Of course, I have to stop in front of the hall mirrors to check myself one last time. I have to make sure I look okay after I put on my coat—a black coat, of course. Nothing has really changed since I checked myself in the bathroom mirror moments earlier. I'm not sure if that's a good thing or a bad thing. *Time to go.*

Out on the street, I get into my quick stride, grateful that the streets are not too crowded and there is no significant wind. I love walking, but I hate being outside when it's windy. Again, it's a hair thing. I spend so much time trying to get my hair to look good, and if I have to walk in the wind, I end up looking like one of those troll dolls with the crazy frizzy hair by the time I get to wherever I'm going. I figure this is God's way of telling me to lighten up. I don't think it's funny.

I know that I really need to just let it go and accept how I look. But not tonight. I have worked too hard at looking good. By all accounts, when I get to this party, I should still look good.

I meet Mike and Peter at the train station, and we only have to wait a few more minutes before Andy shows up in his parents' car. Andy grew up a few minutes away from here, and he was nice enough to offer to drive us. I'm still not sure what town we are even going to. I'm just along for the ride.

About forty-five minutes later, we are pulling up at the address of the party. It's a cute historical row house. Pat, the drag-queen host of the party, lives on the top floor. We make our way up the stairs and knock. Pat opens the door and, surprisingly, he's in street clothes tonight without make-up. At about six-foot-four and more than two hundred and fifty pounds, Pat is striking in a gown and full, glittery make-up as his alter-ego, All Beef Patty. But tonight, he's just one of the guys.

As we make our way in, we are greeted with low lights, which is a must for any gay men's gathering. Lighting is essential, and let's face it, everyone looks better and hotter in low lighting. We are among the first to arrive. I recognize a couple of the faces already here. Some dance music is playing softly in the background, which I know will change as the night progresses. It's not a party until Tina or Whitney are being blasted for all the neighbors to hear.

I feel tense until I notice the table at the back of the apartment: the booze table, my favorite destination at any party, is fully stocked. Since I'm one of the early birds, I can have anything I want. I make small talk for a couple of minutes and then make a beeline for that table.

I've promised myself not to drink too much tonight. I'm working on being good and not getting drunk. I broke this rule already, two weekends earlier, when I got smashed after Mark's hockey game— but justifiably so. That night, I was surrounded by gorgeous, gay, ice hockey players at a small bar in the village that has probably the most stunning bartender I have ever laid my eyes on. His name, of course, is Gabriel—like the angel that he is.

Tonight, I decide I can do better. I won't go overboard. I just need a little something to take the edge off and help me relax so I won't feel so self-conscious. Ah yes, there it is, Kettle One Vodka. The best.

I scan the table; the only cups available are those large, red, Solo plastic cups. *Works for me.* I grab one and pour in the vodka, stopping when the cup is about half filled. Then I add a splash of cranberry juice. *Now this is a drink!* I turn back around and scan the room, which has begun to fill up with guys. I don't know many people here, but that's cool. I'll just stick to those that I do know.

After several sips of my drink, my stomach starts to rumble. Yeah, I didn't eat lunch and barely had breakfast. I notice another table on the other end of the room with some food. Since I don't want to keep drinking on an empty stomach, I decide to get something to eat.

There are more people at the food table. I grab some crackers and cheese. They taste good, but I don't eat much. I feel awkward just standing there, eating. It makes me feel like a pig. *Okay, now it's time to mingle.* I take a few more sips of my drink and head off in the direction of some guys that I know. I stand there in the small group and listen some, and when appropriate, I add something to the conversation. Not much, though …

And that's the last thing I really remember from the party.

BEEEEP … BEEEEP … BEEEEP … BEEEEP! *Oh my God, what the fuck! That sound has got to stop.*

I open my eyes slowly and roll over in bed, slamming my fist onto the alarm clock. The freight train of sound stops. It's 9:30. It must be Sunday. Time to get up for church. *Yeah, right, like that's going to happen.*

Suddenly, it's as if I am watching a spectacular car crash in slow motion. My brain starts to suddenly get some violent messages. Pain, nausea, pain, nausea! My head, my arm, my stomach. My whole fucking body! *I'm dying, I must be dying.* This is crazy. I can't move! It just hurts too much. *What the hell happened?*

I close my eyes again, hoping that this is a dream and I can drift back to sleep. But it's no dream, and my body will have none of it. My brain is now at full alert, getting messages from every cell of my body, messages that are urgent and won't let up. My brain won't let me escape in sleep. *Shit!* I'm hung over, and from the signals my body is screaming at me, I'm in for a long recovery.

I lie still in bed for what feels like hours, trying to stay sane as the waves of pain and nausea crash over me with more force than I've ever experienced. It is unsettling. It's almost more than I can take. I don't do well with pain, and even less so with nausea. I don't like to puke, but at this point, I would welcome it.

As I become more conscious, I notice an unpleasant smell that's all too familiar. Vomit. Yeah, it's puke, but where is it coming from? Slowly, I venture in an upwards direction. *Oh God, this is not fun.*

I somehow manage to prop my torso up against my headboard. My eyes open slowly and start to focus on what's in front of me and the source of the smell. *Yeah, I've done it again.* Vomit is all over my bedspread and—I notice as I look to my left—all over my pillows.

I'm instantly taken back to my freshman year in college, waking up after my first night of hard partying in the dorm. At that time, I had a roommate and I slept on the top bunk. I had somehow managed to puke all over my bed, on the foot of the bed, and onto the floor.

That was my first black-out, the first of too many to count. That was also the night I had proclaimed my homosexuality and my love of Elton John to everyone within earshot—not that I remembered any of this. It was a very liberal college, and everyone thought it was hilarious. Everyone but me.

After that, I had never vomited on myself again. Until now. As I'm tripping down memory lane, my hand makes it way up to my throbbing head. *Nice, I have vomit in my hair as well. Is this what they call rock bottom?*

Now that I'm more awake, my body seems to be in more pain. I lean forward and start to roll up my bedspread. I was able to wash the puke out that time in college, but since I don't have access to a washer and dryer now, I'll just throw it in the garbage. I will have to buy all new bedding.

As I'm gathering up the foul-smelling bedding, I realize my right forearm is killing me. When I look down at it, I'm met with what appears to be the work of Freddy Krueger. My arm is red, bloody, and full of slashes. Twelve slashes to be exact. *What the hell! Surely, I didn't do this again!*

Two years earlier, drunk and home alone, I had taken a serrated kitchen knife and made small slashes on my right forearm. I don't know why I did that, but for some reason, it felt good—even though I was crying the whole time. The next day, when I realized what I'd done, it scared me. I had vowed never to cut myself again. I explained it away as being a drunken rant and decided I was okay. Now here I am, being faced with it again.

Flashes of the previous night snap me back into the present. *The Cointreau bottle that I've had on my kitchen counter for months, left over from my quest to make the perfect Cosmo. Months-old orange juice. My lava lamp sitting on the ledge of the half-wall that separates the kitchen from the living room. The serrated knife. Me sitting on the kitchen floor.*

I hate flashbacks. A sinking feeling starts to overcome me, making the nausea even worse. I don't want to get out of bed to see what other surprises await me.

The gravity of what has happened is slowly starting to dawn on me. The vomit, the self-mutilation, both physically and emotionally. If this isn't rock bottom, then I hope I never hit it.

Slowly, I move my legs to the end of the bed and try to push myself up. My body doesn't agree with my intended path and makes a strong case for me to drop back into bed. I resist. I move forward and shuffle, like an invalid, into the hallway. I cautiously turn right and look into my kitchen.

Shattered on the kitchen tile are the remains of my lava lamp. The red goo that used to bubble inside is clumped next to it. The Cointreau bottle, with the cap off, is turned over. Next to it is the small, serrated knife that I used in a pathetic attempt to dull my inner turmoil.

My stomach starts the heaving motion that I know means it's about to present me with a little present. I turn and rush into the bathroom as fast as I can—which, given my state, is damned slow. I kneel down on the tile and lean my head into the toilet. *Been here plenty of times. Know what to expect.*

I relax as best I can with the expectation that the nausea is about to be relieved. Several moments pass and … nothing. No dry heave, no spit, nothing. Nothing comes up. *Great.* I feel just as bad as before, and now I have to stand up, which isn't going to be fun. As I push myself up, my head throbs in displeasure. I can't believe I did this to myself.

Well, I guess there is no time like the present to start cleaning up my mess. As I try to mop up the kitchen mess, I'm surprised that the insides of the lava lamp are so oily. I realize I have never really thought about what's inside one of those. It proves easier to clean up than I had anticipated, but it still takes a lot of paper towels. I also ruin a large bath towel in the process.

Bagging the bedding helps with the smell. Now that I'm done cleaning, or at least done with what I'm capable of doing, I sit still in my Ikea chair—the one that rocks a bit when you lean into it. I love this chair. It's so comfortable—but not today. My body is still screaming at me and my stomach won't cooperate by puking everything up. I'm afraid it has already emptied all of its contents and I'm going to have to wait this out. *God, I hope I feel better soon.*

The best I can manage is to sit in the chair, quietly, without moving. I'm only wearing my underwear. I'm not hot and I'm not cold. I just sit. Any movement, especially of my head, unleashes waves of discomfort, which I do my best to avoid. Even sitting and not moving, I'm in such pain that I can see how people in chronic pain kill themselves. I couldn't take this if I knew it had no end.

RING … RING … RING … RING. *Oh God, stop that!* My cell phone angers every cell in my body. For some reason, my cell phone is on the book shelf, right next to where I am sitting. I lean over and slowly answer it.

"Hello," I whisper. My voice startles me with its gravelly, low tone.

"Hoyt, how the hell are you?" Mike asks, too loudly.

"Oh God, Mike, I'm dying," I groan. I can hear Mike laughing. I'm glad someone finds this funny.

"Hoyt, I'm just calling to make sure you made it home okay last night," he says between laughs.

"Apparently I did. What happened?" I ask, but I'm not totally sure I want to know.

"Hoyt, you were out of control!" he says with amusement. "You drank so much … and then on the train home"—he pauses to laugh— "oh damn, you were hilarious! On the train, you grabbed the top of the luggage rack above the seats and started hanging from them like a monkey, and then you threw your legs up in the air, doing some sort of weird gymnastics trick. It was impressive."

Mike seems to be getting too much enjoyment out of telling me all of this. "Oh, and get this, when the conductor came by to get our tickets, you were doing all this, and then said you wanted to have sex with him. He just looked at us. I thought we were going to get thrown off!"

Great, I can no longer ride N.J. Transit.

"It was nuts," Mike finishes, "but you were entertaining."

Entertaining. I've heard that before. Unfortunately, when I have, it always seems to be regarding some event that I don't totally recall, because I drank too much. I seem to be entertaining when I drink heavily. Once a friend remarked at a party that was too quiet that, "We should give Hoyt some drinks. That'll liven things up!" I guess I'm not fun enough when I'm sober.

The conversation doesn't last much longer because I can't stand the pain. I thank Mike for calling and hang up. Now I know what happened, or at least the abridged version of what happened. I'm not sure I can handle the detailed version.

The thing that astounds me is that my friends let me walk home alone from the train station. I have no recollection of walking home. It's amazing I didn't get into trouble or walk into a bar for a few more drinks.

Shuddering, I try to stop the feeling that easily engulfs me: shame. I hate myself for acting this way. I feel totally embarrassed. I can't tell now which hurts more, my body or my soul. This is the worst it has ever been. I know I need to stop. *This has to stop now. I can do this.* I've been losing weight and I decide that, if I put my mind to this, I can clean up my act and start acting more mature.

Four days later, I have new bedding on the bed and I've fully recovered—at least physically.

6

"You seem agitated."

No shit, Sherlock. Nothing gets by you. Okay, be nice. "Yeah, I guess you could say that," I say as sincerely as I can.

I like this guy, but he's just so damned calm, sitting there in his chair with his notepad in his lap. I just want him to smile, scream, curse, or something. Show some kind of "normal" emotion. But him being the professional and me being the patient, I guess the "normal" emotions are what I'm supposed to be getting in touch with right now.

He wears that stock therapist expression that conveys compassion and distance at the same time. I don't know whether he's interested or just the counting minutes until our time is up. After several sessions, I still haven't figured out how he knows when time is up, since the clock is on the wall behind him. He must look at his wristwatch when I break eye contact, which is frequently.

This is my first time in therapy with a gay counselor—or social worker, to be precise. I thought when I did my research on this guy that he would be older and not that attractive. Before I made my first appointment, I Googled him and found a picture in which he seemed to be older and not my type. Because the last thing I wanted was to be in therapy with some hot shrink.

Well, that plan didn't work out. My first time meeting him stopped me dead in my tracks. He's not only hot, but he's not a whole lot older than I am. After that first meeting, I re-Googled him and found that photo. Upon closer examination, I realized the photo had been taken outside with the sun shining on him, which for some reason made him look older.

Because I want to be mature about this, I have decided to give Jordan a chance and see where this goes. Lord knows I need someone to talk to. Hopefully, with him being gay and having experience treating gay guys, he will push me in the areas that I need to grow. Today he is proving more than capable in doing so.

He's still just looking at me. He doesn't talk much, nor does he probe with many questions. This silence is annoying. I guess I'd better elaborate. *Damn, he's good.*

"My mom sent me a box of Godiva chocolates for my birthday," I tell him. "I got them in the mail just as I was leaving to come here tonight." I shift my position on the sofa where I'm sitting, not lying down. Lying on a shrink's couch would be too bizarre even for me.

"Okay," he responds quietly.

Okay? That's all he has to say? More silence. I feel him just looking at me. I'm not returning the favor. *Fine, I will keep going.* "The candy annoyed me, for some reason. I took the box and started walking to the PATH station. I didn't leave it in my place. The more I walked, the more nervous and anxious I got."

As I describe this, I suddenly feel that anxiety invading my body again. "Before I went down into the station, I opened the box and ate one truffle. Then I tossed the rest into a garbage can. I was *pissed*," I add forcefully.

"Why?"

"I don't know." *Yes, I do. I just don't want to go there.* Long pause. *I need to go there.*

"I'm mad my mom sent them to me. I didn't want them, and I didn't want to eat them. I ... I just felt out of control. Like out of the blue, this damned temptation just flew in my face, and I don't need that right now. I don't want to be eating anything like that. It's going to mess me up. And of course, now I feel guilty because I threw out a whole box of Godiva truffles."

My monologue over, I shift my gaze from the wall behind Jordan to my left, where I can gaze out the window. Feeling vulnerable, I quickly add, "I just felt out of control."

More silence, which allows the weight of my words and emotions more time to further penetrate the wall I've successfully built around myself.

"You know, you didn't have to eat those," he says with what sounds like genuine compassion in his voice.

"Yes, I know," I quietly agree, still looking out the window.

"You also know it's okay to have thrown them out. They were a gift, and you could choose to do with them whatever you want."

"Yes, I know. That makes sense." *It really does.*

Feeling a bit more reassured, I shift my gaze back to Jordan, making eye contact for the first time in several minutes. The understanding and compassion in his eyes startle me a bit. I'm not sure I like feeling understood. If I'm able to reason all of this away and feel "good," then what will be left to obsess about?

More time passes. I start talking about guilt and the burden I place on myself regarding how I should act and what I should be doing. The emotions that well up are manageable, and we make eye contact several more times. As I spend more time doing this, I feel less self-conscious around Jordan—which is amazing, considering he now knows more intimate details about me than anyone on the planet.

After another long pause, he breaks the silence. "How's the eating?" he asks, changing the subject to something that instantly causes my body to stiffen.

"Okay," I say tersely as I throw my right leg over my left and angle my torso away from him in some feeble, subconscious attempt to let him know that this line of questioning is not welcome.

Being neither dumb nor blind, he takes this as his clue to push forward. "What's a typical day like, in terms of food?"

Ugh, I don't really care what a typical day is like! But I know I should be nice and cooperate. After all, I am paying for this.

"You want to know what I eat?" I ask. I make my voice as naïve as possible, trying to buy some time. I'm hoping that he won't push me too hard to reveal details.

"Yes. Like for breakfast, lunch, and dinner. Walk me through the day," he says clearly, without a tinge of exasperation. I could understand if he was exasperated, because I'm certain he can spot my stalling tactics a mile away.

"Umm, well, I have breakfast at work," I say. "It's usually a blueberry muffin, non-fat yogurt—raspberry flavor—and a large, hot tea." My speech slowly starts to speed up, as though I'm trying to outrun the anxiety that is slowly rising up from the soles of my feet and ruthlessly invading my body, without my consent.

"Lunch some days is a salad and a large Diet Pepsi from this place across this street. And some days now it's just the Diet Pepsi. And I don't eat dinner. I haven't been eating dinner for several years. On the weekends, it's different." I exhale deeply, having recounted all of this in record time. It's as if by getting it out fast, I can't really hear or process what I'm saying.

I don't like talking about food. It makes me nervous. And when I have to talk about what I eat, it always sounds like way too much. *I need to cut back. I should just have that Diet Pepsi every day for lunch. No more salads during the week.*

My body is now completely consumed with anxiety and slowly shaking. My right leg is still crossed over my left, and I shake it in hopes of funneling the anxious energy from my body into one spot. I am hoping Jordan can't tell what's happening. I've dealt with this shaking thing most of my life. By now, I'm pretty adept at covering it up.

I glance over in Jordan's direction and see that his expression has changed. He seems to be deep in thought, although I don't think what I just said was all that interesting. I don't feel the need to break this silence this time. He does.

"How do you feel about what you just said?"

Damn, he just called me out! I realize I'm not as good an actor as I thought. *Good-bye Oscar.*

"Uncomfortable," I say matter-of-factly. As if either of us had no clue. "I don't like talking about it, really." My honesty catches me off guard.

"How so?" He's good at open-ended questions that I can't answer in just one or two words.

"I don't know. I guess it just feels … personal. Like, why talk about food? And I don't like the *sound* of what I'm eating, in terms of … quantity. I don't like it." *Okay, happy now? You got it out of me!*

"You're thinner than you were when you first started coming here, three weeks ago."

I feel a big grin welling up inside me. I've felt this before, that time Tony mentioned my weight. It's nice to know it's noticeable. This fleeting moment of triumph passes and I'm suddenly feeling scared. I don't like the attention to my looks. I know I've lost weight. I could tell pretty soon after I stopped drinking. Totally cutting out all alcohol and not replacing those calories has accelerated my weight loss. It's been great and horrifying at the same time. I don't know what I'll do once I stop losing with such ease.

"Really?" I throw out another naïve comeback. Pathetic, I know.

"Yes. I'm concerned," he says. The compassion is clear in his voice.

"Okay." I don't know what to say to that. That's nice, but I never asked him to care that much.

Jordan shifts in his chair, leans back for a book on his desk, and then redirects his attention toward me. "Hoyt, there's something I want to talk to you about," he says tentatively.

"Okay." I have no clue what subject he is about to broach.

"Hoyt, this type of issue is somewhat new to me, so I've been doing some research. After our sessions thus far and after doing some reading, it's pretty clear to me that you're dealing with an eating disorder." His voice has more authority than I've heard up to this point. He looks up at me.

I meet his gaze with silence. I feel like I've been hit with cold water, which is odd, because what he just said isn't news to me. I'm not dumb. I know I've been obsessing about food and my weight, and I realize I have been nursing this uncontrollable urge to lose more and more weight. I know all of this, but I haven't been able to give a name to it, and neither has anyone else in my life—until now.

An eating disorder. I have an eating disorder. Don't only crazy girls get those? I'm remembering those overly dramatic Lifetime movies from the '80s featuring some young actress "dying to be thin." I think they talked to us about this in health class in eighth grade. But I never heard them mention guys could get this. *Huh, this is a weird feeling. I feel, I feel ... special?* I have something that's not common. I have something that's all my own. I own this.

Snapping me out of my internal monologue, Jordan ventures on. "After hearing you talk about what you're doing, I read the definitions for anorexia and bulimia in the DSM here. I think right now you fall in the N.O.S. category—'Not Otherwise Specified.' It basically means you have characteristics of both disorders, but not enough of either to clearly be classified."

He rambles on and then starts to read to me what the *Diagnostic and Statistical Manual of Mental Disorders* has to say about eating disorders. This isn't my first time in therapy, so I have a cursory knowledge of this bible for the mental health professional. I start zoning out. All I can think about is that I'm not classified. I'm not anorexic and I'm not bulimic. I'm neither. *What the fuck! I'm a freak.*

This sucks. I feel like I'm not good enough to be classified. I don't want to be bulimic. Those people binge and purge. That's gross. I hate puking. Plus, that's just a lack of self-control. It's pathetic! I want to be anorexic if I have to have this thing. *Great, I can't even do that right. Well we'll see.* I'm determined to be good at something. I decide I can do this.

Jordan's done and he's just sitting there looking at me. I feel like he's expecting some emotional outburst from me, as if I should be crying uncontrollably and professing my desire to "live." *Not gonna happen, mister. I couldn't care less right now. I'm just pissed.*

After some awkward silence, we talk more about the next steps to take. I'm on autopilot at this point. It's been an intense session for me, and I'm ready to leave. I pull out my calendar and we schedule another appointment for the following week. I know these sessions are good for me, but right now I just want to get out of here and walk.

I have a lot of walking to do to get home, and the walk helps to burn off more anxious energy. It also provides time for my mind to start obsessing about what just happened. I'm surprisingly mad about the lack of an anorexia diagnosis. Up until this session, I wasn't willing to go there. But now that we have broached the eating disorder topic, I have an unexpected attachment to a label. And now that my therapist has denied me this label, I want it even more.

I want to be anorexic. I want to lose so much weight that I'm the best fucking anorexic that he, or anyone else, has ever seen!

When I get to my apartment, I head to the kitchen, grab a black marker, and cross off another day on the calendar hanging on the wall. All those black x's, twenty-six and counting, are impressive. I feel proud of them. Every "x" represents a day without alcohol. This has proven a lot easier than I ever imagined. I really don't have any desire to drink. Of course, part of my drive to stay sober now is fueled by my desire to lose weight. The thought of drinking booze again and gaining weight is more than I can handle right now.

I get undressed and get ready for bed. No dinner for me tonight, just sleep, which proves elusive. Tossing and turning, my ego really doesn't want to let go of the fact that I've been denied an eating disorder label. I finally placate myself by promising to do some Googling on eating disorders, to see what ideas I can get. This works—for now.

7

It should be somewhere around … ahh, here it is. I walk down three small steps and open the door. Once inside, I'm met with some low-watt lighting and I almost immediately bump into the front counter.

This is a tiny shop. The small bell above the door frame heralds my arrival a second time when I close the door. I notice what seem like endless garments hanging on almost every square inch of wall space. Within a few seconds of entering, a tall, thin man walks up behind the counter.

"I'm here to get some suit pants tailored," I say as I raise my hand, showing off the pants draped over my right arm. "They're too big in the waist." I say this quickly, with a bit of uneasiness in my voice.

"Okay. Why don't you come back here and try them on for me?" the tailor says quietly as he turns around and starts walking toward the rear of the shop. Taking this as my cue to follow him, I pass through the opening in the counter. I walk through an archway of clothes hanging from the ceiling and enter into the back of the shop where there is a small, raised platform in front of a three-way mirror.

"You can change in there," the tailor says as he points to a small doorway to my right. I enter and close the door. It's a tiny room with no seat or mirror, just a small hook on the back of the door. I quickly change out of my jeans and into the pants. I realize that I can slide them on and off without having to unbutton them now.

I open the door slowly, walk out, and step up onto the platform. For some reason, I'm nervous. I don't like being the center of attention. I feel like I've done something wrong, or like I'm trying to hide something.

"I just need the waist taken in," I say to break the silence. By this time, the tailor has his hand on the waist of the pants and is tugging on them to the point that I'm jolting backwards. I try to hold my stance by leaning forward.

"What size are they?" he inquires.

"Thirty-two-inch waist," I reply.

He makes a small grunt, then leans down and starts making marks on the pant legs. This is the first time I've had this done, and all I can think about is whether he's going to ask me which way I hang. The scene from *Friends* where Joey goes to the tailor and gets felt up keeps playing over and over in my mind. It was funny watching it on TV, but I hope this guy really doesn't need to know that bit of personal information. Then again, I think I may be more embarrassed by not knowing the answer to that question. Who thinks about such things? I'm gay, but not that gay.

"You're very thin. And these pants are very big on you. I have to take these in a lot, and I don't know how they will turn out," he says with a furrowed brow, almost as if he's mentally deconstructing the pants in his mind. "I can't rebuild these. I can take them in," he says while tugging again on the waist, "but it may get bunched up here in the back once I do that."

Not really understanding what he is trying to explain, my mind now is totally fixated on his first comment to me: YOU'RE VERY THIN. *Wow, I'm thin and he has to take these in a lot. A Size 32 is way too big for me now. Awesome! I don't care, take them in as much as you have to. It's all good with me.*

"It's good. I'm okay with that," I reassure him. I just need them fixed so I can wear them again. He nods, somewhat reluctantly.

After changing back into my jeans, he gets my information and says I can come back in about a week to pick them up. I take my ticket, thank him, and leave.

As I walk back home, I feel almost like I'm floating. I'm excited to be getting some pants that will finally fit me well, and I'm even more thrilled to have been called "thin." I feel good right now. I feel validated.

RING … RING … RING. I unlock my door as fast as I can and dash into my apartment, grabbing the phone before checking the caller ID. Sometimes I feel like Pavlov's dog when it comes to a ringing phone. It's like I have to answer it just to get the annoying sound to stop. I hate talking on the phone, but as if in a trance, I answer it.

"Hello," I answer, gasping to catch my breath.

"Hey, Jeff," the callers exclaims enthusiastically. There's a slight echo in the background. It's my parents, and I'm on speakerphone. *Great.* I love them, but I hate it when they decide to call and put me on speakerphone. But they are old school and they mean well, so I'll suck it up.

"Hey, how are you guys?" I ask. I haven't seen them in a while. I know it's been tough on them since 9/11 with me living so far away. I'm sure they have some horrible images in their mind about what I've been through and how I'm coping. But being the good little boy that I am, I don't talk about it with them. I have never really elaborated on what I've been through or how I'm actually doing. I just put on a brave front. I basically give them what I think they want. Reassuring people makes me feel more comfortable.

"We're good," they say in unison. It's cute that, after more than thirty years together, they not only think alike, they also talk alike. It's almost too cute. I find my mind wandering, wondering if I will ever find that kind of relationship with a guy. Settling down with a guy and making a life together would be great. I just don't know it will ever happen or that it will ever be as rewarding as what my parents have.

"How are you?" they ask.

"I'm good. Just hanging out. Not much going on. Have you talked to Amy lately?" Now that my older sister knows about my eating disorder, I'm a bit worried that she has told my parents. We're a close family, and usually secrets don't last very long with this bunch.

"I talked to her a few days ago. She seems to be doing well. Staying busy with the boys and nursing school," my mom says. *Ugh, what else did she say?* My mom's voice sounds relaxed and friendly. I imagine she would sound more tense or concerned if Amy had told her anything was wrong with me. I think I may be in the clear.

We spend the next several minutes chit-chatting about my siblings, the family dog, and news from Greensboro that they feel I need to know. All the while, I'm trying my best not to get annoyed that I'm listening to all of this in a wind tunnel. I wish someone would just pick up the damned receiver.

Then my mom asks what seems to be an innocent enough question: "What did you do today?"

"Not much. I just got back from the tailor. I needed to get those new suit pants taken in some."

"Oh, you got a new suit?" my dad asks.

"Yeah. I got this email the other week at work saying we could get a big discount if we bought a new suit from this company. So I just went online and bought a basic black suit. It was a great deal. I had it shipped to me. But the pants are too big in the waist."

"What size did you get?" my mom inquires.

"The usual, 42R and thirty-two-inch waist," I say, as nonchalantly as I can.

"And you have to get them taken in?" she asks, more loudly now. I assume she is now leaning towards the phone.

"Yeah, they are too big. The tailor said he has to take them in a good bit, but it's cool. It's not going to cost much."

"How much does he have to take them in?"

"I don't know. I didn't ask. I just tried them on."

LONG, AWKWARD PAUSE.

Okay, what did I say wrong? I don't like how the energy has suddenly changed.

"Uhh, Jeff, have you lost weight?" my mom asks, tentatively breaking the silence.

I take a deep breath. "Yeah, some I guess," I say, trying to sound as uninterested as possible.

LONG, AWKWARD PAUSE.

Shit! Just stay calm. It's cool. We are not going into this right now.

"How much weight?" she asks with a slight crack in her voice. She sounds almost scared.

"I don't know, Mom. Just some." I feel more annoyed now.

SILENCE.

I refuse to add any more to this subject. I'm keeping my mouth shut.

Breaking the silence again, my mom quietly asks—almost as if she doesn't want to know the answer—"Jeff, do you have a problem?"

"What do you mean?" I'm going to make her work for this one. I'm not confirming anything.

"An eating disorder, Jeff. Do you have an eating disorder?"

Damn it! She's done it again. She's called me out on something I'm not ready to talk about yet. I wanted to be the one to tell them, not hear them tell me. Either Amy told them or my mom is fucking psychic!

I meet her question with more silence. My friend, anxiety, is now completely consuming me. I don't feel well. I can feel the sweat starting to bead up around my hairline. I feel out of control. I'm pissed. Not knowing how much time has passed, I exhale and decide to play nice and answer her question. "Yes. I do." *That's all you're getting out of me.*

I don't like this. It's just like six years ago when, at the end of my summer break after my freshman year in college, my parents took me into their bedroom one night and asked if I was gay. That was totally out of the clear blue! I was shocked and hadn't planned on telling them yet. I wasn't ready to face that with them. And even after a four-hour talk, during which they reassured me that I would not be disowned … to this day, I still wished that I had been in control and had been the one to tell them. I had wanted it to play out differently.

Now here I am again with another shameful secret, and here they are again, beating me to the punch.

"Are you okay?"

"Yeah, Dad, I'm fine. Listen, I don't want you two to worry. You know I'm seeing a really good counselor. I like him a lot and he's really good. We've been talking about all of this. I'm going to be okay," I tell them, although I don't believe a single word that is coming out of my mouth. I'm now numb and just reading my people-pleasing script. I just want this to be over with.

Time passes slowly. We talk and we talk. All on speakerphone. They act like the caring, concerned parents they are, and emphatically deny that Amy told them anything. I act like the loving, appreciative son that I fear I'm not. I reassure them in every way I know how, and they do the same. The game we play feels safe. I know how to play this game.

After this back and forth, they let me know they will be in the city in late April for work and they look forward to seeing me. Even after this conversation, I look forward to seeing them. I tell them that I will think of some fun stuff for us to do.

The conversation ends and I hang up the phone, but I feel physically exhausted. Emotionally, I have no clue. These days, it seems too easy to identify what my body is trying to tell me. My emotions remain elusive.

I hate feeling my body. I hate the signals it keeps sending me. So I do what I do best: I numb out. I stretch out on the sofa, turn on the TV, and start channel surfing.

8

"That was a really good sermon."

"Yeah it was," I say. "I'm amazed at how he never looks at any notes. It sounds like he's just having a relaxed conversation. And his messages aren't just Bible-thumping, either. There's always something that I feel I can apply to my life."

"I totally agree."

Peter and I are critiquing the minister, Dr. Arthur Caliandro, as we walk down the front steps of Marble Collegiate Church into the bright sunshine of a beautiful April Sunday in New York.

I saw an ad in a subway car for this church, and I've been thankful every Sunday since then that I decided to attend. It's a wonderful church, and even more so because it's accepting and open about the gay issue. I'll never forget sitting there one Sunday with Peter and hearing Dr. Caliandro say the word "gay" in reference to a church member. His tone wasn't negative at all. I was shocked, and even more shocked as he went on to talk about his support for GLBT issues. I almost fell out of the pew.

I had never been in a church that was as open as this. I'd never heard a minister who was probably the age of my grandfather speak so lovingly about this issue. It was exhilarating. That's the reason Peter and I have been getting up at nine on Sunday mornings—because

Lord knows, most gay guys are out partying on Saturday nights and they're in no shape to get up that early.

Of course, now that I'm sober, I find myself getting up a lot earlier than I used to. It's weird having so much time on my hands. I never realized how much I slept on the weekends.

Peter and I make our way to the subway. Now that it's noon, most of our friends are willing to meet us for brunch—for church, no, but for brunch with free-flowing mimosas, yes. As we make small talk on the train and check out the hot guys within view, my mind starts its usual obsessive dialogue about food. It's something I have become too familiar with.

This brunch routine has been in place for several months now. A while back, we found a cute little restaurant in the village that serves a cheap brunch and even cheaper mimosas. I loved that place several months ago when I was drinking and eating more, but now, not so much. Now that I don't drink, I'm not having as much fun. Everyone else I know drinks a fair amount, and we laugh a lot, but all I do is think about what I'm eating, what I don't need to be eating, and when I can leave and go home.

So today, it's going to be an omelet. Just an omelet. No cheese. Maybe some bell peppers, because those don't really have any calories. Okay, an omelet with bell peppers. And a Diet Coke. Gotta have that caffeine, and the fizz helps fill up my gut as well. I'm drinking plenty of Diet Coke these days. *Okay I can do this. It will be fun. I need to socialize some.*

To be honest, though, today I can't wait to get this brunch session over with. I've made up my mind that, after brunch, I'm going to buy a scale. How can I measure my success if I can't tell how much I weigh? I'm going to stop off at Bed Bath and Boyfriend—or at least it would be that, if I had a boyfriend—and pick one up.

The Bed Bath and Beyond in the village is a fun place to window shop, but I hate being in there with so many gay guys and their significant others. I feel like I just want to yell at them to get a room and stop flaunting their relationship in everyone's faces. Not that I'm bitter or anything. I'm excited. It will be nice to finally have a scale.

All of this internal dialogue has kept me busy and, before I know it, we are at the restaurant. Several of our friends are already sitting down at a table, so Peter and I join them. Brunch goes well. Everyone seems to have a good time talking, laughing, drinking, and eating. I play along as best as I can. But as usual, my mind keeps me isolated with its obsessions.

I feel I do a good job of faking it. Even though most of these guys now know what I'm dealing with, it hasn't changed anything. Everyone still acts the same around me, and no one has really talked about it.

I'm not sure how I feel about that. Sometimes I'm fine, and sometimes I'm pissed off. I know it makes me feel more isolated, which allows me to retreat more easily into my head.

As time passes and brunch is winding down, I start to feel more anxious. Usually, at this point, I'm feeling calmer, because I know this food and booze-centered event is coming to an end. But not today. Today, I'm excited and anxious because I know what I'm going to do next.

Brunch finally ends and I say my good-byes. I turn down an invitation to hang out some more with Peter and Mike. This may be their way of extending themselves in light of what they know I'm dealing with, but I choose to ignore that fact. I do what I do so well these days. I blow them off.

Bed Bath and Beyond is within walking distance. I enjoy walking, especially when it's so nice out. I'm there within fifteen minutes. Almost floating, I saunter inside.

Suddenly, my heart starts beating faster. I feel like I'm about to commit a crime, as if I'm doing something wrong. I haven't been in this store in a while, so I'm not sure where the scales are located. I just start walking.

Even though I'm on a mission, I can't help but notice a couple of guys I find attractive. I have two eyes and I use them as much as possible. Thank God, today there isn't much eye candy to look at in here.

After several minutes, I find the scales. They all look so pretty sitting there on display. *Gosh, I don't know what kind I want. No, don't think I'll be paying that much for that sleek, modern-looking glass one. I just need it to tell me my weight, nothing else.*

My heart is pounding as I start pacing back and forth in front of the scales. The option of buying one that can tell me my percentage of body fat makes me even more anxious. Deep inside, I seem to know that if I go down that rabbit hole, I'll go crazy even faster. *I just need to know my weight, nothing else.*

So I quell that anxiety by swearing not to spend very much money on a scale. *There's a nice one. It's silver, seems simple, and just does weight. Not too expensive, either.* I grab it and head to the check-out counter. *I must look ridiculous.* Here I am, just after church on a Sunday, buying a scale. Just a scale. Who the hell just buys a scale on a Sunday? I wonder if the check-out girl can tell I'm nervous.

I pay and get the hell out of there. I just want to get back to the privacy of my own home. I feel very self-conscious, although I'm excited at the same time. Soon, I'll know how much I weigh. I'm not sure what it will say back to me: 150? 140? I have no idea. I don't remember the last time I was on a scale.

The train ride back to Hoboken goes by in a blur. I just stand there holding onto the rail with my right hand and hugging the scale under my left armpit, fantasizing about seeing very low numbers displayed. And scared that the numbers I see won't be low enough.

I unlock my front door, rush inside, and slam and lock the door behind me. My heart is now in my throat. I feel like I'm doing something *dirty*. It's the feeling a kid gets when he buys his first adult magazine. It's excitement and shame at the same time.

I rip open the box and pull out the scale. It's beautiful. All silver. I pull off the clear plastic wrap covering the front, then turn it over and open the battery cage. *Damn, I hope I have batteries for this thing.* It takes three AAs. I yank the batteries from the stereo remote control and shove them into the scale. The front blinks zeros several times and then goes blank.

I want this right by my bed. I position it next to my nightstand and I stand there, just looking at it. *Wow. This is for real now.* Any minute now, I can just step on this and see what I weigh. I'm not sure I want to know now. Not knowing has its advantages. I know I'm losing weight, but what if I stop losing? What then?

Suck it up! Just do this. Okay. Naked. I need to strip down to get an accurate reading. I take off all my clothes, including my underwear. I step in front of the scale and stop. Then I take a deep breath, step onto it, and look down. Several seconds pass. Nothing happens. I wait several more seconds. Still nothing. *What the hell!*

I figure I'd better glance at the booklet that came with the scale. I find it in a plastic sleeve in the box. *Oh, I have to tap it lightly first, let it flash zero, and then step on it.* That seems odd, but whatever. Okay, take two.

Throwing the booklet on the floor, I tap the top of the scale with my right foot. Zeros instantly flash a few times and then it goes blank. Guessing that's my cue, I step up and position my feet as close to center as I can. Exhaling, hoping that will shave a few ounces off my weight, I look down.

129. I weigh 129 pounds. I step off.

Wow, that's lower than I was expecting. That can't be right! I tap the top again. It flashes zero and then goes blank. I step up again.

It's still 129. *Huh. I guess that's right. That's pretty damned awesome!* I weigh so much less than I thought. I've lost at least fifteen to twenty pounds. *Holy shit. Just think how much more I can lose.*

My heart begins to pound faster as 129, 129, 129 is streaming through my mind like a ticker tape. I never thought I would get down that low. But I've got to go lower. I decide that 125 sounds nice. *Yeah, it does. I think I can go lower, though. I know I can. I have to go lower.* And I know this scale will help me. It will keep me honest.

The rest of the afternoon is spent avoiding the scale as much as possible. Excitement and fear are now all-consuming. I'm thrilled that I weigh less than I imagined, but scared to death that the scale will flash a number higher than I want. After getting dressed again, I spend the rest of the afternoon numbing out in front of the TV and trying not to think about that silver square in my bedroom, although I want to run to it every five minutes for validation. Before going to bed, I step on it one last time. Again, it flashes 129. It's a good number, but one that will need to go lower in the coming days.

That night, I toss and turn in bed, rolling over numbers in my head. It's all about numbers. The numbers of calories I can cut out, the number of steps I can walk in a day to burn calories, the number of diet sodas I can drink to fill me up, the number on that scale. I finally fall asleep, ignorant of the fact that I've just embraced a new kind of bondage—one that I will allow to dictate my every mood and define my self-worth.

9

Tap.
Step up.
Pause.
Look down.
128.
Step off.
Deep breath.
Tap.
Step up.
Pause.
Look down.
127.
Step off.
Strained, deep breath.
Tap.
Step up.
Pause.
Look down.
128.
Step off.
Slightly relieved, deep breath.

*O*kay that's my three weigh-ins, now it's time to get in the shower. I turn around and head to the bathroom. The water is already running, and since I only weigh myself naked, I step into the shower, slightly annoyed. I've been doing this routine now for almost ten days, but I'm still not totally satisfied. I weigh myself three times before I get into the shower and then three more times after I get out. I have to force myself to stop at that many times. I'd never leave the house on time if I didn't.

But of course, because it's a cheap scale, every time I step on it I get a slightly different reading. This doesn't help my mood any. That's the reason I need to weigh myself six times every morning and six times every night. I have to ensure that the number on the scale is going in the right direction.

Since I've had the scale, the number has been going down. At first, it felt pretty good—not great, but good. Now, after several days of this, it's not enough. I want more. I want that number to be lower and lower every time I weigh myself. But life being what it is, that number is not lower every time. So in those moments of panic, when I'm convinced that I won't be able to keep losing, I try to talk myself down off the ledge I've willingly forced myself onto by remembering that the number has never gone up. Staying the same, for a short while, is okay. It's gaining weight that's not acceptable.

I step out of the shower, grab my towel, and thoroughly dry myself. I'm convinced that any extra moisture left on my body will be reflected by that number on the scale. I then throw the towel over my head and rub furiously, knowing that my hair is the biggest culprit in trapping excess moisture weight. When I feel satisfied with my dry job, I start to head back into my bedroom for the second half of my morning routine. But I suddenly feel this pressure in my lower abdomen.

I stop in the hallway and pause. *Hot damn, I have to go to the bathroom!* I turn around, walk back into the bathroom, and sit on the toilet. This is an unusual event for me these days. My bowels don't seem to move frequently anymore, and it's nice having it happen without me having to take anything. Also, after taking a dump, I should weigh less.

After finishing in the bathroom, I head into my bedroom, feeling a bit lighter and slightly excited. I know that anything and everything that I can get out of my body before I weigh myself will make a difference. I take a deep breath and start my ritual again: 127 glares back at me. Then 128. And finally, 127.

I take another deep breath. I'm not elated, but I'm not upset either. I'm numb, I think. It could have been worse, but at least the scale has validated a new low for me. 127. I can live with that, for now.

I get dressed and head out the door. I'm going to be bad today, skipping church and just meeting the guys for brunch. For some reason, someone suggested another place to eat. I've been there many times for dinner, but not for brunch. Not knowing what to expect in terms of their brunch menu makes me nervous. I don't like not being able to plan—or obsess—about what I'm going to eat. So to distract myself, I start to run down all of the things I'm doing right in terms of my weight loss.

I now pretty much just eat at work. I have the muffin, yogurt, and hot tea for breakfast. For lunch, I now just grab a large Diet Coke or Diet Pepsi and go sit by the Hudson River, looking at the yachts and watching the birds. I love doing that when the weather is nice. I skip dinner on week nights, and on those rare occasions I need something, I've taken a liking to rice cakes and hummus. I no longer drink alcohol and I pretty much have not replaced those calories.

On the weekends, my meals vary. I will eat lunch and dinner sometimes when I'm out with the guys. Sometimes it's just one meal. Sleeping has become harder. For some reason, my mind doesn't like to shut down, so I take Benadryl.

As proof of my weight-loss success, I note that I start to black out now if I stand up too quickly—which of course, I try to avoid. I can see almost every rib when I look in the mirror, without having to raise my arms to stretch my skin. My clothes are too big for me now;

I finally broke down and got some new black pants with a 28" waist, a size that surprised me.

And last but not least, there is that number on the scale. As of today, it stands at 127. My B.M.I. now clearly places me in the underweight, or "not normal," category. So I'm not like everybody else.

This internal checklist continues for a while as I make my way onto the PATH train and then hop off at my stop in the city. Once outside, I'm able to walk fast and my mind starts a quick transition from self-satisfaction to panic. It's great that I've done all of these things, but what happens when they stop working? I've got to be able to show something for my efforts.

I'm able to somewhat calm that fire by noting that I've spent countless hours on Google researching eating disorders. I'm amazed at what I've learned. One phrase keeps running through my head. It has proven very helpful when I feel like I'm going to slip and eat too much: "Nothing tastes as good as thin feels." How true that is! Even more surprising is that the website I got that little ditty from credits it to Weight Watchers. That's hilarious to me, given the fact that the only people that phrase will ever motivate are people like me, anorexics who will stop at nothing to lose weight.

It's ironic that many websites out there about eating disorders are trying to be helpful and provide information to those suffering from these ailments, or the loved ones of those suffering—but what they are really doing is providing me with great ideas and tricks about losing weight that I never knew about.

I had never heard of using Ipecac syrup until I found a site that had articles written by a woman who recovered from an eating disorder. She detailed her use of Ipecac. It sounded like a great tool to use when you need to get rid of some food.

Yes, I've lost some weight, but I'm not one to sit on my laurels. I have decided that after brunch today, on my way home, I'm going to stop at the pharmacy and buy some Ipecac. I figure it will be perfect timing. I can eat brunch and then use the Ipecac to get rid of it.

This plan seems to appease my mind for now, but my body isn't so sure. I choose to ignore my discomfort and focus on the present, enjoying the weather as I approach the restaurant.

I'm relieved to find several of the guys inside. There is no wait, so we are soon making our way to a table upstairs. We have a great view looking out the front window of the place. As nonchalantly as I can, I sit down and open my menu. I need time to read the menu options so I can choose the least destructive item. My goal is to get something that isn't too fattening or too tempting.

Eating safe foods keeps me on track. If I get something that tastes too good, there is the possibility I'll fall off the wagon and just keep eating like a gluttonous slob. By choosing safe foods to eat, I know what to expect and how I will feel eating then. This provides the control I need.

I notice the usual fare of omelets (a safe food, depending on the ingredients), French toast and pancakes (hell no!), sausage (no), frittatas (no), and some lunch items. After several minutes, the waiter comes back to take our orders. I'm the last to order.

"I'll just take some scrambled eggs and whole wheat toast, please."

"Is that all?" the waiter asks innocently.

I say yes quickly, somewhat annoyed. What did he mean by "Is that all"? Was he implying my choice wasn't good enough or that I need to eat more? *Whatever.*

I try to listen and participate in the conversation at our table, but unfortunately, I don't do a good job of it. I'm physically present, but my mind is miles away. I'm nervous about what I just ordered. I know it's safe, but it still causes me unease. I'm not big on eating in a social setting. I would much rather be at home, alone.

I'm also nervous about what I'm going to do after this. I want to try the Ipecac, but part of me is scared. I'm afraid that this is another big step. This seems akin to buying the scale, but somehow even more serious. The scale just displays a number. The syrup will make me puke, which really is the root of my concern. I honestly don't like puking. I never have. It just freaks me out. I haven't done it since I was hung over, more than two months ago, and I didn't even remember doing it that night.

Even as a kid, if I ever got sick, my first thought would be: Please don't let me puke. And thankfully, I never really did. I don't have any memories of puking when I was sick. My body seems to just take it and force it out the other end. But I know if I want to keep being successful and to keep seeing that number drop, I'll have to try new things. I can't keep doing what I'm doing and expect it to keep working.

By now, my body is doing its usual anxious routine of thundering heart, clammy hands, and racing mind. I respond with my usual deep breathing, numbing out routine. I just sit there and smile and nod every so often until the food comes.

Once the plate is in front of me, my choice doesn't seem that scary. I play around with it on my plate. I end up eating half of the eggs and both slices of the toast. I even splurge a bit and put jelly on the toast. It tastes wonderful, which causes me to panic slightly. I reassure myself that it doesn't matter because it's all going to come back up anyway.

Brunch ends soon. We give our parting hugs and I'm off. I move quickly to the PATH station and get on the train. I'm doing my best not to overthink what I'm about to do. I'm afraid if I allow my fear to keep obsessing about this, I won't go through with it. So I numb out again. If I just keep moving and go through the steps without thinking, I can do this.

Once I'm up out of the PATH station in Hoboken, I head to a CVS that's close by. I've been in here a million times, but I have no idea where to find Ipecac. I hope they stock it and it's not some special item you have to order.

I start roaming the aisles. I'm certainly not going to ask for help in finding it. That would feel too creepy. The salesperson would probably wonder why I would need something like that.

After several minutes, I get lucky and find it in the first-aid aisle. The bottle is tiny. *This little bottle doesn't seem like it could make you burp, let alone puke.* I decide I need to buy something else with it, so I don't look too weird. I grab several items of lip balm to round out my purchase. I'm addicted to lip balm and I know I will use it.

I check out without much acknowledgment from the young cashier. She probably sees people buying odd things all day long.

As I head home, I pick up the pace. It's been a while since I ate, and I know I need to get home and take this stuff before there isn't much left in my gut.

At my house, I head into the kitchen and place the tiny box on the counter. I just stare at it. I freeze. *I'm not sure I can do this.* I'm really scared. After that brief moment of fear, I snap back into autopilot and start chastising myself for being pathetic. I pick up the box and read the directions. It says one dose is just half the bottle. So this bottle is two doses. It says to take one dose, and if it doesn't work, to take another.

I contemplate taking the whole bottle at once. That way, I know it will work. But I discount this option as overkill.

I slowly open the box and take out the bottle. *This is wild! I can't get over how small it is.* I open a drawer and pull out a large measuring spoon, then unscrew the bottle's cap and pour half the bottle into the spoon. I take a deep breath as I lift the spoon to my lips and … ugh! It's disgusting. I swallow what tastes like the most concentrated, sugary, maple-syrup-tasting mess I've ever tasted. I'm not a big syrup fan. *If this stuff doesn't work, I'm going to puke anyway. That was nasty.*

The taste wears off in my mouth quickly and I'm left standing in my kitchen, alone. It's quiet. All I feel is this dread slowly rising up from the floor, filling my body. It feels like the anticipation you get when you know something painful is about to happen. That's the feeling I get when I know I have to get blood drawn—but this dread is about twenty times worse. I'm afraid I've started something that I'm not sure I'll be able to stop.

I don't like the fact that, once I start puking, then I've started being bulimic.

Walk. Just walk. Walking seems to help everything. I start pacing around my apartment, and even though I can't get into a good rhythm, staying in motion does help calm my mind somewhat. I look up at the clock and note it's been almost ten minutes. *I thought this would be working by now.*

And then I feel it. *Damn it! Here we go!* A small bubble in my gut is slowly rising up into my throat. I rush into the bathroom and kneel down in front of the toilet. Noting the familiarity of this position, I grip the sides of the bowl in anticipation of seeing my brunch again, any second. Slowly, I feel the bubble continue to rise and then ... BURP! A sickly sweet, syrupy burp comes up.

That's it? A burp! I stay put for a few more minutes, even though my knees are yelling at me for some relief from the hard tile. Finally, I stand up and return to the kitchen. I feel defeated but somewhat relieved.

After waiting another fifteen minutes, I decide to take the other dose. Again, I play a cat-and-mouse game, both wanting to puke and not wanting to. My mind wins out in the end. After another thirty minutes and several more horribly sweet burps, I have nothing to show for my first attempt at purging. *Great, I let myself splurge today at brunch and I haven't been able to get rid of it. Now I'm going to have to compensate and cut back even more tomorrow to make up for this.*

Having a rare moment of clarity that one day I'll want to read about what I have just put myself through, I turn to my journal:

Sunday April 28, 2002
Hell of a lot has happened! Therapy is going well – we meet once a week. He's still cute!

The eating disorder has gotten worse and I am now down to 127 pounds (I bought a cool silver scale!) Still not drinking – not because I don't want to but now I'm so scared of the calories and gaining weight.

I just tried Ipecac syrup – took two dosages and no luck! I swear I guess I am not meant to puke. So of course that has made me more upset, scared, and depressed. I have to be more determined now, because if I slip, I have no way of getting rid of what I put into my body!

I'm pretty moody and tired – just par for the course. It's a long race and I'm in it for the long haul.

I see my Dr. tomorrow to get blood tests done so I know where I stand. I really don't think anything will be low or bad. Part of me though wants the numbers to be in the toilet, just to show everyone and myself! I really don't know why I just said that.

I told everyone what I am dealing with and of my friends, Andy and Peter were the only ones who acted even slightly concerned. Everyone else acts like everything is okay. I know they don't know what to do or what to say. It would be nice if they said at least something! I get pretty pissed off.

The whole family knows and of course is supportive and nice about everything. I feel like I'm in my own little world sometimes and am so isolated from everyone, even when I'm out with the gang.

This is definitely the hardest thing I have had to deal with. Sorry this is so short but since I can't puke, my body for some reason has decided to get the runs! So until next time . . .

10

Leaning over the kitchen counter I grab a pen and start writing:

1 can Diet Coke = 0
3 rice cakes = 150

My left hand, my writing hand, is sweaty, and my heart is beating faster than I would like. *I hate doing this. I don't know why I agreed to do this. Yes, I do.* My therapist is hot and I'm a people-pleaser. I can't say no. And on some level, I guess keeping this list is supposed to help me. But right now, it feels like all it's doing is making me obsess even more about what I'm eating.

Last week in therapy, Jordan suggested that I start keeping a food journal. Because I didn't want to question him or be difficult, I agreed to the plan. Now, almost four days into this crazy-ass exercise, I don't think it's helping me one bit.

Just as I always did in school, I take this assignment very seriously and make sure I do it perfectly. I took a clean sheet of paper and drew very neat grid lines so that each day has a column. Each time of day—breakfast, lunch and dinner—has its own row within that day. It looks great and it's easy to read. Or at least Jordan will find it easy to read. I find it anything but.

Ever since I started doing this, I'm more anxious when I eat because I know I will have to write it down in this damned journal. The act of writing down what I eat and seeing it there in black and white makes it more real. All I can see are these words with huge numbers next to them: rice cakes = 150, muffin = 250, yogurt = 90, sandwich = 300, Balance Bar = 150. The numbers translate to me as failure and a lack of control. The numbers mean I will gain weight and become fat. They take away my success and my sense of self.

That's it, I'm done. I'm not doing this anymore! This is fucked up, and all I want to do is not eat a damn thing for the next week. Grabbing the pen again, I scrawl a big X across the sheet. Of course, I don't totally ruin all of my work, because I still have to take it to Jordan to show him the effort I made. I want him to at least tell me I did a good job. For some reason, I still need his validation. I still need to be told I'm good and what I did was good. I have to be good. I can't be anything else.

B. I have to take the B train. And then I get off at 86th Street and walk up one block to 87th and then turn left. I go over and over these directions in my head. I memorize things easily, because the last thing I want is to have to break out a map and look like some lost tourist.

Jordan has moved his office to his home, and I'm still having to refresh myself on how to get there. It's a beautiful walk-up and his office is very nice. Because it's on the upper west side, it takes longer for me to get there than it took me to get to his old office.

I reach around for my messenger bag, open it, and look down to check—for the third time—that I have my half-completed assignment. It's still there.

For some reason, the more nervous I get, the more obsessive I get. I find myself checking and double-checking on things that I know are okay. This doesn't make sense, but checking makes me feel better. I really think it just gives my mind something to obsess about so it doesn't have to think about more important things—like the fact that I didn't or couldn't complete the food journal.

I'm nervous about going to see Jordan with a half-completed assignment. For some reason, it makes me feel like I'm bad. I'm scared of disappointing him and getting in trouble. All of this is laughable, since I'm the client and I'm paying him.

The B rolls into the station; I'm thankful that it's not too crowded. The doors open and I find a seat against the wall that faces out into the aisle. These days, I'm pretty tired, and I don't feel great, so I sit down when I can. I have a pretty good view out the other side of the train, so I should be able to read when we reach the 86th Street station. I relax somewhat and zone out the best I can.

Several stops come and go. I blankly stare as people enter and exit the train quickly. I'm somewhat amused by the lone person who always seems to be running down the stairs yelling at the train to wait for them while flailing their arms in the air. This odd display reminds me of some strange mating ritual that I've seen on Animal Planet. Soon, I'm back in a haze, lulled there by the vibration of the train. I start to feel really tired, even more than usual. I take a deep breath and try to ignore it, like I do with any signal my body tries to convey these days.

Another stop comes and goes. Now I'm not only feeling tired, I'm also light-headed. I can feel beads of sweat forming on my brow. My legs feel weak and shaky. My heart starts to pump faster. *I don't like this at all.*

I look around and realize I don't recognize any of the people in this car. *Where did they come from?* I don't remember seeing any of them get on this train. I try to look out the window, but it's all black and I can't see anything. I'm not sure what stop we just passed. *Damn, where am I?* I have no idea what stop is next.

My heart is beating faster now. My anxiety has turned into full-fledged panic. I suddenly can't remember where I need to get off. *Shit! What stop is it again?* I try to take a deep breath and calm down, but my body won't have it. It's freaking out, and my mind is playing along. *I don't know. I don't know. I can't think. I can't think.* Now I have no idea what stop I need to get off at or where I even need to go.

The train roars into a station. The conductor announces the stop and, as always, I can't understand a damned word. I look up and I can read embedded in the tile: 81st Street. I have no idea if this is where I need to get off or not. *I can't think.* But without warning, my body launches itself up and out the open door.

On the platform, I follow the throng of people. *Just move and get outside.* I know once I am outside, I will be able to figure out where I need to go. I keep my head down and follow the crowd.

Soon, I see the glint of sunshine streaming down the corridor. Within a few steps, I'm outside. I'm met with a rush of fresh air. I look up and, almost instantly, my mind reboots. I'm facing the park. I turn left and walk a few feet and look up at the street sign. I'm on 81st Street. *Thank God, I only got off one stop early. I can easily walk the rest of the way.*

My mind is now cooperating and functioning again. I know where I need to go and, better yet, I know how to get there. But when I look down at my watch, I realize I'm running late. I push my body as much as I can. I hate being late. I pride myself on always being on time. But now I'm afraid that, given my physical state, I'm going to be late. I can only walk so fast, and right now I don't feel like I have enough energy.

After several minutes, I arrive at Jordan's place. I'm only eight minutes late. I walk in and his door is open. He's waiting on me. *Great, just my luck. I see the one therapist who runs on time.* Trying to catch my breath, I stand in the hallway for a few seconds. I take a deep breath and walk through the doorway as confidently as I can.

As I enter, I see Jordan sitting at his desk on the other side of the room with his back to me. He hears me and turns around.

"Hi," he says without emotion.

"Hey. Sorry I'm late," I try to say without a hint of breathlessness.

He nods and I sit down on the big, comfortable leather couch. I sink into it. It feels great. Right now, I would love just to curl up and fall asleep, or at least try. His office is so inviting. It has ceilings that are at least twelve feet high. The walls are a pale white and the whole room is furnished in a minimalist modern motif. I find it soothing.

I also find myself wondering what's beyond the door behind him. I assume it goes into the rest of his place. Does he live here with anyone? Is he single? I can only imagine, because he's very professional and has never revealed anything personal about himself.

This mental masturbation is fruitless. These days I'm so numb, physically, that even if he came onto me—or hell, even if Hugh Jackman showed up at my door wearing nothing but a small towel wrapped around his waist and a big grin on his face—I wouldn't feel anything. I don't think I'd be able to perform. I haven't felt anything physical stirring below my waist in at least three months. In a way, it's been nice. I have felt calm, and I haven't had to deal with any of those feelings that seem to mess up life for so many of us.

I look up and he's just staring at me. *Ah yes, here we are again, just waiting for me to start things off.* As always, I don't want to. I feel myself tensing up. I'm not going to mention the assignment until he does. But I need to break the silence, so I attempt to explain my lateness.

"Sorry. I got turned around and got off at the wrong stop. Still getting used to coming up this way, I guess," I say sheepishly. I am looking down, trying not to catch his gaze and hoping he buys my story.

"It's okay," he says.

Relief slowly settles over my body. *Good, he's not mad.* Then again, why should he be? I'm paying him for an hour whether I'm here the whole time or not.

"So, how was your week?"

"Fine," I reply quickly, without thinking. This is my stock answer to this question. Just keep it short and simple.

He does what he does best: nothing. He just sits there and let's my glib answer linger in the air. After feeling annoyed long enough, I decide to go there—partly because I want to please him, and partly because I've been doing this long enough to know it will be good for me.

"The week was okay. I struggled some with that food journal."

"What happened with that?"

"I just ... I found it hard. I used a sheet of paper and blocked off the days. At first, I just started writing everything I was eating." As I speak, I feel anxiety slowly start to rise from my feet, trying to consume me.

I continue. "I found myself getting more and more anxious when I ate, because I knew I would have to write it down. Then seeing it there, all written down, just drove me nuts! I felt like I was slipping and eating too much. It felt like too much pressure. So I stopped. I couldn't do it anymore. It just made me want to restrict more." Exhausted, I push my back more firmly into the couch, wishing it would swallow me whole.

I glance up quickly, hoping not to be noticed, and I see Jordan intently contemplating all of this. He seems to really be processing what I just said. I don't know if this makes me feel good or more scared. He might be thinking how messed up I am and what assignments I need to do next.

"I have to admit, I didn't want this exercise to cause you any undue stress or anxiety. I was hoping it would help you see how little you were eating, and help us come up with plan to move forward," he explains. His tone is almost apologetic.

I'm not prepared for this. I figure that, being a therapist, he has all the answers. Hearing him admit that this exercise may not have been the best idea almost makes me feel happy. Like I won. Like what I knew from the start of this was true, and this was not going to help me.

"It's okay. It's no big deal," I say reassuringly. "I've got what I wrote. Do you want to see it?" I unzip the top of my bag, pull out the sheet of paper, and hand it to him.

He skims it quickly and then looks back up at me. "What caused you to be late?" he asks out of the clear blue, "That's not like you."

Anxiety is now completely pulsing through my veins. I do my usual stalling tactic. I shift my weight to my left butt cheek and fling my right leg over my left. I don't know what he is trying to get at with this line of questioning, but I guess I can play along.

"Like I said, I got off at the wrong stop. For some reason, I just blanked out on the train."

"What happened?"

"I don't know. It was weird. I was sitting there and suddenly I just felt this drop. It was like my mind just went blank. I didn't know where I was going or what stop to get off at. I totally forgot everything. I felt so out of it, it was scary, actually. But once I got off the train and got outside, I snapped out of it."

Admitting my fear makes me feel a bit calmer. I uncross my leg and reposition myself to face Jordan more directly.

He pauses in thought for a bit and then continues. "Do you think the fact that you were nervous about the food journal and not wanting to talk about it caused you to be late?"

That's an interesting thought. "No I didn't think about that," I say honestly. "I guess that could be a reason. I know I didn't like trying to keep that journal, but I also know I honestly just blanked out on the train. So I don't know if they're connected."

What I honestly think is that he's trying to give too much credit to my subconscious. It's true, I didn't like trying to keep a journal of what I ate. But could that have made me completely lose it on the train, so that I would be late to this session? *I showed up, didn't I?* If I really wanted to avoid things, I would not be in therapy right now.

We talk for several more minutes about what happened to me and about my next steps. Jordan asks about my weight and says he can tell I'm getting thinner. I give him my deflective answer, saying I'm "around 130." He pushes like a good therapist, and I end up answering with the exact number that I know I am—as of this morning, it's 126.

We talk about family and my support system. I confess to feeling pretty angry and isolated most of the time. I mention that I'm going home for Mother's Day at the end of the week. I tell him I'm looking forward to it but also feeling anxious, since I won't be in my routine. I'm afraid of eating more than I want to and gaining weight. Then the conversation shifts.

"Hoyt, by now you know you have a problem. You're clearly suffering from anorexia. You're continuing to lose weight, and you look sick. I've talked to some colleagues and have found a resource that I think will be helpful to you. There is a center here in the city that treats individuals with eating disorders. It's called Renfrew. They have a really good reputation. How would you feel about talking with someone there?"

"Sure, that's fine," I answer. I agree without even realizing it. *Just say yes to anything and everything.*

"So you would be willing to go into their offices and speak with someone?"

"Yeah, sure." *Damn it, I did it again!*

With my eagerness to please in full force, I watch as Jordan pulls out a contact name and phone number for me to call. He asks that I call this Rosie woman to make an appointment, and then call him to let him know I did that. Of course, I agree to all of this. We set our next appointment and I leave.

On my way home, I keep trying to pronounce the name of this place in my head. Renfew. Renfert. Renfrew. *What the hell kind of name is that?* I've never heard of this place. Jordan says it's well-known and supposedly very good at treating people with eating disorders. I don't know how I feel about this. I guess it can't hurt to go and talk to someone with knowledge about this issue. But then again, I'm not sure I want to. I don't know if I'm ready to give this up.

I'm a gay guy with anorexia. I can't imagine there are many patients out there like me, and probably even fewer therapists out there who know what I'm going through. I don't think I want to open myself up to being let down.

My long commute back to Hoboken provides plenty of time to weigh the pros and cons of going to this strange place. Once I get home, I decide that I will call and make an appointment because I told Jordan I would, and I need to keep my word. Plus, I'm not committing to anything.

I'm exhausted from my outing. I do my usual six weigh-ins and get an overall reading of 126. Feeling somewhat relieved that the number hasn't gone up, I lie down on the couch and turn on the TV. Time to numb out.

11

"Hey, how you doing?" I ask as I lean in and give Amy a hug, not really feeling her touch.

"I'm good. It's great to see you," she says enthusiastically.

"Hey, Jess." I let go of Amy and do my one-armed hug around Jessica. Looking up, I notice they are the only two here to meet me. For some reason, Mom and Dad aren't here. That's not like them. Usually, being picked up at the airport is a whole-family affair.

"Did you check any bags?" Amy asks.

"No, I'm good— unlike some people in this family," I say sarcastically. "I have everything I need in my book bag."

"Let's go, then," Jessica quickly blurts out. She turns and starts heading for the front doors. Amy follows, and I bring up the rear.

Amy and Jessica are walking together in front of me for a bit, but then Amy falls back to join me. Jessica keeps up her pace in front of us. I start to feel a bit awkward, like the odd man out. For some reason, there seems to be tension or unease in the air.

Amy breaks the silence. "She's upset," she says, pointing to Jessica. "She's been crying."

"Okay," I add, not knowing what to say. Since I'm not the touchy-feely type, I figure it must have something to do with a guy, which I really couldn't care less about. I've never been overly protective when it comes to either of my sisters. They both are so capable and strong-willed that I tend to be more concerned for the men in their lives.

"You look really bad," Amy whispers. "It shocked her. She thinks you look like one of those people from a concentration camp."

This direct, unsolicited statement by my older sister just lands in the air with a big thud. I don't know what to say next. All I can manage is an eloquent, "Huh."

"How does that make you feel?" she prods. I can always count on Amy to just lay it all out there and to keep pushing until she gets what she wants. She definitely is protective toward me.

"I don't know. She'll get over it. I'm fine," I say as strongly as I can. I feel defensive.

"Mom and Dad didn't come because they are watching the boys … and they were scared, too. I thought it would be good if just Jessie and I came."

There she goes again. Now, not only do I look like death, but my own parents don't want to see me. This is turning out to be a fun-filled trip. I can't wait to see what's in store next.

They are parked nearby, and when we get to the car, Jessica says she'll ride in the back. This is somewhat amusing, given the fact that all three of us as kids fought like cats and dogs to get a front seat in the car. Since Jessica has barely spoken to me or really looked at me, I guess she doesn't want to be that close to me in the car, either.

Amy drives us home and we make small talk along the way. I assure Jessica I'm fine and she tells me that I look like crap. I thank her for her honesty—not meaning it, of course. Amy preps me for the boys and how hyped they are that I'm coming to visit. I'm really looking forward to seeing them, but I start to feel this knot in my stomach as we get closer to the house.

Now that I know how bad everyone thinks I look and that my own parents are nervous to see me, I'm starting to feel really self-conscious. I'm even more worried about the boys. I love them more than anything, and I just want to have a fun time while I'm home for a few days.

Amy pulls into the driveway and, as we get out of the car, I make an effort to walk through the back door last. I just need a few extra seconds to gear up for my entrance.

"Hey," I say sheepishly, with a faint smile on my face.

"Hey, Jeff." My mom stands up from the bar stool she was sitting on and walks over and gives me a hug. This one I purposefully try not to feel.

"Hey, Dad."

"Hey, Jeff. How was your flight?"

"It was fine. Thanks. On time, which was nice."

"Uncle Jeeeefffff!" I hear in unison the sound of two little boys' voices before I ever see them. Suddenly rounding the corner of the family room and entering the kitchen are Kellen, four years old, and Brooks, two years old, coming at full speed toward me.

"Hey, you two!" I exclaim as I lower myself down to their level, preparing for a full, head-on collision. They slow down a bit and just bump into me without knocking me over. I give them a big hug and notice that they are hugging more tightly than I am.

They let go, and I use my right hand to steady myself and push up. I start to black out, as I normally do these days when I stand up, so I try to compensate by reaching for the kitchen island to my right. I'm pretty adept now at covering up my physical limitations. I'm hoping no one notices.

Once fully upright, several seconds pass before my vision is back to normal. Everyone is making small talk while I stand there pretending to pay attention. Then, out of the blue, this smell just crashes into me. It feels like this immense wave washing over my entire body. *What is that? It smells like, like … butter, sugar, cream, yeah, and I smell … salt? Oh my God, it's amazing! I can almost taste it!*

I start to sweat as this aroma invades every pore of my body, tempting me to seek it out and devour it. I must find where this is coming from. I glance to my left and right, but I don't see anything out of the ordinary that would produce such an amazing smell. Then I snap back into reality and the conversation piques my interest.

"We're going to celebrate your mommy's birthday tomorrow night. It's going to be fun," my mother says to the boys. "And I got a big, special cake from this really good bakery in town." She points to a box on the counter behind me. "It's vanilla cake with butter cream icing. Yummm!" She smiles when she sees their eyes widen at the mention of cake.

Cake! That's it. It's a cake. I swing around and there, to the left of the sink, is a large, brown box. *That's it! That's the source.* My heart starts to race a bit faster. By now, the smell is almost overwhelming. I've never experienced anything like this before. This must be what a bloodhound feels like. I swear I could close my eyes and name exactly what's in this cake and taste it at the same time.

I don't like this at all. I don't trust myself around this temptation. I slowly make my way around the island to the other side. I need as much distance from this thing as I can get.

The rest of the evening goes smoothly. Everyone is on their best behavior. That's one nice thing about the South: people down here know how to pretend that everything is fine, even when it's so obviously not.

As I get ready for bed, all I can think about is that damned cake. I get undressed and crawl into bed. I stare up at the ceiling seeing that brown box in my mind. I imagine sitting in front of that cake and eating it. To make matters worse, my room is directly above the kitchen. I swear, I can still smell it.

I haven't made up my mind yet whether I'm going to eat any of it. On the one hand, I really want to, because it just smells too good to pass up. But on the other hand, it's *cake.* I'm terrified of eating it and then not being able to stop. I'm afraid it will taste too good. I don't know how to deal with being overwhelmed with a sensation like that.

For the next thirty minutes or so, my mind does what it does best: I obsess. Without making a resolution one way or the other, I slowly drift off to sleep.

∿

"Hey Uncle Jeff, watch this!"

Emerging from a fog, I turn my head to watch as Kellen races down the driveway on his tricycle at full speed. I smile when I see him pass. He is staring intensely over the handlebars with what looks like all his might, trying to steer the tricycle in a straight line down the driveway. It's cute. I love seeing the boys play so hard with what seems like such a carefree attitude. I feel a twinge of sadness when I realize that I am long past the carefree days of youth.

I clap my hands. "Awesome job, K-dog! That was impressive!"

"I can do that, too," Brooks claims in his broken, two-year-old talk. He doesn't want to be outdone by his older brother.

"Okay, just be careful," I say. I feel more and more paternal toward these two as they get older.

"You feel okay, Jeff?" my mom asks as she walks over to where I'm sitting.

"Yeah, I'm fine, Mom, thanks." I feel slightly annoyed. I know she's worried about me, but I can't look *that* bad. I'm tired and a little bit cold, but I'll be damned if I let her know that. Plus, sitting on this wrought iron bench is killing my ass. *I don't know why anyone would want to sit on metal like this.*

I stand up slowly and notice Brooks is making his way down the driveway. He gets about halfway and putters out. His little legs just can't get enough momentum to take him the entire length of the driveway. My first instinct is to go over to him and push him the rest of the way, but I reconsider once I realize that I'm slowly blacking out from standing up. I just don't have the strength.

My mom and I stand outside making small talk while we watch the boys play hard. It's nice being outside and watching them. I love spending time with them, even though talking with my mom feels strained.

After several minutes and a couple of fights between the boys, my mom suggests a change of venue. "Hey guys, why don't we walk down to the pond and feed the ducks?" She holds up a bag of old bread. Like a good grandmother, she has surprised us all with her idea—and with the fact that she has bread. I never saw her bring the bag out. But then again, she's always prepared.

"Oh yeah, mama, that would be fun," Kellen squeals.

"Yeah, I want to go," Brooks adds breathlessly as he runs up to where we are standing.

"You up for walking down there?" my mom asks, turning to me.

"Yeah, Mom. I'm fine. Let's go."

I start to walk down the driveway. We cross the street and make our way to the lot next to the neighbor who lives across from my parents. Our neighbors own the lot, which has a pond where ducks and geese like to hang out. For some reason, kids never seem to be able to resist water and animals.

Once we're at the water's edge, it doesn't take the ducks long to figure out they are in for a feast. Like a good uncle, I stand there and hand the boys a steady stream of bread so they don't run out. The ducks consume the allotment in just a few minutes.

"Mama, do you have anymore?" Kellen asks with longing in his voice.

"No, I'm sorry, honey. That's all I have."

"We can get more and come back tomorrow," I suggest.

Brooks and Kellen just stand there and watch as the ducks finish the last scraps and then start to waddle back to the water.

"Quack, quack, quack."

I look down at Brooks, who is making duck noises. "B., what are you doing?" I ask, trying my best to stifle my amusement.

"They're leaving. I want them back," he blurts out in between quacks.

I can't help but laugh as I marvel at his innocence. He's the animal lover in our family. He never fails to stop and inspect any animal that crosses his path, no matter how small.

Once my mom convinces Brooks that the ducks need time to rest, he reluctantly agrees to walk back to the house with us. The neighbor who owns the property happens to be standing at his mailbox.

"Hey, Beth, how are you today?" Mr. McGee asks.

"Oh, hi, Gerald. Doing well, thank you." Without skipping a beat, she adds, "Gerald, I don't think you have met my grandkids."

"No, I don't think I have."

"Well, this is Brooks and this is Kellen." She proudly points to each as she calls out their names.

"Nice to meet you guys."

"Hey," the boys respond shyly.

"We were just down feeding the ducks," my mom explains.

"Hi, I'm Gerald McGee," the neighbor says as he turns to me, extending his hand.

I'm startled at this introduction, given the fact that I've met this man many times before and have even been in his house. The best I can muster is, "Hey, I'm Jeff. We've met."

"Oh yeah, hey," he says, stumbling over his words.

"Well, I guess we'd better get back to the house," my mom announces, trying to end the awkwardness that has now enveloped this odd interaction.

"It was nice meeting you guys," Gerald says to the boys.

"Good to see you, Gerald. Tell Debbie we say hi," my mom says. Finally, we all start walking across the street and up my parents' driveway.

Once inside the house, the boys run upstairs and my mom turns to me. "You know, he didn't even know who you were."

"Huh?" I grunt, feigning ignorance. I don't want to go into this right now.

"You look so different that Gerald didn't recognize you."

"Whatever, Mom. It must be old age. He just forgot. It's been a while," I say quickly, even though I know that he's younger than my parents.

I'm grateful when my mom drops this conversation and I can head upstairs to rest. I'm wiped out and need to crash before dinner. I don't want to really believe that Mr. McGee had no idea who I was because I look so different.

I lie down on my bed and shut my eyes, trying to tune out what just happened.

"I'm ready," I announce to my dad, who is sitting in his chair in the family room reading one of his many religious-themed books. Once I make it down the stairs and into the room, he looks up.

"Okay. You're mom and sisters, of course, are still getting ready."

"Of course they are," I chuckle. I start to walk through the room on my way to the kitchen. I've been able to avoid the kitchen—and therefore the cake—for most of the day. But since I'll be faced with it fairly soon, I want to make a pass by it to see if it still has such a strong pull on me.

As soon as I pass my dad's chair, he stops me. "Hey, wait. I need to talk to you for a minute," he says matter-of-factly.

Immediately, the hairs on the back of my neck stand up. *Oh shit!* I know what this means. He never says that line unless it's something bad. I stay facing the center of the room. He stays seated to my right, also facing the center of the room.

"You're mom's worried about you. You don't look good," he says. He pauses as if waiting for me to interject. I don't.

"You're really thin, and I know you're not eating," he says, pausing again, "We just need you to get well and eat. Okay?" This last statement falls out of his mouth less as a request and more as an order not open to discussion. This is a skill I'm sure he honed while in the military. I'm not open to discussion either, so I give him what he wants.

"Fine. I'll eat," I blurt out, hoping to shut down any further need he may have to continue this conversation.

"Good."

Well, that was easy. I love it when I can just tell people what they want to hear and they buy it. Like it's just that easy. Just eat and everything will be okay. *Yeah, right.*

Still marveling at my dad's misguided attempt at an intervention, I continue my trek toward the kitchen. I stop at the sink. *Huh, that's weird. I don't really smell the cake as strongly now as I did last night. Maybe I'm getting used to it.* Relieved that I'm not feeling so overwhelmed by the cake, I go upstairs to the rec room to hang out with the boys before we leave.

Dinner goes fairly well. I eat a grilled chicken dish, which is safe, but I eat more than I normally would on a Saturday night. I'm pretty quiet. I feel isolated, even with my own family.

Everyone else seems to have a decent time, and the boys are entertaining, as usual. We make it back home for dessert and to finish the birthday celebration. Once home, I can feel my anxiety slowly start to kick back up again. It's countdown time. I'm getting more and more nervous about the prospect of coming face to face with that cake.

Of course, Amy wants to do gifts first, so I have to wait even longer, dragging out my misery. The boys, like normal kids, are more than willing to help their mother rip open her gifts. Upon inspection of each gift, they lose interest fast and turn to the next one. Because of the boys' help, the gift-opening session is short

Then my mom announces, "Time for cake!"

My heart skips a beat.

The cake comes out. It's beautiful, mostly white with some pretty, decorative scrollwork in pink and a birthday greeting on the top. The smell is nice, but not overwhelming anymore. Someone dims the lights and we all sing—or at least we do what is supposed to be singing. No one can accuse our bunch of being able to carry a tune.

The lights come back up, the candles are taken out of the cake, and the big knife comes out. My mom proceeds to cut slices for everyone, even me.

I want it, I really want it, but I don't want to feel it. I don't want to feel out of control. Sitting next to the boys at the kitchen table, I place the plate in front of me, pick up my fork, cut off a small piece and put it in my mouth with enormous anticipation of an out-of-this-world experience.

I close my mouth and wait for it. And ... nothing. It's just cake. I don't taste the incredible butter, sugar, or salt that I so acutely smelled the night before. It's just a nice-tasting cake. It's good, but it's not what my mind had made it out to be.

I feel some energy quickly drain from my body as I pick up another bite and put it in my mouth. Again, the same taste. Now totally disappointed, I shift into autopilot and just eat the rest of the piece without much thought or feeling. I want it because it tastes good, but I'm also pissed because I had such great expectations and the payoff wasn't what I had hoped for. *All this time spent obsessing about this damn cake was for nothing.* Of course, when I get back home, I will have to compensate for all the eating I'm doing now.

In bed that night, I lie there staring up at the ceiling again. This time, I'm not obsessing about what's below me in the kitchen. I'm scared about what's inside me. I feel more full than I have in ages, so my mind is totally tuned into my gut. I'm worrying about what the food I ate today is going to do to that number on the scale.

Luckily, I don't have access to a scale here. Well, that's not totally true. My parents have one in their bathroom, an ancient scale they've had for thirty years. It's one of those with a dial on it that turns. But I haven't had a chance to sneak in there to use it when no one is looking. Plus, I don't think I have the heart to weigh myself right now. I don't want to see what that number is going to be.

My thoughts then turn to the next day and the additional food I will be faced with. Tomorrow is Mother's Day, and we are going to brunch at the country club. *Fun! I can't wait to be around a huge buffet of food.*

I really don't want to eat anything else for a while, and at a buffet, it's more noticeable when you're not eating much. At a regular restaurant, you can order a little bit of food, get served with everyone else, and then eat as little as you want. No one really notices. But at a buffet, everyone seems to notice whether you make a trip to the buffet and how much you get to eat. People like talking about what you got and what you should try. I hate it. Life shouldn't revolve around food so much.

After getting myself worked up about the outing tomorrow, I attempt to calm myself with the fact that, once I get back home Monday night, I can do whatever I want to do. Sleep doesn't come as easily as I would like.

Salad. That's safe. I can eat that, and if need be, I can make another trip up to get more salad. It will look like I'm eating normally. As I walk up to the buffet, I'm running through my head as quickly as possible what I can and cannot eat. When we walked in, I did my best to eye what was on the buffet. Salad is always a safe choice.

After putting enough salad and other toppings on my plate to pass for a normal portion, I make my way back to our table, which is in another room. An older woman passes me on my left and stares at me. Or does she? Maybe not. It's probably just in my head.

I keep walking and make it into the other room. Again, another woman passes me—this one probably middle-aged—and she stares at me. I glance away quickly and then look down. *That's weird. Why are these people staring at me?* Maybe I remind them of someone.

At that moment, Amy has made her way back from the buffet and is standing next to me.

"You know people are staring at you?"

"Uh, no. I don't think so," I say. I'm confused. I have no idea why she just said that.

"You look really sick. You're gray."

"Okay, whatever."

I choose to ignore our little exchange and head back to the table. The brunch is tolerable. I don't like all the people that are there. It's too crowded, which makes me feel uncomfortable. But I'm able to get by with eating mostly salad and some chicken. I feel pretty good about what I eat, or don't eat. I'm grateful that we don't stay very long.

Once we're back home, my mom opens some gifts. Then the cake from the previous night is brought out. The boys dig in, but I easily refrain from eating again. *It wasn't that great last night, and the more I eat, the more I'll have to compensate when I get home. Nothing tastes as good as thin feels.*

Later that afternoon, my mom pulls me into her bedroom. After the talk from my dad, I guess it's only fair that my mom gets her shot. Feeling dread, I sit down in a chair by the window. She seems withdrawn. I ignore it.

"Jeff, I know you're struggling. And I'm scared for you. You look really sick," she tentatively begins. "I was wondering if you wouldn't mind, if you, uhh … well, I found a really good contact here in town who specializes in treating people with eating disorders. I was wondering if you would like to see him. It might help to talk to someone who has knowledge in this area." She looks at me with an expression that seems to be begging me to agree to her request.

I don't make eye contact for long. Anger begins to surface. I hate feeling like I'm obligated to do something, but she's my mom, and I have never been able to say no to her. Of course I'm going to agree to this, but I hate feeling like I have no choice. After a long pause, I do what I do best.

"Yeah, fine. I'll go."

"Oh, good." She exhales a sigh of relief. "His name is Dr. Hugh. He's a psychologist and has a great reputation. Since you don't leave until tomorrow evening, I figure we could go tomorrow afternoon."

"Sure, whatever." *Wait a minute, did she say "we"?* Great, I guess this will be a group outing. Now I can assume everything I say to this guy will be told to my mother. *Wonderful.* It doesn't matter, I guess. I'll do this to make her happy and then I'll get on a plane back to my own life.

"Nice to meet you, Jeff."

"Thanks. Nice to meet you. I go by Hoyt. Only my family calls me Jeff," I add tensely.

"Oh, okay. Have a seat," he says as he motions to the sofa on my left.

I sit down and he sits in front of me in a big office chair. There is a large window behind him and to my right, behind where he is sitting, is his desk and a massive bookshelf.

Once I'm seated, he just sits there and stares at me. *Great, another one.* I really don't feel up to this whole cat-and-mouse game of the shrink being silent and waiting for me to talk. I don't know this guy, so he's going to have to start things off—which he does.

"So, you're not eating?"

He's direct, that's for sure. I feel myself stiffen. "Yeah, I guess," I say nervously, letting out a slight laugh.

"How much do you weigh?"

Ugh, he doesn't ease into anything, does he? "I'm not sure," I lie.

There's a long pause. He just looks at me. *I don't think he's buying this.*

"How much do you weigh?" he asks again, as if he hadn't just posed this question. Long pause again.

I guess I'd better 'fess up. "126."

"That's low," he says somberly, with a bit of an edge to his voice. I can't tell if he's mad, shocked, or just annoyed. "Do you know what your B.M.I. is?"

"No," I reply, lying again.

He grabs a chart off his desk. "How tall are you?"

"Six feet."

He scans down the chart for several seconds before he looks up, "Your B.M.I. is about 17," he says. He's leering at me, almost sternly. "By the looks of you, you're clearly anorexic."

Damn, this guy doesn't pull any punches. For the next several minutes, he questions me about my eating and living habits. Then he starts telling me how I'm feeling. He tells me about feeling isolated, alone, scared, and out of control. He describes obsessing about the number on the scale.

It's almost too much to take. I've never had anyone—a therapist, a friend, anyone—tell me how I was feeling and actually be right. I'm excited … I think. Someone actually knows what I'm going through!

"You know what's going to happen if you keep doing this?" he asks. Then he continues without waiting for my reply. "Your hair is going to fall out."

I make a mental note that he's hit a bull's eye with that one. Every time I wash my hair now, enough comes out in my hands that I have to ball it up and throw it away because it would clog the drain.

"Your nails will turn black. Your bowels will stop working. You will become more isolated and will lose most of your friends." He goes on and on, and I do my best to tune him out. I can't relate to most of these bad things he is saying.

"Have you had vivid dreams about food?" he asks.

"Not really," I reply, lying again

"Have you taken Ipecac?"

"Yes, but it didn't work. I only tried it once."

"Good, don't do it. It will kill you. It's what killed Karen Carpenter."

The rest of the session consists of us going back and forth. He's direct and doesn't seem to buy any of the diversions I try to throw his way. Because of his directness, I find myself feeling less and less guarded. I start to answer his questions honestly, and it feels nice.

But I'm still not buying this whole idea that I have to change and have to get better. I don't want to—and I tell him so.

Toward the end of our session, he asks permission to invite my mom and dad into the room. I allow it. Like I have a choice.

"Well, Beth and Hoyt, I've talked to Jeff. He's a smart guy and he's sick. He knows that. We all know that. But in the end, he's going to do what he's going to do."

My mom is sitting to my right on the couch and my dad to my left. I don't look at either of them. I can feel my mom's sadness.

"Okay ... but I don't think it's such a good idea for him to go back to New York. I don't think he should go back alone," my mom pleads.

"Well, I don't think you have much choice in the matter. He's an adult," the shrink says. Turning to me, he adds, "You're going to do what you want to do, aren't you?"

"Uh, yeah," I mutter. I'm somewhat perplexed at this line of questioning.

Turning back toward my mom, Dr. Hugh continues. "You can't make him get well. When he's ready, he will. When he hits rock bottom, hopefully, he will. I don't think he's hit rock bottom yet."

I can feel my mom stiffen the instant he finishes this statement. *Rock bottom. I don't know about that.* I don't know if I've hit it or not. I don't really care. I just want to go back home and be left alone. I just want everyone to leave me alone. I'm tired.

The session is over soon after that. I don't feel much, but I know my mom is feeling enough for the both of us. As for my dad, I have no idea. None of us talk during the car ride home. I'm grateful that my flight leaves in a few hours.

The rest of the afternoon goes quickly. I pack my book bag and, when it's time to leave for the airport, I ask Amy to take me. I don't feel up for any long good-byes. I'm in my zone now, not feeling, just moving. *If I move fast enough, I can't get caught.*

I automatically hug my mom and shake my dad's hand. I hug the boys and Jessica goodbye, and then get in the car, thankful that I've made it through the farewells unscathed.

We drive off. On the ride to the airport, I start feeling anxious about going back to an empty apartment. I'm not sure I want to go back, but I do know that I want to be left alone so I can keep losing weight. This tug-of-war in my mind helps to mask the feeling that, deep down, I probably want someone to take charge and tell me what to do. I want someone to save me from myself.

Once inside the airport, I head for the ticket counter. Amy decides to come in, which annoys me. I'm feeling a bit smothered, and

I'm already in my check-out mode. I don't want to feel anything, because I know I'm leaving and I'll have to say good-bye to her.

At the counter, I'm met with the news that most travelers dread, no matter how seasoned they are.

"I'm sorry, Mr. Phillips, but your flight has been cancelled because of the weather. Since this was the last flight out today, we can reschedule you on the first flight out tomorrow morning," the counter agent says robotically, without any hint of remorse in her voice. I don't believe that she is really sorry.

All I hear is "cancelled." *Cancelled? My flight has been cancelled? You have to be joking! I have to get out of here. I have to get out of this hell and get back to my life! I can't stay here any longer. I'm back-sliding and I need to leave, now!*

I try my best to smile and not get too outwardly upset. I stand there while she types furiously and issues another ticket. Then I skulk out of line and head back to where Amy is standing.

"It's cancelled."

"Oh gosh, I'm sorry! Well, on the bright side, you get to stay another day," she adds, smiling.

"Yeah, that's great, but I have my Renfrew appointment tomorrow. Great. I guess I have to miss that," I say with more than a touch of anger in my voice.

"It's okay. You can call and reschedule. I'm sure people do it all the time," she says, trying to comfort me.

I'm having none of it. I'm ignoring her now as we start walking back to the car. I'm just pissed. I want out of here, and now I can't even go to my appointment tomorrow. I guess I'm not meant to go. I guess God is telling me that I'm not sick enough and that I don't have to go.

Everyone is surprised to see me back home. My mom lights up so much that I get this feeling she wants to make this permanent. She is seeing this as a chance to keep me here. That scares me. *I'll be damned if she'll trap me here.*

The rest of the evening goes by quickly and without mention of my situation.

I'm up at the crack of dawn and, after packing again, my parents take me to the airport. This time the flight is on time and I do my usual good-byes, all on autopilot. The anger has subsided somewhat and given way to annoyance. I should be home by now, but I guess one extra night isn't that bad.

Doing my best not to think about anything, I go through security and board the plane as soon as they start calling sections. I want to be on that plane as fast as possible. I'm afraid that if I don't get on, I will be stuck here even longer.

As soon as I'm on board, I just sink down into my hard seat. At that moment, images of my empty apartment start flashing in my head and anxiety slowly creeps back into my consciousness.

I've been so angry during the last few hours that I never stopped to think that the cancellation was my out. It was God's way of providing me an opportunity not to go back. I could have used it as an excuse to stay and get help. But then again, no one told me to stay. No one told me that they would take care of everything. *No, God can do better than that.*

My anxiety then turns to fear as I realize that I might not come back here again. I feel paralyzed. I don't know what to do anymore. I feel like shit all of the time. I'm mad most of the time, and all I can think about is how much more weight I need to lose. This is so messed-up, but I don't know where to get off this ride from hell or how to stop this insanity. I'm not sure I need to go back to New York, but I feel really scared about the thought of not going back to my life.

Lost in thought over my doubts and apathy about my life, I look out the window and realize we are already airborne. The choice has been made for me. I'm going back to my empty apartment and to my scale.

I hope it will tell me that I'm still good.

12

Wow, she's gorgeous.

My head turns as my eyes follow this statuesque, very thin young woman as she walks by me. She's carrying what looks like a clear plastic lunchbox and she glides down the hall with a slight spring in her step. She's almost childlike. I may be gay, but I can't help but notice beautiful women. My mind begins to imagine why she is here. But given the fact that I'm sitting in Renfrew's waiting room, I have to assume she's sick.

I glance down at my watch and notice that I'm about fifteen minutes early. I've already checked-in and given them my insurance card, and I've filled out pointless paperwork. Now I get to sit here and wait and obsess about what is waiting for me.

It was my dumb luck that they were able to quickly reschedule my appointment, but I still don't know why I agreed to do this. *I'm not sick enough for this.* I don't think there is anything these people can do for me. Plus, I've only seen women around here. I haven't seen even one other guy. The story of my life. I'm always the lone guy. I have only sisters, no brothers. I was the only guy in my high school honors English class for three years. Now I have a woman's disease. *Just my luck.*

I shift my weight to my right butt cheek and flip through some magazine I pretend to be reading. I've been home almost two weeks, and I've barely heard from anyone. Everyone knows I've got this appointment, but no one has called to check on me. I know I'm not the easiest person to get along with these days, but it kind of pisses me off. I would think my own family would want to know how I'm doing, and would take comfort in the fact that I'm going to a clinic that treats what I supposedly have. Then again, maybe it was the way I told everyone not to worry and to stop being overbearing. Maybe that has something to with it.

I choose to ignore my own role in my isolation. I just get mad at everyone for abandoning me. I am mad that I'm sitting in this stupid waiting room in some random clinic waiting for some "therapist" I don't even know to tell me that I'm sick. *This is messed up. I don't need this.*

"Hoyt," a female voice announces, shocking me out of my internal dialog.

"Uh, yeah. That's me," I say with a half-smile. I stand up—slowly, of course.

"Hi, I'm Rosie. Nice to meet you." She smiles as I walk towards her to the other side of the room.

"Hi, nice to meet you," I mumble, returning the smile but not the eye contact. I feel more comfortable noticing the bland carpet on the floor.

I follow her down the hall and we turn into her small office. There are books everywhere. I like the feel. I've always loved reading.

I sit down on a small sofa and she sits in front of me in her desk chair. Her desk is behind her and to my left is a large window overlooking a nondescript section of Midtown. This place wasn't too far from the PATH station.

"So, how are you?"

"Fine," I answer, glancing toward her and then looking away quickly. She seems nice enough, but I'm not all that comfortable. This is my first experience with a female therapist.

"Well, I'm the intake counselor here. And I know your therapist, ummm ..." She pauses, looking down at her notes. "... Jordan referred you here."

"Yeah," I say, nodding.

"So what's going on? Why did Jordan feel the need for you to come here?"

Ugh. I hate these reflective questions so early in a therapist relationship. I barely know this woman, and she wants me to be all deep and open up for her. *Well forget that, honey.* She is the damned therapist! She should know why I'm here.

I feel my body stiffen as my mind starts racing, trying to come up a short and sweet, but noncommittal, response.

"Well, I guess ... Jordan wanted me to see someone with more knowledge about eating disorders. I'm, umm, not eating much." I stammer on the last part, still not able to verbally announce that I'm anorexic. I'm afraid that if I say that to a therapist, it will make it more real. It will also make me a fake, since I know I'm not that sick.

Rosie furrows her brow as if she's deep in thought. I just sit there, gazing out the window, and then snap back when she starts talking about the center and what is does and how it helps people. I try my best to pay attention and nod when appropriate. I notice that she does not mention male patients, even once. She mentions women and having day groups for them—but not men.

Then Rosie proves her therapy chops by lobbing out my favorite inquiry: "How much do you weigh?"

I shift my weight to my left butt cheek and fling my right leg over my left without even thinking. It's automatic. My body and mind are trying to stall. I should be used to this question by now.

"About 130," I say calmly, trying not to sound too eager and hoping she will buy this obvious lie. Of course, I'm not 130. I'm 123, but I hope she doesn't know that.

The expression on her face is blank. I can't tell if she knows I'm lying or if she's confused.

"Okay," is all she says.

Wow, that was easy. She's not a tough sell at all.

"I wonder what that would make your B.M.I.?" she asks out loud. I'm not sure whether she expects an answer from me, so I just sit there, silent. I'm not dying to jump in to answer her question that my B.M.I. at the moment is 16.7.

She turns around and reaches for a piece of paper on her desk. Looking at it, she furrows her brow again. "I've got the B.M.I. for women, but it doesn't look like I have one for men. Since we don't really work with men, I don't know what that makes your B.M.I. I don't really know what a healthy weight would be for you."

Wow. I'm so stunned, I just stare at the wall behind her. This woman bought my crap about how much I weigh. She knew she was meeting with a guy with an eating disorder who was referred by a therapist, yet she doesn't have a clue about guys with eating disorders.

The rest of the session is spent with Rosie telling me about some guy at the center who is starting to work with males. There is a new group he is trying to start up that would be like a support group for guys. For some reason, when she asks me if I want this guy to contact me, I agree. She says there isn't much else that the center could offer me directly, since they don't really treat males.

I'm amazed at the lack of preparation this woman did for this session. She has no clue how to help me. She also has never once validated that I'm sick or that I need help. I come to realize, toward the end of my appointment with her, that this whole experience has been a complete waste of MY time. She's getting paid for this. What the hell am I getting out of this?

Slowly, my numbness and the defenses that are always present start breaking away, and I feel anger start to overtake me. I'm polite as we end the session, and I quickly make my exit out onto the street, where I start walking as fast as I can.

I'm pissed. Very pissed. *This is so fucked up!* I feel like my time was wasted, but worse yet, I feel like it was wasted by some nitwit who didn't know what the hell she was doing! I understand if someone like Jordan doesn't have the expertise in a given area and admits it. But this moron, who works at an eating disorder clinic, just sat in front of me and admitted that she doesn't work with males and has no idea what I should weigh.

I'm no genius, but if you know you're going to meet with a guy who has an eating disorder, is it that hard to go online and just print off a B.M.I chart? *God, how stupid do you have to be to work there?*

It's a beautiful day, and the more I walk, the more I feel my anger being burned off. The sunshine and fresh air help calm me back down. The unnerving side effect of this is that, right before the anger dissipates and numbness takes back its helm over my body and mind, there is a brief window of clarity regarding my reaction to all of this.

I can't help but notice that I got what I thought I wanted. I sat in front of someone who was supposed to be an expert in this field, and I was able to lie to her about my weight and my problem, and she believed it. Not only did she believe it, but she never told me I was sick and that I had to change. She never said anything! She just sat there and tried to pass me off to someone else.

In essence, she validated for me that I'm not that sick and that I don't really need help. I don't even need to gain one pound! I should be thrilled by this turn of events ... but I'm not.

Somewhere inside my screwed-up mind, there is a voice that I haven't managed to kill yet. This voice knows that what I need is for someone to tell me that I'm sick and that I need to really hear it and to believe it. I need to get help. Using this "expert's" lack of concern for me as an excuse to stay sick will only further my decline into a hell that I seem so bent on getting to.

I don't like this voice or the feelings it's trying to make me confront. With all the strength I can muster, I take a deep breath and successfully silence it—for the time being. The numbness that I too easily embrace envelopes me again, just as softly as the warm sunshine that I'm enjoying on my walk to the subway station that will take me to work.

I'm good. Thanks for checking. It went okay but doesn't look like they can do that much. They don't really treat guys. So right now there is nothing more planned.

> *Hope you're having a good day. I just got to work. Fun*
> *fun*
> *Talk to you later,*
> *Hoyt*

I review my message for spelling errors and then click SEND. I'm replying to an email from Peter asking about my appointment. I'm a bit annoyed because now I have to talk about it, or at least think about it, but it's nice that he asked.

After sending the mail, I check some more messages and then do my best to get some work done. About an hour later, I get a reply from Peter.

> *I'm at a loss for words (I've just sat here trying to figure out what to say). Not quite sure how to understand what's going through your head. I was looking through photos from my birthday in Jan., Vermont in Feb., and Austin in May. In each set you look progressively worse.*
>
> *Your friends love you greatly, but we're all very concerned. At what point does your body simply shut down and stop responding? You seem to know you have a problem but still don't think anything needs to be done. Saying that you have nothing more planned in getting help, to me at least, says that you don't understand that this situation is becoming very grave.*
>
> *I'm here for you. Even if you don't want my help, I'm still here for you. I do feel like this is getting beyond control for you.*
>
> *Realize that I'm trying to not be nagging about this but trying not to take this issue lightly. I'm trying to find the right balance. If I'm failing, let me know*
> *Love,*
> *Peter*

I read this email about five times. I'm not sure what I'm looking for by reading it so many times. I think I want to believe it. I want to feel it, but I don't. Nothing is getting through. Since the fallout of this morning's session, my defenses have been well fortified, and I'm on autopilot with no desire to disengage it.

Of course, the goal of my reply is to reassure Peter. I don't want him to feel bad. Heaven forbid I think about myself and how I feel. I've got to make *him* feel better. So I do just that. I thank him for his concern and let him know I do have a therapist who is working with me on this. I tell him that everything will be okay. I'm not sure I believe what I'm typing, but it sounds good, anyway.

Peter and I exchange a few more emails. He asks if we can hang out after work and get something to eat. I laugh to myself at this request, knowing that I want to do anything but eat. But in a moment of weakness, I agree, and we make plans to meet in the village at a small Mexican place. It's a restaurant where I used to love to eat when I first moved here.

The rest of the day goes by in a blur, not because it's all that busy but because I'm usually in a fog these days. I do my best to look busy, all the while obsessing about what I'm going to eat next and what I'm not going to eat. I keep trying to psych myself up for the night so I won't eat too much.

At five sharp, I'm out the door and on my way to meet Peter. I feel settled in my numbness now. I'm somewhat heartened that I don't feel all that anxious. Usually, the idea of meeting someone for dinner during the week would send me into a tailspin of anxiety, terrified that I would be faced with eating a normal dinner. But for some reason, I'm not feeling that right now. I feel almost light. I've burned through my quota of intense feelings for the day, and my body and mind are blessedly quiet.

After riding the train for a while, I notice that the lightness I was feeling minutes earlier has now given way to hunger. Instantly, my mind flashes on a cake. I close my eyes and shake my head slightly.

There it is again—a flash, in color, of a cake. I shake my head again, hoping the image will break loose and leave me alone. But now my mind won't let it go. I want some cake. *I really want some cake.*

Without fail, my body starts its usual reaction when I'm faced with food obsessions. Sweat begins to slowly bead around my hairline, my heart starts pounding faster and harder, and anxiety snakes up from the floor, invading my body. In a New York second, that lightness I was feeling has been completely devoured by anxiety.

I do my best to stay calm in the midst of this mental shit storm. When I get off at my stop, I race as fast as I can to the restaurant, where I find Peter waiting for me. We are seated immediately.

During the whole dinner, I obsess about cake. I do my best to pay attention to Peter. I order an enchilada and some rice. I cut up the enchilada and eat one bite along with several spoonfuls of rice. The rest of the time, I play with my food, drink a lot of water, and just stare at Peter, nodding when I think it's appropriate. I do my best not to let on that I wish I was somewhere else. I hope it doesn't show on my face that I'm obsessing about cake.

The dinner ends with me thanking him again for his concern but reassuring him that I will be fine. This, again, pisses me off. I'm supposedly the sick one. Why do I have to reassure anyone?

I can't get out of there fast enough. I race to the PATH station and jump on the train. I'm almost giddy. Intense fear and uncontrolled anticipation are coursing through my body, and I feel like I could take off into flight at any moment. I can't wait to get back to Hoboken and get a cake! But at the same time, I know I don't want to! I don't want to eat cake, but my mind is demanding nothing less than a delicious, moist, sweet cake.

I give in to the inevitable and my thoughts turn to the kind of cake I'm going to consume. My taste buds start to awaken with the possibilities. The next twenty minutes are an endless mirage of images and aromas parading through my mind. I'm oblivious to the hell that I'm about to unleash on my body and the emotional chaos I'm about to embrace.

13

As I round the street corner, I pick up steam and swerve around several people. I'm just hoping it's still open.

I see the bakery to my right and notice the lights are still on. *Great, I'm in luck! They haven't closed yet.* I pass the first window, which is filled with beautiful wedding cakes, and push through the door. Inside, I'm met with a huge rush of cold air. It feels nice and startles me at the same time, effectively knocking me out of my daze.

I stand there for a brief moment before making my way to the counter. It's beautiful, with rows and rows of delicious treats. I'm doing my best to breathe deeply, hoping to cover up the fact that my heart is in my throat. I'm scared, but I really want to do this. I really need a cake.

Ahh, there they are. One section of the counter has a few small, round cakes. I lean in and read the tags in front of them. Then, before I know it, I'm pointing at the one I want. Chocolate Cannoli Cake. I have to have that six-inch, round cake.

I quietly tell the salesperson what I want, and she smiles. She places the object of my desire in a tiny box. I pay and thank her. Then I gently pick up the box and bolt out of there.

I can't get home fast enough. *God, I wish everyone would just get the hell out of my way!* I'm walking as fast as humanly possible without running. I feel like an animal that has just been set free, like I have to get away. I have to move fast and just get home, where it's safe, where I can do what I want to do and no one can judge me.

My heart is pounding harder and harder with each step I take. I'm scared, anxious, and nervous all at the same time. I feel like I'm doing something wrong—almost like I'm about to break the law—but I don't care. I want to—I *have* to—eat this cake.

I also can't help but imagine how I must look to everyone else. Can they tell I'm out of control? Can they see that I'm about to be bad? Do I look ridiculous?

I get inside my apartment fast, slam the door behind me, throw down my bag, and walk into the kitchen. I set the box on the counter and open it. The aroma almost knocks me down. It smells wonderful. I swear, I'm gaining weight just by smelling this thing. Without taking my eyes off the cake, my left hand opens the drawer and pulls out a fork. I carry the box and my fork to my favorite Ikea chair.

I can't allow myself to pause too long, or else I may not follow through with this craziness. I'm mostly numb, but my mind has one clear intention: EAT!

I squeeze my fork tightly and, very carefully, I dig in. As I lift the fork up to my mouth, I take one last smell of the cake, which is now ever-so-close to my nose. It still smells wonderful. I place that bite in my mouth and pull out the fork, closing my eyes. I start to chew and chew and chew. Then I swallow.

It tastes sweet. It tastes nice—but something is missing. I don't feel that *different*. But I choose to ignore anything I'm feeling. Instead, I plunge back into the cake with my fork and take another mouthful. Again—nothing all that great. So I take another mouthful and then another and then another. I just keep shoveling it in. My heart is still pounding as if it thinks I'm running a marathon, and my mind is just commanding me to keep eating.

Several minutes pass before I'm able to gain some measure of self-control. My left hand falls down, exhausted and limp, onto my left thigh with the fork dangling from my fingertips. Tension is slowly starting to fade from my body. I peer into the box and am amazed to see that half the cake is gone. *Damn, I don't remember eating that much.*

I just sit there staring into what feels like a black abyss. *What am I doing? This is ridiculous. I can't do this and still expect to stay thin.* I know that eating half a cake will make me gain weight.

Now total terror consumes me. *I can't believe I just did this! This is so fucked up! I can't gain weight. I won't allow myself.* I leap to my feet, rush into the kitchen, and drop the box onto the counter, tossing my fork into the sink. I reach into the drawer again and grab the wooden spoon, and head into the bathroom.

I kneel down in front of the toilet and shove the handle of the spoon down my throat. Gagging on the taste of wood in my mouth, I press the handle against my throat, hoping it will trigger my gut to empty itself. Nothing. Nothing happens.

I wiggle the handle and try to push it further into my throat. Still nothing. Knowing full well I'm not sold on the idea of forcing myself to puke, I pull the handle out my mouth and throw it down on the floor in disgust. I can't even purge correctly. *I'm such a fucking pathetic failure! This is so messed up!*

After another useless attempt to purge, this time with my fingers, I stand up and head back into the kitchen. The box is sitting, open, on the counter top. I hate it. I hate that box and what's inside of it! It doesn't like me, either.

I grab my window glass cleaner and start spraying the cake. I squeeze the bottle as if my life depends on it, and I keep spraying and spraying as if I'm trying to kill some poisonous insect. After several moments, I stop and just stare at it. It still looks normal. It still looks like a cake.

Out of the corner of my eye, I notice the dishwashing liquid. I grab the bottle from the back of the sink, pop the top, and turn it upside down over the cake. I squeeze again for dear life and cover the cake in the blue liquid. I'm able to cover it quickly. I stop and stare again. Now I feel a bit more satisfied that it doesn't look as tempting. I know what I must do next.

I lean down and pull the bag out of the garbage can, grab the cake box, and toss it into the bag. I pull the drawstrings tight as I tie off the bag, and then I walk it downstairs and set it at the curb. As I climb the stairs back to my apartment, I feel a little bit of relief. At least this evil temptation is out of my place now, so I don't have to worry about messing up again.

Once back inside my apartment, the ease I was feeling melts away at the first signal my gut sends to my brain. It's a signal I don't feel often anymore, and it's a signal I don't like to feel, because it's only purpose is to let me know that I'm not losing weight. I hate feeling full. I hate it.

Now I feel just as anxious as before, and I know I have to do something to get rid of this feeling. I have to get back on track for losing weight. I can't stumble like this, or else that number on the scale is going to go up. I can't let that happen.

Luckily, I have tools to help me. After my disappointment with Ipecac, I did more research and found another trick of the trade: Fleet Phospho-Soda. It's a saline laxative, and it's supposedly very strong. This should do the trick in getting my gut to empty itself. I haven't tried it yet, but I'm hopeful it will work.

I reach under the bathroom counter and grab the small bottle, then back to the kitchen for a spoon, and then I'm ready to read the directions. It says I can take up to nine teaspoons in a twenty four hour period. Well, that's what I'm going to take then. This is serious, and I need the maximum benefit.

I pour the dosage into a glass and then mix in some water, as directed. The consistency is odd. It's very oily. But this can't be as bad as the Ipecac. I take my first sip.

UGH! Oh my God, this is atrocious! I slam the glass down on the counter and stomp my right foot in an attempt to alleviate the pain my taste buds are experiencing. *I can't believe they can sell this shit for consumption.* It's worse than the Ipecac. It's rancid. It's horrible—and that's good. This is good punishment for what I just ate. I like the fact that I don't like this crap, and I hope my body won't like it either.

After several seconds of shock, I take a deep breath and try to muster enough strength to swallow another mouthful. I hesitantly lift the glass off the counter and bring it to my nose. I pause. Briefly, that voice in my head asks why I am doing this to myself. I shut the voice down and gulp the remaining liquid in the glass. It doesn't go down any easier the second time.

An hour passes before I find myself in the bathroom again. It's quick, and my body's violent eruption on the toilet does what I was hoping for: it calms me. My gut is convulsing, and I like it. It's violently emptying everything that I violently shoved into it.

This goes on for the next sixteen hours and prevents me from going to work the next day.

By 10 a.m., I can't believe my body has been going to the bathroom since seven the previous night. *I didn't know I had that much in me.* But most of it is just water now.

Ice cream. Chocolate peanut butter. *Yeah, I really want some chocolate peanut butter ice cream.* My mind starts playing the flashing game and images of ice cream are now running through my mind. I can't shake them. I feel like it's yesterday all over again. *It's okay, I can handle this. Just one pint won't hurt. I could probably use it, since I've emptied everything out of my system.*

Feeling nervous, I get dressed and decide it's safe enough to venture out to get some ice cream. I make my way to the A & P, several blocks away. I don't waste time. I go right to the ice cream, get what I want, check out, and leave.

On my way back, about two blocks from my place, it starts. The cramping and then the dropping feeling in my gut. *Damn, it's not done! I've got to go again.*

I hustle back as fast as I can. Once inside, I throw the ice cream into the freezer and head to the bathroom. When I'm done, I inhale the pint of ice cream without really tasting it. It's gone in less than ten minutes. Gone. All of it. *I ate an entire pint of ice cream.*

My mind is berating me for being so weak. First it wants me to eat, and now it's telling me to stop or else I'm going to gain weight. And again, I go back to the bathroom. Shoving fingers to the back of my throat still doesn't work. *It's okay, this won't derail me. I can always take more laxative to get it out.*

After an unconvincing attempt to calm myself, I crash in front of the TV.

Donuts. Powdered. Cream-filled. Apple-filled. Donuts. I want donuts. It's like watching an old film strip. It just starts playing in my mind in vivid color, and I can't turn it off. It's only been about two hours since I inhaled the ice cream. My body is still feeling the effects of the laxative, and now my mind has decided on another food group to obsess about. *Donuts. Yeah, that does sound good.*

I can go get just a few. They will taste so good.

Before I know what's happening, I'm out the door and walking down Washington Street. Dunkin Donuts is several blocks from me, but I'm there in just a few minutes. I get six beautiful donuts and storm out of there. Again, people can't get out of my way fast enough. I'm holding the box like it's my firstborn and we are fleeing some war-torn country. I have to get home where it's safe.

That voice pops up and wonders how crazy I must look. *People must know I'm bingeing. Who buys donuts in the middle of the afternoon?*

Back in my favorite chair, I open the box and close my eyes. The smell. *Oh, the smell.* It's great. These six beautiful donuts. I can't wait to eat them. Then again, I don't want to eat them. This isn't healthy. *I can stop doing this. I can get help. Nope. Shut up. Just shut the fuck up!*

Silencing that voice again, I reach in for a powdered donut and . . . they're gone. Looking into an empty box, all I see are crumbs. As if in a dream, the six donuts are gone, just like that. I know I ate them, but I don't really remember. In fact, I feel like I could eat six more.

That feeling is there again, but I don't want to acknowledge it. *I'm full. I feel it.* I don't want to face the reason I'm full, and I definitely don't want to face the scale. *Shit, shit, shit! Stupid, fat pig!* I can't believe I have done this.

My pulse races. My heart's in my throat. My mind is berating me with every four-letter word I've ever heard. I slowly get up and throw the donut box in the trash. *I have to move. I can't sit still, or else I'll die.* My mind, if it had its way, would kill me right here.

As I walk down the hall, I take off my shirt. Then I stand in front of the full-length mirror in my hallway. There, halfway down my chest, on the left side, is what appears to be a small softball. It's just sitting there, protruding from my gut. My stomach is full, and all around it the skin stretches to cover that softball, which further exposes my ribs. I can see all of them now.

Then I turn my gaze to the right of my gut, to where my breastbone comes together in the center of my chest. If I stand really still—*ahh, there it is!* The skin is moving up and down, very slowly. My heartbeat.

Looking at my body relaxes me some. My mind is relieved that I can still see my heart beat. That must mean I'm still thin. *I'm still good. I wasn't that bad.*

Not content to be at peace for any length of time, my mind orders my eyes to focus on what I don't like. My gaze slowly drifts down to the area I avoid truly looking at, my waist. Staring back at me are large love handles. I have fantasized taking a chainsaw to them and chopping them off my body. I can feel their weight pulling me down. I hate them. I wish they were gone and my body had that nice V shape that you see on male models in magazines.

I take my hands and wrap them behind me and grab the love handles from the back, stretching them out. I like that look, the look of having nothing at my waist. I want that look. I guess I will just have to lose more weight. But now I'm starting to feel uneasy in front the mirror, so I fall into bed for a nap. I'm surprised that sleep comes so easily.

Chocolate. Truffles. Godiva. Shit, I can't believe this! More flashes. I've barely awakened from my nap when my mind starts in again. Now, of course, I *really* want this. I love truffles. My mind is in total control. I don't physically feel anything. I'm numb, but my mind sure isn't. Again, before I realize it, I'm skulking down the streets of Hoboken is search of truffles. I don't know where any may be. After searching without success, I pass a McDonald's.

Oh, that sounds good. My mind instantly switches gears, and I'm inside McDonald's ordering two double cheeseburgers, medium fries, and a Sprite. All to go, of course. I can't eat in public. I'm being bad, and I can't do that where everyone can see.

Fuck. Fuck. Fuck. It's all gone! Why the fuck did I eat all that food? I can't believe this. I'm anorexic. If I can't purge, I can't eat. This can't be happening. My body is tense. I feel fat. I can feel the fat just attaching itself to me. I don't like it. I can't have it. I have to get back on track and just stop. I can't keep doing this! *It's okay. My body just needed some food but now it's done.*

I walk into my kitchen, throw away all the McDonald's wrappers, and grab a piece of paper and a pen. I furiously start scribbling down numbers. I run through everything I ate in the last twenty-four hours and give it a number. It's a high number—a bad number, if you ask me. Looking down, I see the total but I can't believe it. I've eaten 6500 calories. *Holy shit! That is obscene.* My body just goes numb. Totally numb.

I back away from the counter and just start walking around. I walk down the hallway, turn, and walk back. I do this for several minutes, almost as if in a trance. I just have to move. When I move, it helps me not to think about what I've just done to myself.

It's okay. It's okay. It's okay. I'm afraid if I don't tell myself this and if I actually think about what's happened during these last few hours, I will totally lose it. I'm afraid that I will want to just check out, for good. I can't let myself truly face this. It's too scary and overwhelming. *It's okay. It's okay. It's okay.*

After several more minutes of reciting my mantra, my thoughts slowly turn back to restricting. I focus on my past success and realize that I can get back into the routine of restricting and that I can make up for all these calories I just ate. The calories I ate are still less than what a normal person would eat during a whole week. So I'm still ahead. I just have to get back on track and restrict. *Okay, this is good. It's all good. I'm good.*

After my little pep talk, I head down to get my mail. As I sit on the couch and go through it, I notice a card. I open it. It's from my family. Everyone has signed it. It's their version of a pep talk. I freeze. I sit back and … I cry, hard.

The defenses that I've had up for the past day, during my binge, get blown apart just as violently as I've tried to blow my body apart. Everything comes rushing in. Loneliness. Fear. Sadness. Anger. Shame. I want someone to reach out to me, to hug me and tell me everything will be fine, and that I'll be okay. I want someone to call. I want someone to show up, but no one does. I'm alone in my apartment with this card, and my garbage can is full of the remnants of bad food.

After spending the next few hours in front of the TV, attempting to disconnect from reality, I go to bed. This time, sleep doesn't come. I get back up and take a Benadryl. Once back in bed, I lie there reassuring myself that tomorrow will be better. I tell myself that once I get back into a routine, I will be able to keep losing weight. I fall asleep feeling stronger in my resolve.

I have no idea that the next few days will prove to be anything but routine.

Saturday, May 25, 2002

So on Thursday, after my binge of cake, ice cream, donuts, McDonald's and laxatives, I was down to one hundred and twenty pounds according to the scale. I had my first total blackout. I lost my sight for a good ten seconds. Jordan called during all of this mess trying to schedule an appointment. I agreed to see him next week just to get him off the phone.

If you think all that was it, you are mistaken my friend. Oh yes, now it's Friday, flash forward to end of day. I stop by a market after work to buy rice cakes. I now have to severely restrict all weekend. There I see the Godiva ice cream that I love more than an orgasm – White Chocolate Raspberry!

127

I buy it. I go to another store for something else and see soy ice cream – Chocolate Peanut Butter. I've never tried soy ice cream and it's low in calories, and so I buy a quart. Go home and in ten minutes I eat a partial pint of the Godiva and three quarters of the Soy ice cream. Now I really want to pump myself full of laxatives, but I have to talk myself out of it, because I have to meet a friend to see 'Star Wars.'

It's a hard, thirty-minute battle not to down a bottle of laxatives, but I don't and then I break down and cry. Again, I yearn for a phone call.

I go out and during part of the movie (which was slow, by the way) I think about cake. There's another bakery I have never tried. Well, on my way home, I am once again like a rabid man trying to score his heroin! Of course at 11 p.m., nothing is open, so I go to A&P again and buy a carrot cake. Ashamed and heart pounding, I pay for it (who the hell buys a whole cake at 11 p.m., and do they know I am going home to binge?) I storm home and eat half of it in about eight minutes. It tastes wonderful.

Now I am too exhausted to do the laxatives now. I feel kinda at peace now. I gather up the garbage and throw out the rest of the cake and now feel my binge is totally over. I mentally put the monster back in his cage and know in a few hours I will pump myself full of laxatives. That comforts me.

With Renfrew a bust and now my folks not calling – it drills into me I am now on my own with this, and yes, I have no reason to trust anymore. Why should I, when it just ends up hurting me and letting loose this monster?

So now it's Saturday morning (the next day) and I am writing all of this just before I take the bottle of laxative. I wanted to get all this down just so I never forget. Don't forget those out-of-control feelings and that the food never tasted that good. You have to keep the monster caged and have to stay in control! Never let go!

This has only strengthened me. From my setbacks and failures I will learn and go on to be more successful, for this journey is truly a journey of one.

14

Blackout. I start to feel the familiar sensation of losing my sight and the dropping feeling, like I could pass out at any minute, as I climb up out of the PATH station. I pause and start to take the steps more slowly. I automatically compensate, before I even realize what I'm doing. This event has become routine for me now. Luckily, I make it to the top of the stairs and get outside before the episode becomes worse. The fresh air seems to have a calming effect on me and I don't experience a total blackout—this time.

After regaining my sight, I set upon my usual path back home. I feel like a robot these days, just walking along without seeing anything. I'm not really enjoying the beautiful summer evening. All I know is that I want to get home and just be alone. But I need to make one stop first.

Rounding the corner, I walk into the CVS. I'm grateful the doors are automatic. I don't have enough strength these days to open heavy doors. Once inside, I'm met with an overpowering rush of cold air that instantly chills me to the bone. I'm pretty cold most of the time these days. I just need to buy two things, and then I can get out of here and get home.

Luckily, I've done this routine many times before, so I know exactly where to find what I need. Weaving around people, down one aisle and up the next, I stop in front of my intended target. The first time I bought this, it terrified me. But this time, I'm so numb I don't feel much at all. I now know what to expect, and I'm confident that this item will be more than adequate in helping me stay on track.

It pisses me off that they place things so fucking low. I kneel down so I'm facing the bottom shelf and reach in for the small box of Fleet Phospho-Soda. I have to put my right hand down to steady myself and take a small breath in and then exhale as I slowly stand up. *Nice, I didn't black out at all.*

Okay, now just one more thing to buy, and then I'm done. The other item is close by and it's on an upper shelf. I'm able to buzz past and grab a package of toilet paper as I'm walking down the aisle. I've always been embarrassed buying toilet paper. I know everyone poops, but it just feels weird to buy the supplies for it.

As I approach the front checkout, it suddenly dawns on me that I've got a laxative in one hand and toilet paper in the other. That's it. I'm buying something to make me shit and something else to clean it up. *This is fucked up.* Here I am, a rail-thin, pale, anorexic guy, and I'm buying a laxative that I shouldn't need until I'm like ninety years old. I must look ridiculous! If I felt anything these days, this would be funny to me. Maybe one day it will seem funny.

I try not to feel too self-conscious as I stand in line for what feels like an hour. I hide the Fleet under one arm so people in line can't see it. When I finally get to the counter, I look down, never making eye contact with the check-out girl. I pay cash and then storm out of there as fast as I can.

Thank God, I'm home at last! These days, work is driving me nuts. It's all I can do just to stay awake. I know my coworkers know something is going on with me, but nobody at work—not even my boss—has said anything or even asked if I'm okay. On one hand, this relieves me, because it allows me to keep doing what I want to. But on the other hand, it's shocking to me that no one has said anything. For all they know, I could be dying.

But today is Friday and I don't have to worry about work for two whole days. I'm going to do what I love to do: take this Fleet, enjoy the violence it unleashes upon my body, and stay inside all weekend with the anticipation of seeing the number on my scale go down even further.

I'm hungry. I'd better eat a little something just so I can make it through the evening. I walk over to the cart in my kitchen and grab the bag of rice cakes. My heart starts pounding a bit faster as I open the bag. These days, the only strong physical reaction I get is when I decide to eat anything. It makes me nervous, because I know I don't need to be eating if I want to keep losing weight. But sometimes I give in and eat. I don't like it, but I know if I don't eat something, I risk the monster getting loose and creating havoc again. I know I don't want that to happen. Never again.

I down about four rice cakes without thinking. It registers in my gut, which I don't care to acknowledge. I decide to watch a movie before I take my allotment of Fleet, so I lie down on the sofa and turn on the TV. About an hour into the movie, I'm restless, so I decide to take the Fleet. By the time the movie is over, it will be in full gear, and then it should run its course pretty quickly. I've done this several times now, and it doesn't take twelve hours to go through me like it used to.

I choke down the oily sludge and chase it with a full glass of water, which tastes heavenly. *I don't think I will ever get used to the taste of this shit.* I'm glad that one dose is all it takes. I crash on the sofa and settle in for the last half of the movie.

I'm tired, really tired. It's been three hours and I've gone to the bathroom about twelve times. My body is exhausted. I strip down to my underwear and crawl into bed. Looking forward to some sleep, I curl up on my side. Instantly, my knees start yelling at me. I keep forgetting that I can't stack my legs on top of each other anymore—my knees are too bony for that.

I grab a pillow and jam it between my legs. I sink into my queen-sized bed and fall asleep, faster than I have in weeks.

Ugh. Damn it, I'm tired! I roll over to my right side and swing my legs off the bed. As I slowly start to sit up, my stomach starts to churn more and more violently. I squint at the clock; it's 1:12 am. This is my first time up tonight. I'm thankful my gut hasn't awakened me before now.

I push off the bed with my eyes half shut. Suddenly, my stomach does that gurgling sound, and I feel more pressure deep inside. I know what's coming next. I race into the bathroom as fast as I can.

My right foot steps onto the cold tile, my left foot follows, and then ... *Oh my God! The pain! It's it's it's* ... My body lurches forward as my right arm grabs the edge of the sink and I fall to the floor.

The pain is excruciating. It feels like a knife has been plunged into the left side of my chest and is being pulled down my left arm. My knees hit the tile with a small thud and I throw myself forward, grasping the sides of the toilet. My eyes are clenching, waiting for complete darkness to take me at any moment.

My breathing slows, and before I know it, the pain is gone, just as fast as it appeared. And all I'm left with is ... nothing. I don't feel anything but sweat trickling down my forehead. It's gone. *Oh my God, what the hell was that?*

I can't move, so I just sit there until the feeling slowly starts to return to the rest of my body. The feel of the cold tile registers on my knees, and soon the pain of kneeling becomes too much, so I push myself up. My stomach gets back into the action and reminds me why I'm in the bathroom in the first place. I spin around and pull down my underwear, and I sit on the toilet.

While my body does what it needs to, all I can think about is what just happened. I feel okay, I think, but I'm scared. That pain was overwhelming. It was really bad, and I don't know what it was or why it happened. My mind is racing, trying to come up with some explanation.

After several minutes, all I can come up with is the Fleet. I've been downing this crap and it's been taking a toll on my body. I know it's getting rid of not only waste, but also fluid. I like it, I like how I feel when I take it, and I like what it does to my weight. But now I'm not so sure I should be taking it. My mind flashes images of me hunched over the toilet in just my underwear, dead. *I don't want to die like that.*

HOYT J. PHILLIPS, III

I stand up, wash my hands, and head back to my bed. I can obsess about this more later. Now I just want to go back to bed and try to forget this ever happened. I crawl into bed, sprawl out on my stomach, and turn my head to the left. I notice the time on the clock. It's 1:18 a.m. *Wow, all that took place in six minutes. It felt more like an hour.*

I feel a chill run through my body at the thought that my life could end so quickly, without warning. In the blink of an eye, I could be gone—*if I keep up this madness.* I'm scared by the thought that I may no longer be able to keep taking Fleet, so I shut down. I don't want to think about what is happening to me.

I'm tired. I'm exhausted. And I'm grateful when my queen-sized bed swallows my tiny frame once more and I fall asleep—quickly, without warning.

15

"You're parents are worried about you."

I choose not to fully take this statement in. Without thinking, I state the obvious: "I know."

"How are you doing today?" Dr. Baranoff asks with quiet concern in his voice.

"I'm fine." Again, I'm not thinking. I'm just saying what I think is expected.

It's been a little more than three weeks since my binge episode, and I've gotten back on track. I am in full restricting mode, though the fear of dropping dead from a heart attack is now invading my thoughts on a daily basis. My body is still hovering in the low 120's; as a result, I'm pretty beaten down and don't feel much of anything.

This is my third visit with this new psychologist that my parents have asked me to see. Somehow, my mom was able to find this guy who has experience treating both women and men with eating disorders. I agreed to see him. I guess it's to make my parents happy—and maybe, deep down, I know it would be good for me.

So far, the jury is still out on him. He's nice enough, but he doesn't push much. I also feel a little bit guilty, like I'm cheating on Jordan. I'm still seeing Jordan sometimes, but I don't know—it just feels weird. And, truth be told, Jordan is gay, younger, and better to look at than Dr. Baranoff.

"Hoyt, things are bad," the doctor is telling me. "The tests you had done at the doctor are okay, for now. But if you keep doing this, you're going to do some real damage to your body."

I just sit there on his couch and look at him. I've given up shifting my weight or throwing my right leg over my left anymore. It's useless. I don't care anymore. I just sit there. I hear what he's saying, but I don't really care. I don't know what to do or how to stop. He doesn't wait for a response.

"We've talked about Rogers Memorial Hospital before."

I nod in recognition at the name, trying to remember what he has said about it.

"It's a good place, and they treat men with eating disorders," he says. "I've had several patients go there and do very well."

"How does that work? Are the guys in with the women?"

"Everyone is in the same building, but the men are treated separately from the women. Your treatment is completely separate. You don't have to interact with them." He pauses for a while to let me process this information.

"I've called, and they actually have room. They have a space for you."

Wow. I wasn't prepared for that. A space for me. For me. I think I should be feeling something right now, but I don't. I just sit there, stone-faced. I'm not sure what to do. I know if I don't do anything, I'm agreeing to my death. I won't stop on my own. Amazingly, that voice still has something to say—and because my body and mind have pretty much shut down, the voice has my attention.

"Hoyt, will you go?"

As I sit there, looking at him, my mind jumps back into the game to protest. *You're not sick enough. You can't go. You can't leave your life, you're job. No.*

Dr. Baranoff waits, looking at me, not breaking eye contact. It makes me uneasy. I know he won't say anything. He's waiting for my reply, and we will sit in silence until I speak.

Feeling defeated, I whisper, "Yes … I'll go." My body, out of sheer exhaustion, slumps deeper into the sofa.

I'm tired. I just need a break from my life.

PART II

Rehab

16

"You want one?" she asks.

"What?" I mutter, turning from the window to face her.

"A Xanax. It will help with your nerves." *She's got to be joking. I'm on my way to rehab, and she's asking if I want to pop a pill.* Then again, pills were never my thing.

"No," I answer, annoyed.

I turn back to staring out the window at the baggage handlers loading the luggage into the underbelly of the plane. It's daybreak, my favorite time of day. Sunlight peeks over the horizon, casting an orange-yellow glow that demands the world's attention—a reminder to everything in its path that it's time to start another day.

My heart floods with guilt.

Damn it. I was too harsh. Mom was just being nice. I shouldn't have said no. Maybe I do need a Xanax. Maybe that's why she offered it to me. Of course, I did the polite thing by refusing the first offer—just as I had been taught from infancy. Always say no at first, so you don't seem rude or too eager. But a second offer—that's fine to accept. My brain volleys with the temptation. I know this day is going to get more surreal, so taking the edge off might do some good.

"Actually, if you don't mind, I'll take one."

She smiles, reaches under her seat, and grabs her behemoth purse. Why she carries such a huge thing around, I'll never know. But as a true Southern belle, fashion always trumps comfort.

She finds her bag of goodies —an overly-used, gallon-sized plastic bag packed with pill bottles, both over-the-counter and prescriptions ones, including some that have no doubt long expired. For a moment, I wonder how she got all this past security. My mother never ceases to amaze me.

"One or two?" she asks as she snaps the cap off a bottle and points it toward me.

"I have no idea," I answer. I'm still surprised by her willingness to let me have at her pill stash. "How many should I take?"

"One should be good," she says. "It will just make you relaxed. Maybe a bit tired."

Peering into the bottle, I'm amazed at how tiny the pills are. I poke a finger in and somehow manage to slide a single tablet up the side of the bottle. I pop it into my mouth and wash it down with a sip of water. I can't drink too much. I refuse to use the bathroom on this trip.

My personal flying game of never leaving my seat has now started. I usually win this game, and I'll be damned if this flight will be any different.

After screwing the top back on, I lean down and slide my Deer Park water bottle back into the mesh pocket on the side of my book bag, which rests against my feet. I know I won't be drinking for the rest of the flight.

Just then, the flight crew gets on the intercom system and starts reciting their script about emergency exits, the speech that most people hear as a signal to tune out and try to get some sleep. Since I got up at four to catch this eight a.m. flight out of Philadelphia, sleep sounds like a great idea.

Unfortunately, sleep is not on my mind's agenda. In true, obsessive fashion, my mind starts racing. What awaits us once we touch down in Wisconsin? Why, again, am I doing this? For how long? *I really don't need to go away; I'm not that sick.*

Of course, all of this preoccupation is totally self-serving. It allows me to hide in my own world, ignoring the woman sitting next to me who is suffering in silence, as only the mother of a sick child can. Her beautiful exterior—with its impeccably styled, blond-highlighted hair, black pants, red silk blouse, just the right amount of make-up, and her elegant-but-eye-catching, three carat, oval-cut diamond engagement ring—masks her inner turmoil.

I know I'm the cause of that turmoil. I can feel the pain, uncertainty, and fear radiating from her, but I don't want to deal with it or acknowledge it. That's one great thing about being an addict—it's always all about me.

Mom sits there quietly, letting me stay in my own little world. She knows that soon the Xanax will do its job for both of us and help us to at least start this journey a bit desensitized—or in my case, even more numb than I usually am.

Before I know it, a fog descends. I'm feeling out of it. My mind, still racing to come up with answers, surrenders to my body's overwhelming demand to shut down for a while. With protest, my mind relents.

We land in Milwaukee. Never been here. I loved *Laverne & Shirley* as a kid, but I know that what I'm embarking on is going to be anything but a zany sitcom.

After retrieving my suitcase, we make our way outside to the taxi stand. It's the end of June, hot and humid outside, and yet I feel cold. I zip up my grey hoodie, attempting to insulate my frail frame. The worn-out Gap jacket is too big and it looks like hell on me, but I couldn't imagine not bringing it with me. I feel safe wearing it. I feel protected.

Great, I'm trembling. Nerves are a bitch.

A late-model, white Ford min-van pulls up and we slide in while the driver loads my suitcase in the back.

"Rogers Memorial Hospital in Oconomowoc, please," my mother says in her soft, Southern accent. She flashes a smile, the one that denotes neither pleasure nor fear.

The driver nods and we speed off to nowhere—nowhere that I've ever been. I've never visited this state, and I've never heard of where we are going. Hell, I can't even pronounce the town's name.

I'm suddenly self-conscious. *Does the driver know why we are here? Does he know that I'm the sick one? Is it that obvious to other people?* During the past nine months, I've worked so damn hard presenting a healthy front. Now it occurs to me that maybe it was all in vain—that if anyone really looked at me, they could tell.

No, no, he can't tell, my ego protests. I look okay. Even though I'm growing out my hair, it still looks good. Under my hoodie, I've got on a dark blue, striped Polo shirt, and I am actually wearing jeans that are the correct size. Thankfully, Mom insisted that we go shopping, since I didn't have many clothes that fit anymore.

"The ride should only be about forty-five minutes," Mom says casually, trying to make small talk.

"Cool." I don't know what else to say. I really don't want to say anything. I know I should be grateful. After everything I have put my parents through, my mother is escorting me to rehab. She also made all the arrangements for me. She worked with my therapist and the rehab center to get me a bed there, found out what needed to be done, and made sure it was done. All that is expected of me is just to show up.

For some reason, though, I can't help but resent her. It's like my life hasn't turned out the way I planned, and now for me to get better, my mom has to do all the dirty work. I'm not even grown up enough to help myself.

In a few minutes, we are off the freeway and driving along scenic roads. I assume we have reached the destined town, whose name it will take me more than two weeks to learn to spell correctly.

It's so warm out my mom cracks open her window. I'm struck by the aroma that floods the car. The air is wonderful—so sweet and fresh. It smells like fruit, mint, and something else I'm not really sure of. I know I like it, though.

We pass by enormous farms. I've never seen such large swaths of land up close. I also notice the massive, metal arms that stretch across the land, spraying water like a jumbo sprinkler. I feel like a kid at the zoo seeing some strange animal for the first time. I'm amazed at the scale of everything here. It's all just so large.

"Look at all that," I comment. My mom just smiles.

"Smells good, doesn't it?"

"Yeah, it does. I've never seen stuff like this before."

She laughs. "You've been in New York City too long! I used to love to visit my grandparents in Boone every summer. Walking around their farm and picking strawberries ..." she says wistfully. For a brief moment, we are just a mother and son having a lighthearted conversation about nothing significant. And for a brief moment, I feel at peace. Her smile is comforting. Her love warms me. I unzip my hoodie.

Then the sign appears, shattering that moment: Rogers Memorial Hospital. It's real. We're here. My heart beats faster.

The driver makes his way down a long drive. We pass a big, sterile-looking building on the right as we make our way behind the building and down the drive, pulling up in front of a house. It looks like any generic house you would see in a mountain vacation community. Muted colors. Pretty drab. We get out and my mom pays the fare.

I'm standing there holding my suitcase and book bag, staring at the front door.

"Come on. We can do this," Mom says as she gently squeezes my left arm, motioning me forward.

We? Interesting choice of words. Deep breaths, deep breaths. I focus on reminding myself that I don't have to do anything. I can pretend this is all a movie. *Put on your game face.*

We walk through the front entrance, and there it is: the front desk. No one is there. *Hot damn! We can leave.*

No, we can't. My mom walks up to the desk, and suddenly a friendly-looking, middle-aged women appears and smiles.

"Yes, Hi. I'm Beth Phillips. I'm here to check in my son," my mom says. I can't help but smile at her need to always introduce herself before talking to someone new. She even does it on the phone.

"Oh, Hoyt Phillips. Yes, we've been expecting you. I hope your trip went well," the woman says, too enthusiastically. *Why is she so happy?*

"It was fine. Thank you."

The receptionist picks up the phone and taps some numbers. I ignore what she says, because by this time, I've begun inching toward the front door, in case I need to make a quick escape. I'm reading a small flyer posted by the door that cautions people about the wind chill factor. It warns me that proper clothing must be worn to prevent frostbite. I've never seen such a thing. Then it dawns on me: I'm in Wisconsin and it gets cold here. Just how cold, I hope to never find out.

Before I know it, on my left, elevator doors open and a young guy walks out, along with a young woman. They both appear pleasant enough. I smile and lower my head.

"Hoyt?" the woman asks.

"Yes," I reply. I look up but avoid eye contact.

"Hi I'm Lori. I'm a tech here. It's nice to meet you," the woman says. Her voice is cheery. She seems too damn happy and friendly. *Am I in rehab or in Mr. Roger's Neighborhood?*

"Nice to meet you too," I say quickly. Actually, I think I could have been perfectly happy having never met her—but why start telling the truth now?

"This is Cesar. It's his last day here. He's leaving now," she says, still smiling brightly. Cesar also smiles, but somewhat awkwardly. I don't know what to say. Is it a good thing or a bad thing that he's leaving?

I settle on, "Congratulations."

"Thanks. I'm a bit nervous," Cesar says. *Oh, it's a bad thing, I take it.*

This whole exchange lasts about one minute but it feels painfully longer. Cesar says good-bye to Lori and then walks out the front door, hauling his suitcase. I would kill to follow him right now.

Lori then turns to me. "Well, you ready to go down to the unit to get checked in?"

"Yeah, okay," I say tentatively while my heart skips several beats. As I turn around to my mom, Lori says, "Mrs. Phillips, you can come down as well."

We all board the elevator and the doors close. The elevator seems huge and I'm alone in the top half of it, since I'm taller than Lori and my mom by at least five inches. As we ride, Lori enthusiastically gives me the run-down regarding the house and its three levels.

The main level, which we were on, houses the teenage girls and the dining room. The top floor has other rooms for art and individual therapy. And the bottom floor, where we are headed, houses the men and the adult women—in separate rooms, of course. *Of course.*

The elevator doors open and I'm met with a view of the bottom floor. A small, upholstered chair sits to the left, underneath a pay phone. You don't see those anymore. *No one has cell phones around here?*

"I'll show you the guys' day room first," Lori tells us. "Follow me." She turns right and, a few steps later, opens a door on the left. Wow, the guys have their own day room—not bad. We follow her into the room. Once inside, my expectations are not upheld. The room is painted up to chair height in a color that looks like a cross between Pepto-Bismol and vomit. That colorful area is topped off with a lovely floral border that makes me think I'm in a retirement home. Above that is your standard *One Flew Over the Cuckoo's Nest* white wall.

The room is furnished with items that, from the looks of them, were yard sale bargains. Two old, blue sofas line two different walls. There is a worn-out, wine-colored recliner in the corner. And opposite the recliner, on the other end of the room, is a small entertainment table with a TV and DVD player on it. Some kid is sitting facing us with his head down, writing in a notebook.

"Kyle, this is Hoyt. He's joining us today," Lori tells the kid.

Kyle halfway looks up. "Hey," he says in his not-yet-settled-in post-pubescent voice.

"Hey," seems like an appropriate response. *Great, I'm going to be with a kid who seems to be missing his skateboard and cigarettes.* Kyle is sporting a major emo look, wearing mostly black, baggy clothes and some weird-looking, smiley-faced wrist band. The phrase "nothing in common" keeps running through my head. After that stimulating interaction with another patient, Mom and I follow Lori back into the hall and into the office, which is just past the pay phone.

The office is cramped with two desks forming an L. I notice a big, beautiful window opposite where we are standing and a large, doctor office-style scale to my immediate left. I also spot an open door leading into what looks like a supply or medicine closet to my right. At the other end of the office there is a guy, probably in his early thirties. He smiles and reaches out his hand to me.

"Hi, I'm Steve." He looks and sounds like he could have just stepped off a movie set, acting as a double for Arnold Schwarzenegger. His yellow t-shirt is pasted on him, stretching over muscles that look like balloons inflated under his skin.

"Hi, I'm Hoyt," I respond returning the handshake with as much force as possible. *This isn't real.*

I've been met by an overly happy, middle-aged receptionist; a perky female tech who should be on *Sesame Street*, teaching kids how to count; and now I'm meeting a guy who looks like he should be wearing ripped jeans and gliding down the Santa Monica boardwalk on roller skates. I lower my head, biting my tongue and try not to laugh at what is turning out to be a more surreal day than I had bargained for.

Steve mentions he has some paperwork that needs to be completed. He asks my mom some questions. She answers. I stand there awkwardly, trying not to look around. I'm afraid if I really notice anything, it will make all this too real.

Turning to me, Steve asks, "Do you like to go by Hoyt or Jeff?"

Here we go. I'm surprised it took this long. Yes, my first name is Hoyt, but my whole life, until college, I was called Jeff—my middle name. I'm the third Hoyt in the family, so my parents thought it would be less confusing to call me some other name. They didn't expect me to start using my given name—and truth be told, they still seem put out by it.

"Hoyt," I reply tersely.

My mom smiles and rattles on. "We call him Jeff. We just never thought he would go by Hoyt. His father and I still haven't adjusted to it, I guess," she says with a nervous chuckle.

Thanks, Mom. I feel a knot rise in my stomach. *Anything else we need to talk about? Is it time for family therapy yet?* That would be a great way to top off this day. Steve just keeps writing his notes.

I'm feeling more and more jittery, and I just want to get it over with. What "it" is, I don't know. But things seem to be moving at a snail's pace here. I have this sinking feeling that my mom won't be staying much longer, and this makes me both agitated and scared. I want to be here alone, but at the same time, I don't want to be alone. I've felt this push-pull with her most of my life.

It's this tension between us that will prove to be fruitful ground for self exploration over the next several weeks.

"Well, I think that's about it," Steve says, looking up at me.

"If you want, you and your mom can say good-bye and then we will get you settled into your room," Lori chirps. This chick only seems to have one mode, and it's getting on my nerves.

I was right—it's time for Mom to go. I suddenly feel her energy shift. It's startling, and I do my best to ignore it. Her vulnerability scares me and my desire to protect her exhausts me, so I numb out to it.

We walk together out to the hallway and stand in front of the elevator doors. She looks at me while I stand there frozen. I know that, deep down, all she wants to do is hold me and take me back home. We both know she can't. We exchange awkward smiles, stalled in our valiant attempt to reassure one another. She hugs me - initiating it as she always does with me. She squeezes tight.

"It's going to be okay. This is good. You know I love you so much," is all she manages before she has to stop herself to prevent from breaking down.

"I know. I know. I love you, too. And thank you," I say sincerely as I reach around her to push the UP button. "Have a safe trip home. I'll talk to you soon."

The doors open much more quickly than either of us anticipates. She looks at me and steps into the elevator. Turns around and looks again. I do my best to hold her gaze, but eye contact for me feels so electric. It makes me feel too vulnerable. She pushes the button and the doors close with merciful speed. I stand there. *Now what?*

"Ready?" *Oh yeah.* It's Little Miss Susie Sunshine, Lori, standing at the office door. I step back into the office. "Let's go get you settled into your room, okay?" She starts to leave the office, lugging my large suitcase and calls over her shoulder, "Follow me. Bring your book bag."

We turn left out of the office and go down this long, generic-looking, hospital-like hall. It has that thin carpet that provides no cushioning but is so durable it will probably end up sitting in a dump until the next dinosaurs roam the earth.

"J.R. is your roommate," she's telling me. "He's a great guy. Nineteen and from Pennsylvania. He's been here about six weeks now. He's doing great. I think he's at rec right now, so you'll meet him later." She rattles on more about how wonderful a guy J.R. is and how much I will like him. *I'm twenty-five, and I get to share a room with a nineteen-year-old. It's old college week. Whoo-hooo.*

She turns the handle on the door to room 502AB and leans heavily into it. I reach in to help her. *Damn, this thing is heavy. Are they trying to keep people in the room, or out of it?* I help her by wheeling my suitcase into the room.

Directly in front of me is a simple, single bed with a wooden nightstand next to it. Above the bed is a cork board with a photo of a dog and a small cross. *Interesting.* Is J.R. a holy roller? That will make for some intriguing conversation.

I turn to the left, and there is my bed. Empty. Some sheets folded on top. Oh yeah, and the color of the room is just plain, old-fashioned Pepto-Bismol—no vomit mixed in.

"I've got to go through everything and make sure you didn't bring anything that's not allowed," Lori says. Now her voice sounds somewhat apprehensive. It's nice to see she does have some other mode.

Everything? She has to go through all of my stuff? I didn't know about this part of the fun. She won't even let me open my own suitcase. She opens it on the floor and—wearing gloves now—starts to take everything out, piece by piece.

"Yeah, we have to do this for everyone. We just have to make sure you didn't bring any contraband. Oh, like this," she says, holding up my razor. "I'll take this and put it in the office. When you need it, just grab one of the techs and they will check it out for you. We have some cutters, and so we can't have these laying around."

Cutters! Is that something I have to worry about J.R. doing? My mind suddenly jumps to the Sandra Bullock movie *28 Days* where her roommate was a cutter and it didn't turn out so well. I'm not loving the thought of being in a movie anymore.

As Lori is on the floor going through everything I brought with me, I just stand there, towering over this scene that doesn't seem to be happening to me. My mind races back to my mom, hoping she got back to the airport alright. Then I start to wonder what fun is in store for me next. And then back to the nagging statement my mind keeps playing over and over again: *I'm not sick enough. I'm not sick enough!* And then to the final thought, the one I'm not sure I'm ready to face: *How did I end up in a place like this?*

17

"I'm glad you didn't bring any contraband. You'd be surprised what some people try to sneak in," Lori says as she rolls her eyes.

"What? Oh, Oh yeah," I mutter, not really listening. My mind is still trying to gain some sense of control over this situation. I don't know what to do or say.

I lean against the wall while Lori, with excruciating slowness, goes through all of my stuff. *This is so messed-up. Oh great, now she's got my underwear.* I do my best to stifle a smile at the irony that this is the most action my underwear has seen in months, and it's being instigated by a female. This whole scene is *so* not my idea of fun.

"I'm glad you're here. It's a good place," Lori says. She pauses and looks up at me with a soft face. I feel uncomfortable at the amount of sincerity directed my way, so I look down.

"Thanks," is all that comes out. *What do I say to that?* "So ... how did you end up working in a place like this?" I blurt out, doing my best to change the subject.

"Oh, I've had a personal experience with this," she quietly answers as she resumes searching through my suitcase. There is a silence that I don't feel like breaking. Apparently she has dealt with an eating disorder, but she looks healthy now.

"I had a good friend a couple of years ago die from anorexia."

Okay, now I feel awkward. "Oh, I'm sorry," I say. It's all I can manage. I don't like having to feel like I have to comfort someone. *I just met you, girl, and I don't need to know this personal stuff.*

"Thank you. It's tough, but I feel led to help other people so that they don't have to suffer like that," she adds. A hint of cheeriness is slowly starting to come back into her voice.

I watch as she finishes with my suitcase and starts pulling things out of my book bag. I slowly become anxious at the thought of what's inside my book bag. I'm not ready to reveal anything too personal—just yet, or possibly ever—to this girl. Dread is now completely consuming me. I'm resigned to the fact that I can't stop her from pulling everything out of my bag, but I hold out hope that she won't make a big deal out of anything.

I gasp as I see in her hand the one item that I've most feared her discovering. *Wait a minute, I don't think she even really looked at it. Awesome!* All she does is flip through the pages of the book and then, just as quickly as she picked it up, she places it down on the ground, with the front cover down on the floor, which would prevent anyone from reading the title.

It's a title that, in conjunction with the photo of the gorgeous guy on the cover, would probably tell even the most clueless that I'm gay. *Assuming the Position* by Rick Whitaker just sounded too good not to read. It's a memoir about a guy who used to be a gay prostitute. I'm looking forward to reading this, and Lord knows I could use some escapism right about now. As soon as I'm able, I will put the book in a safe place so no one can find it.

"Well, everything looks good," Lori says. "Why don't I let you put everything away, and then after you're done, just come back to the front station so we can get your vitals. Then it will be time for lunch," she announces as she stands.

Lunch. Did she just say lunch? There is no way that you are expecting me to eat now. I just got here. No. No lunch.

"I'll see you in a few," she chirps as she walks out, leaving me just standing there in shock.

Lunch. I will have to eat lunch with all these people! *Damn it, I'm not ready for this! I don't want to do this.* I see all of my stuff sprawled out on the floor and figure I'd better put it away. I can't stand things being out of their place. I can handle this one little task, and maybe it will take my mind off what is waiting for me.

After placing all my clothes in the small, wooden dresser and stashing the book in my nightstand, I shove my suitcase and book bag in the closet that is close to the door. I want to escape. I notice that there isn't much in this closet, which leaves plenty of room for me to crawl in and just shut the door. *Oh, how I would love that!* Just get in there, close the door and shut everything else out.

Then again, this eating disorder has pretty much forced me to live in a dark closet for a long time. And there is a real possibility that I will be placing myself back in another kind of "closet" during my stay here. It's weird. I thought there would be plenty of gay guys in a place like this, but by the looks of things, I'm all alone on that front.

I walk back toward my side of the room and flop down onto the bed. It feels fairly comfortable. I haven't slept on a twin bed since college, but I'm sure I will get used to it again. It's probably like riding a bike. I lie there, staring up at the ceiling. *I'm here. I'm really here in the middle of Wisconsin in a rehab facility for people with eating disorders.*

Rehab. I never in a million years thought I would ever be in rehab. My mind is doing a superb job at keeping me stuck in myself, which prevents me from really feeling my fear of what's coming next. Lunch.

After what I'm sure is too long, I exhale and stand up. This isn't going to go away, so I decide I'd better get my butt down the hall and face the music.

I step out of the room and find the hallway is quiet. No one really seems to be around. *Stall. I need more time. Yes, bathroom. I'll go to the bathroom.* I noticed one when we walked this way before. I look to my left and notice a very wide door opening. I can see a sink. *Okay, this will work.*

I hesitantly walk up to the door way and peer inside. *Wow, it's huge in here.* I lean in trying, to see if this is a men's or women's bathroom. There isn't a sign on the door. I step in, turn around and close the door. Then I look at the wall above the sink in disbelief. *That can't be! No. That's the mirror?* Above the long counter top hangs a tiny square mirror, smaller than a dinner plate. *This is nuts. How am I supposed to see myself in this thing? Ugh, whatever.*

I pace back and forth, noticing that on one side behind a door is the shower and the toilet is behind another door on the opposite side. I realize that this is a communal bathroom where someone can be using the toilet and someone else can be in here washing their hands or whatever else they need to be doing.

I pee, walk back into the main area, and wash my hands. The tiny mirror is hung so low that I'll have to bend my knees to see my face in it. I hate not having a large mirror to see myself. It's going to make obsessing about my appearance so much harder.

After stalling for a couple more minutes, I leave the bathroom and walk down the hall to the office. I can feel my muscles tense. They contract so hard that I have no option but to stop walking for a moment. I'm nervous. I don't want to go into the office.

"Hey, there you are. Come on in," the familiar, friendly voice exclaims.

I walk in. It's just me and Lori. She motions to a chair by the door and I sit down. She pulls out a blood pressure cuff and quickly fastens it over my left arm. I just sit there, staring straight ahead. It seems like she has to pump a lot just to get the cuff to inflate over my thin arm. Next, she takes my temperature.

"Okay, the last thing is your weight. You need to turn around and face into the room. So basically, stand on the scale backwards," she instructs.

I have to stand backwards on this thing? That's weird. I would really like to see what the scale says. My heart starts to beat a little bit faster. I really want to know what this says. I *need* to know what this says. I feel terrified now, afraid that I've been bad and will weigh more than I should. I step onto the scale and turn around as instructed.

She reaches around me, turns the scale on, and leans over to see what number it spits out. Then she quickly turns it off and makes notes in my chart. As nonchalantly as possible, I lean forward and crane my neck in her direction, but she has the chart slanted towards her so I can't see what she is writing. *Oh, she's good.*

"So in the mornings before breakfast, you need to come down here and the tech on duty will weigh you," she explains.

"Okay," I say. I'm somewhat confused. I'll have to stand on this scale backwards *every morning*? *Fun.*

"So now it's time for lunch. I'll take you up and show you where the guys sit," she says lightly as she files my chart away and heads toward the door.

My heart hasn't slowed down. I was nervous enough about the scale, and now she has launched right into lunch. I don't like this one bit. I guess they like to do things as a baptism by fire around here.

With my head down, I follow Lori onto the elevator like a lost little puppy. There are stairs right next to the elevator, but for some reason, we take the elevator. *This is so stupid. I can walk. I like to walk.*

Lori seems to have read my thoughts. "Since you are new, we need to take the elevator. In fact, for the next seventy-two hours, you are on observation. That means you need to stay on the unit. We need to keep an eye on you to make sure you're okay. It's just for the next three days. And so, for the time being, you need to take the elevator and you can just go as far as the patio that is right outside the lower unit that you are staying on," she explains with a twinge of apprehension in her voice. I get the feeling that she's had a bad reaction to this news from previous residents.

Three days. I can't leave the unit. *Great. I get to be the lab rat that everyone stares at, watching to see if I keel over or something.*

Just then the doors open—yeah, this elevator is so slow—and we get out. I follow Lori again with my head down, thinking that if I don't really pay attention, none of this will sink in. Then I can pretend it's all a dream.

We go through a doorway and I'm suddenly in a large room filled with round tables. All the tables are encircled with chairs topped with mauve-colored cushions. To my surprise, on the opposite wall is a massive, floor-to-ceiling window. In fact, the entire back wall of this place is made of windows that overlook a wooden patio. It's pretty, but so very bright. This place is so well lit that I'll be able to see my food very clearly, and everyone will be able to see me eating. *Wonderful!*

"Oh, there's Steve," Lori says. She motions and Steve gets up from the table where he is sitting with Kyle.

"Hey, Hoyt," he says, which startles me. I'm still getting used to his voice. It's so deep.

"Hey."

"Well, since you haven't met with your nutritionist yet, we've just got you a general meal card today. Basically, the exchanges you need to eat are two grains, two fats, and two proteins for now. Once you meet with the nutritionist, she will put you on a formal meal plan," he rattles on. While he talks, I just stand there, frozen with apprehension.

All I hear is the phrase "need to eat." I don't *need to eat* anything. I don't want to eat anything. So I just stand there. He continues.

"Here, follow me," he says as he starts to walk toward an inset in the room that has a long table top lined with plates, bowls, and trays of food.

"So you just get a plate, and here it tells you what a serving will be made of," he says, pointing to a sheet of paper displayed at the front of the line. I look down and see words and numbers. I'm slowly starting to realize that numbers will become my focus from now on. *Ugh, I hate this.* I've been obsessing about numbers in relation to losing weight, and now I will have to obsess about more numbers with the goal of gaining weight.

I follow Steve through the line and take as little food as possible, hoping that it will pass muster with him. I feel this incredible push/pull inside. I want to be the good little newbie and do what I'm told, but at the same time, my mind is screaming for me to flee. *Stop getting food and just get the hell out of here!*

We sit down and I notice that another guy is at the table. After brief introductions, I'm now acquainted with J.R., my roommate. I don't want to be here, and I don't want to be nice and make small talk. For several minutes, it seems I'm going to get out of this without having to talk too much. But then the inevitable happens.

"So, where you from?" J.R. asks, attempting to start a conversation.

"I live in Hoboken, New Jersey, and work in Manhattan," I quickly answer without looking up. I don't want to engage with him.

"Oh, cool. How do you like that?" J.R. asks.

"It's okay. The city is fun, but it's expensive," I answer. This time I lift my head and make eye contact so I won't come across as a total asshole.

"So, were you there during 9/11?" Kyle asks, out of the blue.

Shit! Here we go. I don't want to talk about this! Suddenly I experience this drop in my gut and it feels like the room temperature just shot up fifteen degrees. *It's okay, just take a deep breath and answer.* It's not like this is the first or last time I'm going to be asked this.

"Yeah, I was there. I worked next door to the towers," I say as calmly as possible, even as I feel my pulse begin to race.

"Wow, that must have been crazy," Kyle comments.

No shit, Sherlock! No, in fact, it was a walk in the park. I'd like to do it again. After my brief mental temper tantrum, I decide I'd better play nice. So I add, "Yeah, it was nuts."

I have no idea what to say, really. When people bring this up and find out I was there, I feel totally awkward. I feel like they want me to recount some harrowing, life-threatening story of that day. But I'm not into reliving that event with people who weren't there because I know they can't relate.

Thankfully, that part of the conversation ends quickly, and the rest of lunch goes by in a blur. The guys make small talk with each other while I do my best to swallow my chicken sandwich one miserable bite at a time. My mind isn't happy, and neither is my body. I feel so awkward and scared that I just keep my head down most of the time. There are other people in the dining room, but from what little I notice, everyone seems somewhat normal. And, as I suspected, everyone else is female.

After the horror of lunch is over, I follow the guys back down to the unit. I take the elevator while they take the stairs. I guess once I'm here longer, I can be trusted to walk down one flight of stairs.

My afternoon is spent in an endless maze of paperwork. I'm given questionnaires to complete. Some are about mundane things, but others are more in-depth and cause me to actually think. I have to answer questions about how I'm feeling and what I think about my eating disorder. They ask about any other addictive or self-destructive behaviors, about my sexuality, and if I'm suicidal. *If I wasn't suicidal before lunch, I could be tempted now.* My mind and body have pretty much decided to shut down, which is helpful in getting through this phase.

As I sit on my bed with all these papers, I can't help but stare out the window. It's beautiful outside. All I can think about is being anywhere but here. I would love to run outside and just get away. But I can't. I can't leave this unit—or else. Of course, I'm paying to be here, so I'm not sure what they would do if I fled. Plus, I'm an adult. I can do whatever I want.

Always the obedient one, I nix the idea of running. I don't want to be bad. Instead, I buckle down and get all the paperwork done. I end up answering more questions about myself than I care to know the answers to.

Then I decide there is no rush to get all this back to the office. Plus, I'm not dying for anyone to read everything I wrote. Since I confirmed that I'm a raging homo on one of these forms, I know it will only be a matter of time before my sexuality comes up in conversation. I have a schedule for the house that Lori gave me after lunch, and so I pull it out and decide to see what this place is going to make me do on a daily basis.

The sheet is neatly organized into a grid pattern. The top row lists days of the week and down the side are the times. Breakfast starts at 7:40 am. That's not too bad, since I'm an early riser. Doing the math in my head, I realize I will have to get up about 5:30 or six to have time to shower and get some alone time to watch the morning news. I hate being around people first thing in the morning.

I scan down further and notice a term that makes my stomach lurch. *Group therapy.* Visions of sad people sitting in a circle bemoaning their tough lives race through my head. I realize that I will get to experience this fun five times a week. *Great, I can't wait!*

Not wanting to be outdone, Check-in Group happens every single night after dinner. Not just five times a week, but every damn night— and right after dinner, at that. That just sounds like too much fun for one day. At least the time allotted for that activity is only thirty minutes.

Food. That's the real reason I'm looking at this. Breakfast, lunch and dinner. Okay, no surprises there. I figured we would be expected to eat three times a day. *But wait! Snacks?* We have snacks. *What is this, kindergarten?* We have snacks three times a day. *Oh, this just keeps getting better and better. They feed us six times a day. That is fucked up!*

I'm anorexic. I don't even eat six times in a week.

When I can't take anymore and feel like I have to get the hell out of my room, I gather up all the papers I've completed and head to the office. I'm informed that this evening, Kyle and J.R. get an outing, so they'll be gone. Since I can't leave, I get the evening to myself. I take a nap for the rest of the afternoon and shrewdly avoid my first snack time.

Dinner is just as hellish as lunch, or even worse, since Kyle and J.R. spend it talking about their outing. Bowling, I think. I do my best not to pay attention. I just keep my head down.

I watch some TV after dinner and then go to my room to be alone. Everyone seems nice enough here, but I feel pretty lonely and out of sorts. It's not so different from the feeling a kid gets during his first night away from home. Even though you're at a friend's house and his parents are nice, you still feel lonely.

I turn to my journal, wanting to capture some of what I'm feeling.

Thursday June 20, 2002

    Well, I am here at Rogers Memorial Hospital—in Oconomowoc, WI, that is. It honestly doesn't seem real. Mom and I woke up at four a.m. for an eight a.m. flight. I just can't keep from laughing – this is just so freakin' surreal.

My roommate is J.R., a nineteen-year-old from Pittsburgh who goes to Yale University and has been here for six weeks. He's also anorexic. The only other guy is Kyle, who is fifteen years old. He's from Albuquerque and is anorexic, bulimic, and a drug addict. This is his second time here.

Everyone so far has been really nice. I just feel like I'm in la-la land. I am pissed, though, because I've had to eat lunch and dinner. We use these exchange cards. I was thrown for a loop. So I have eaten more in these two meals than I usually eat for two days! Plus, the food sucks so far. Kinda funny. Being picky is not good for an anorexic.

I am looking around and am just in awe. How did I get here? I still don't feel sick enough to be in a place like this. I do feel better that the girls and guys I see don't look much different from me. So I am not the fattest nor the skinniest. I do still feel like a fake, though. I know intellectually this will be good, but emotionally, I am screaming for some control!

It's kinda weird being on the same floor as the older women, but they are all so nice and I think it will be an interesting learning curve.

I really don't know what else to write because I am so in shock. So until next time:

"Just like a dream, you are not what you seem."
– Madonna

I feel some relief after writing. It dawns on me that every night I should write down a recap of my feelings for that day. I can use it as a barometer of how I'm doing. So, in true perfectionist style, I grab the empty notebook I brought and turn to a back page. I neatly draw a grid of twelve squares on a page. I label each square with the dates for the next twelve days, starting with today. The top of the page is simply titled: Daily Wrap-Up.

> *Day 1: Thurs. June 20:*
> *In shock! Everyone nice though. I'm not sick enough!*

18

I roll over and squint to see the red numbers on the alarm clock I brought. I hate not being able to see well. Slowly, my eyes begin to focus on the time: 5:25 a.m. It's early, but I can't really sleep anymore, so I throw the covers off, sit up in the bed, and swing my feet around, lightly placing them on the floor. I sit there for a minute trying to determine if J.R. is still asleep. I don't hear anything, so I figure he still is. This is good. I love having time to myself in the mornings. I hope it's still early enough that I won't run into anyone.

I stand up slowly and pick up my towel, toiletry bag, and the clothes I laid out the night before. I like being prepared so I don't have to rummage around for stuff. I'm grateful for light penetrating the crack under the front door, which enables me to navigate across the room and out into the hallway. *Ah, nice. It's quiet out here as well.* I turn left and make my way down the hall and into the bathroom that I discovered the day before.

I wash my hands and put in my contacts. Now I can really see. I hunch over to look at myself in the tiny mirror. *This is so ridiculous.* As I stare into the mirror, I suddenly realize I need to shave. I open my toiletry bag, but then it dawns on me. Lori, that cheery little tech, took my razor. *Great, now I have to go to the front and ask for it like some little kid.*

I head down the hall to the front office area and realize I have no idea who I am going to meet. I don't like meeting new people, especially at 5:30 in the morning when I look like hell, so I approach the front door slowly. Sitting at the table is a woman I don't recognize.

"Oh, hey," she says looking up. She is pretty, probably not much older than I am, and has long, dark brown hair.

"Hey, I um, just came in to get my razor," I say.

"Oh, okay. What's your name?"

"I'm Hoyt."

"Nice to meet you. I'm Rose. Just a minute." She walks into the room that has plastic bins for each resident.

"Here you go. When you get done, bring it right back. Then I'll get your weight."

"Oh, okay," I mumble. I'd forgotten the obligatory morning ritual. As I walk back down the hall, I notice my mind is more awake now, and it's starting its usual morning routine of thinking about food and how I need to avoid it. I've got almost two hours before I have to face my first breakfast here, but my body is already pulsing with anxiety.

I shave quickly and return the razor to Rose, as requested. She weighs me just like Lori did, and I do my best again to steal a glance at what she writes. Again, I'm shot down. These techs have some damned good training. All of this, of course, is done in silence. Neither of us acknowledges what's happening.

Nice, this shower has great pressure. I close the shower curtain and enjoy the hot water pouring over my body. It feels wonderful. After shampooing, I have to gather all the hair that falls out and place it on the ledge in the shower. I need to throw it away. It would be disgusting to just leave it. Now that I have to share a bathroom, I guess I'd better leave it clean. I hate sharing bathrooms. That's one more reason I enjoy living alone.

After getting dressed, I quietly go back into my room and return my things. J.R. is still asleep. I sneak out, hoping not to wake him, and head to the guys' day room. Since I have the place to myself, I settle in on the blue couch and turn on the TV. I channel surf for a while, then stop on CNN and watch *American Morning*. This show has a hot male anchor. It makes the time go by faster.

"Hey."

Startled, I look to my left to see J.R. coming through the day room door.

"Oh, hey."

"How'd you sleep?" he asks. He's so damned nice.

"Okay, I guess—considering it was my first night here," I add with a slight laugh.

"You'll get used to it," he says sleepily. I can tell he's still waking up.

He sits down in the wine-colored recliner and just stares at the TV. Before long, it's time for breakfast. I follow J.R.'s lead and this morning I follow him right up the stairs. None of the techs are around, and I figure I can break the rules this one time.

But once I'm inside the dining room, I freeze. I don't know what to do. I don't know what to eat or what I'm supposed to eat. I hate breakfast, probably more than any other meal of the day. I don't know why, I just do. Breakfast foods scare me the most. I think it's because they tend to be sweet and taste too good.

"Good morning, Hoyt."

"Hey, Steve."

"Well, this morning for breakfast, just eat two grains, two fats, and one protein," he says.

"Oh, okay, thanks."

I guess now I know what to do. I walk up to the line and grab a plate. I intently scan the sheet posting all the exchanges. My heart is racing and I feel like I'm on display, like everyone is watching me—like they are waiting to see what the new guy is going to do. I don't know what I'm going to do! I do know I don't want to be in here with these people.

I'm sweating now. My heart is racing. I'm frozen in front of this sheet of paper. I need more time to read it, but more people are coming into the room. The energy is shifting and the room is coming more alive. I don't like this.

As I try to breathe, my brain goes into hyper-drive, and suddenly it just jumps out at me: yogurt, cereal. That's it! I can do yogurt and cereal. Feeling relief, I move forward and spot the small cartons of yogurt. I grab a blackberry one and move down the line, picking up a small box of Special K. I smile. These little cereal boxes remind me of being at summer camp.

I carry my tray of food back to the guys' table, where Kyle, Steve, and J.R. are sitting. I slump into my chair, exhausted from the mental energy that has exploded inside of my brain. With my head down, just like the day before, I proceed to eat. I mix the cereal into the yogurt. It tastes good. I like the crunch.

My mind doesn't like this. *I can't enjoy this food! I shouldn't be enjoying this. I need to stop eating and to keep losing weight.* I can only imagine how much I've gained, given how much I have eaten already.

The guys aren't morning people, so talk is sparse. I love it. I stay in my head for the entire meal. After a while, my mind has moved from what I'm doing now to what I will be doing next. Group therapy. *Whoa, what's that going to be like?* I'm not sure I'm ready to open up to anyone. I can feel my anxiety rising and I realize I need to break some of this internal tension I'm feeling. I need to know what to expect. These two guys sitting here with me are the best ones to ask.

"So, what's after breakfast?" I ask, knowing the answer.

"Oh, group therapy with Sue. She's nice. You'll like her," J.R. informs me.

"Yeah, she's okay," Kyle adds, although he has a slight edge to his voice, as if he doesn't want to give her too much credit. Somehow, I don't think Kyle would give a second thought before voicing his honest opinion about anything, no matter how brutal is was. J.R., on the other hand, is probably too nice to say anything bad about anyone.

"Yeah, I won't be there this morning. I've got class," Kyle says, rolling his eyes.

"What's that?" I ask.

"I'm still in school, so they make me do schoolwork around here. It fucking sucks," he grumbles with disgust in his voice.

"Well, I'm done. I'm out of here," Kyle announces as he stands up. He's out the door before anyone can say good-bye.

A few minutes later, I follow J.R. as we leave. This time, we take the elevator down. Steve is with us, and J.R. seems to know that is what I need to do. He seems so thoughtful. It's hard to imagine he is sick enough—or was sick enough—to be in a place like this. He looks good now. He's several inches shorter than I am, but he looks healthy. In fact, both guys look good.

Kyle is also shorter than I am, and he's thin, but not painfully so. They seem pretty normal.

Well, maybe I'll get like that after a few weeks here. My body tenses at that thought.

I sit on the blue couch in the day room, but this time I have my grey GAP hoodie on and my notebook and journal are in my lap. I look up at the clock on the wall and notice it's 8:30 a.m. *Time for therapy. Fun. Let the games begin.*

J.R. enters and sits in the recliner. I'm guessing that is his chair. I'll have to remember that. I don't want to do anything wrong.

"Hey, guys."

A short, middle- aged women bops into the room. She has short, sandy blond hair and a round face. From her enthusiastic greeting and the way she is walking, I surmise she is perky. She and Lori must get along great.

"Hey, Sue," J.R. replies, smiling.

"You must be Hoyt. It's nice to meet you," Sue says, walking over to me. She smiles as she reaches out her hand.

"Hi. Nice to meet you, too," I say. I stand up—the way I was taught to—as I shake her hand.

Sue makes her way across the room, pulls a chair in front of the TV, and sits down facing the two of us.

"Kyle has class today," J.R. informs her.

"Oh, okay, so it's just the three of us today," she says. "So how are things going? How are you doing?"

There's a long pause. I'm not sure who that question was directed to, so I look down at the cover of my notebook. I don't feel comfortable. I certainly don't want to start things off.

"I guess I'll start," J.R. says, breaking the silence. My body relaxes more into the couch, grateful that I've been spared—at least for now—from having to talk.

J.R. goes on to talk about how he has been struggling with living in his head. He says he has doubts about his recovery. I sit there enthralled and horrified at the same time. Here is this guy who is dealing with what I am dealing with and he's talking about it. Actually talking about it. I've never heard another guy talk about things like this. It's exciting but scary at the same time. I sit there silently and do my best not to make eye contact with anyone in the room.

"Hoyt, so how are you doing?" Sue asks me. "I'm sure there's a lot going on for you, this being your first day and all."

What? Me? Damn, is J.R. done already? Can't he talk some more? I don't want to talk. My body stiffens. My right leg comes to life and is about fly to over my left, but I stop it. I can't do that. It's too gay. I look too gay when I cross my legs like that, and Lord knows, I just met these people. I don't really want to come out right now. *Okay, okay I can do this. Just keep it short and sweet.*

"I'm okay. Everyone has been really nice so far," I answer, looking up at Sue and hoping she approves. I think that was a good reply. It sounded good and it was actually sincere. Everyone has been nice so far.

There is a pause. She just looks at me. I look down. "How do you feel?" she asks. *Damn, she's good.*

I don't really want to feel anything, but now I've been cornered. "Umm, I'm in a bit of shock. It doesn't really feel real, actually," I reply with a nervous laugh.

"That's normal. You'll get used to everything. J.R. and Kyle are great guys. I know you all will learn from each other and help each other," she says. It sounds like she has genuine admiration for J.R. and Kyle. It's nice, but feels weird.

"So, just to let you know, this is our group therapy time. We meet here together Monday through Friday, and then you and I will have private sessions as well that we will schedule throughout the week. Group therapy is a time for you guys to talk as a group and hopefully open up. There are some assignments—I will give you one today— and once the assignments are done, you will present some of them to the group," she says.

I start to numb out. *Assignments. Present to the group. She can't be serious.* I don't like presenting anything, and I especially don't like the idea of presenting therapy assignments.

My body hasn't relaxed since the spotlight was pointed at me several minutes ago. Now my thoughts are racing. All this new information is wreaking havoc with my brain. *I can't do this. I'm not sick enough.* I don't need to do this. I just need to be alone and stay the way I am.

Sue turns the conversation back to J.R. and I'm able to settle down. But the dread of what will be expected from me is now firmly entrenched in my psyche, and it's all I can do to pay attention to what J.R. is saying. I perk up when he starts to elaborate about how he lives in his mind and goes over and over everything. Basically, he obsesses. I can relate to that too well, I'm afraid.

The time goes fast. Not much of the conversation is directed toward me again. I think they both may be treating me to a honeymoon period, which I appreciate—although somehow, I'm afraid that this period will be short-lived.

"Well, looks like time is up," Sue says, looking up at a clock that reads 9:58 a.m.

J.R. and Sue start to stand. I feel perfectly content sitting, but I reluctantly stand so I won't feel left out of what is coming next.

"We hold hands at the end of every session and say an affirmation," Sue informs me. *Okay, this is starting to feel a bit too touchy-feely for me.* J.R. grabs my right hand and Sue grabs my left and then, without warning, they both speak in unison.

"God grant me the serenity … to know the difference." Then my hands are being squeezed and shaken up and down. "Keep working … it works … work at it."

I have no idea what the hell they just said. I only caught bits and pieces. It sounded somewhat familiar, though.

"Okay, great jobs, guys. Snack time," Sue says, smiling.

Snack time? Already? Shit, I can't run to my room and pretend I'm asleep. I follow J.R. out of the room and down the hall. We head into the women's day room area on our floor. Right at the doorway, there is a cabinet and a tech is there unlocking some doors. As we get closer, I see the shelves are full of snacks. J.R. walks up and grabs an apple. An apple. Well, that doesn't seem so bad. I can handle that. Several women choose snacks after him. I'm the last one.

I walk up and scan the shelves, my heart pounding and my eyes furiously darting back and forth. *I have to get an apple. I can handle that. Oh, thank God, there's one left.* I reach inside the cabinet and snatch up a small red apple.

Feeling some relief at getting what I wanted, I turn around and follow J.R. back down the hall and into our day room. He sits down in the recliner and I sit down on the blue couch. All I can do is look down at the apple in my hands. I felt relief a minute ago but now I feel ashamed. I don't want to eat this. I feel like I'm being bad in eating this.

There is total silence in the room except for the crunching sound of J.R. eating his apple. I take a deep breath and put the fruit up to my mouth and bite. My mouth is filled with wet sweetness. I take big bites, chew as little as possible, and swallow as fast as I can. I don't want to taste this.

All this happens without talking. J.R. is in his world and I'm in mine.

"Oh, Hoyt. I forgot to give you these," Sue says as she enters the room, breaking the silence. I stand and meet her across the room, where she hands me some papers.

"These are a couple of assignments I would like for you to start working on. They are pretty self-explanatory. They will help you to start thinking about how your eating disorder has affected your life. If you have any questions, just ask. And there is no deadline in getting them done," she tells me.

"Oh, okay. Thanks."

Sue leaves just as quickly as she entered. I toss the apple core in the trash and then head to my first art therapy session, alone. J.R. has a private session with Sue. He gets back-to-back therapy fun today.

Once I'm up on the third floor of the house, I have to walk down a long hallway. I feel lighter now that my first group session and snack are behind me. I have survived both experiences, and I'm glad I now know what to expect.

I get to the end of the hall and apprehensively enter the room. I'm instantly transported back to elementary school. I spot craft paper lining the walls, a sink in one corner cluttered with dirty brushes in old glass jars, a brown table in the middle of the room that has paint spots all over it, and another table in the back of the room with small plastic containers full of brushes. Beneath the table, colored craft paper has been stacked up in piles. And the smell! It's a smell that only exists in an art room.

I smile. I have nice memories of being in art class as a kid. I'm not that artistic, but I enjoy it.

"Oh hey, you must be Hoyt," is the greeting that I'm hearing a lot lately. On the other end of the room, a tall, round woman with brassy yellow hair pulled back into a bun turns around and is smiling at me. She appears to be only a few years older than I am and she's wearing stylish, black-rimmed glasses. I notice she is wearing clogs. Clogs! The woman is wearing ugly, brown clogs. *I guess I'm not in New York City anymore.*

And to my surprise, she is very round. Actually, she's fat. I've got a fashion-challenged, fat art teacher at an eating disorder clinic.

"Yeah, that's me," I say.

"It's nice to meet you. I'm Melissa, the art therapist," she says, keeping the table between us. We don't shake hands. I like her already.

"Nice to meet you," I add.

"Well, this is the art therapy room," she says with a slight giggle in her voice. It's kind of cute.

"Cool."

"Why don't you sit down, and we can get started."

I sit at the table facing into the room and she sits down on the other side, catty corner from me.

"So what's your experience with art? Do you like it?"

"Yeah, I do. I always liked it in school."

"Great!" she exclaims with what sounds like a sigh of relief. I guess some of the people in here aren't that into this part of the program.

I turn my head to the left and notice, for the first time, a couple of large pieces of paper that are hanging on the wall. Each piece contains a painted outline of a woman. Each outline is disturbing in a violent way. Both pictures are large with dramatic brush strokes creating lots of curves. I don't feel comfortable looking at them. It feels like I'm invading someone's privacy. I glance away quickly and focus my attention on Melissa again.

"So today, basically, I just want you to do a collage. And the main purpose of it is to show who you are and why you're here. It's a way for you to express yourself, and you will be able to present it in group."

Present it. In group. My body stiffens in the hard, wooden chair. Instantly, I know what I need to do, but I don't want to do it. I'm scared. I don't want to come out yet, but I'm being presented with an opportunity to do it through this collage. *Okay, I can do this.*

After more explanation, Melissa lets me get started. There are tons of magazines to choose from. Of course, at this place, most of them are for girls. I smile to myself, knowing it won't be hard to find images and words in these rags that will help me come out to these people. *Cosmo* alone has more photos of gorgeous men than most gay porn magazines.

I spend the next ninety minutes flipping through magazines, cutting out words and images that resonate with me. The background
of the entire collage is a pride flag. I don't want to be subtle about
my intention. As I work, I feel somewhat calm. The room is soothing
with its abundance of sunlight, and Melissa is fun. The fact that she
is overweight puts me even more at ease. I'm still the thinnest person
in this setting, and that feels nice.

I finish the collage in the session and fold it up, knowing that it
will be up to me to decide when to pull it out in group. I know it will
make me feel vulnerable when I do. My mind screams that I don't
have to show it to anyone, and that I shouldn't. I'm in here with two
younger guys who are obviously very straight and they're probably not
going to take it well. I don't want to be treated differently, and I don't
want things to become awkward. As I walk back down to my floor, I
decide that I don't have to show off my collage any time soon.

"So, who wants to start us off?" Ray, the evening shift tech, asks.

There's a long pause. I'm back on the blue couch, J.R. is in the
recliner, and Kyle is on the other couch. Ray is sitting in the chair Sue
was in earlier, facing all of us.

This is my first check-in group after dinner. The night before,
there wasn't a check-in, since the guys were on their outing. I'm not
feeling well. I've just eaten dinner, and I'm not happy. I feel fat, bloat-
ed, and just plain scared. This isn't fun.

"I can," J.R. announces. I notice that he's more than willing to
break the silence. Me, not so much. I can sit in silence for hours.

J.R. goes on to talk, again, about being in his head and struggling
with the program. It's heartfelt but it makes me nervous. If he's struggling so much, what does that say about my chances?

After several minutes, Kyle chimes in and opens up about his
struggles. Struggle seems to be the word of the day.

"Hoyt, how about you?" Ray asks, directing everyone's attention
my way. I don't appreciate this. I glance down. I don't have my journal
or notebook with me. I've got nothing with me. I feel naked.

"I'm okay," is all that comes out. I don't feel okay, but I don't know how to put it into words yet.

"And? This is your first day. How do you feel?" Ray prods. He must have gotten a script from Sue.

"I, uh, umm, I'm struggling." My mouth blurts out the one word that seems to be permeating the conversation. "It's hard. I don't like the fact that I'm eating. It's scary, and I really don't feel like I'm sick enough to be here," I confide, surprising myself with my candor as my body slumps deeper into the couch. It relieves me, getting it out, but I'm also feeling vulnerable. I place my right leg on top of my left knee, forming a square. This doesn't seem gay, I tell myself.

"Thanks for sharing, Hoyt. Guys, what do you think about that?" Ray asks, looking at Kyle and J.R.

"Hoyt, it's normal. I was really scared and mad for a while when I first got here," J.R. says.

"Yeah, me too," Kyle says with a sadistic laugh in his voice. "You're doing really well. You're eating, which may not feel good, but it is good."

"Yeah, I've noticed you're pretty quiet at meals. That will get better," J.R. reassures me.

"And you *are* sick enough to be here," Kyle says. "You're really thin." Kyle instinctively seems to know that I needed to hear that. It makes me feel good. I'm thin. Yeah, I am, but I'm not sure I'm thin enough.

The attention focused my way is scary. These guys are so open and honest, and they seem to really care. Guys. I wasn't prepared for this. I expect caring from women, but not guys—especially not straight guys. I shift my weight again and place both feet on the floor.

"Thanks," is all I offer. The check-in wraps up. To my surprise, I got through it without falling apart. I didn't run away screaming. I guess I can handle this part of the program as well. Not bad for a day's work.

"Okay, now let's have some fun. It's been a heavy day," Kyle says, smiling.

"Sounds good," J.R. adds.

"We watch a lot of movies around here to pass the time. J.R. and I got some last night," Kyle informs me.

"Yeah, what do you want to watch?" J.R. asks Kyle.

"*Orange County* sounds good. I could use something funny," he says.

Yes, something funny would be nice.

We set up the DVD player and turn off the lights. Kyle, J.R., and I settle into the darkness and escape. We escape into laughter, with the darkness providing the cover we all crave, the cover that allows us to hide and not be truly seen. But the one thing we cannot escape is each other. We're trudging through this hell together, whether we like it or not.

19

I need to get the hell off this floor. I can't stand this! Feeling like a rat trapped in a cage, my anxiety and just good old fashioned anger are boiling over. This is Day Three, and I'm still not allowed to go anywhere. Of course, the fact that I've eaten breakfast—again—and my stomach feels somewhat full isn't helping matters either.

My mind is screaming for some control and is daring my body to run. Run anywhere, it doesn't matter where, just run. I need to get the hell out of here and to get moving so that I can shed some of the weight I know that I am gaining. It's also not fair that J.R., Kyle, and most of the adult women are on a Walmart run while I have to stay here in case I keel over.

I walk back to my room and try to slam the door, but I can't even do that. The damned door has one of those automatic closers that won't let you push it closed. *These people thought of everything around here.*

I slump down on my bed, propping my body up against the wooden headboard. This is just weird. It's a Saturday afternoon, I'm an adult, and I feel like I'm grounded. I can't go anywhere. I can't just hop on the subway and go meet some friends or go shopping. Nothing. I have to stay here in The Middle of Nowhere, Wisconsin. *Fine. Fine, I can do this.*

I look to my left and gaze out the window across the room. It's a beautiful, sunny day. *Yeah, let's do that.* I am allowed to sit outside, and I can work on the assignments that Sue gave me yesterday. Working on a Saturday. This is priceless.

I grab my notebook and journal and head down the hall, crossing through the women's day room to get to the patio door, I grab a chair and drag it onto the lawn so I can sit in the sun.

This is nice. I unzip my hoodie but don't take it off. I'm still a bit chilly. I take one of my assignments from my notebook. *Personal Autobiography* is in big letters across the top. The instructions say I need to write about my life from birth up to this point. I decide against it. That's way too much work, and I don't feel like thinking that much right now. So, on to assignment Number Two.

The instructions say this one has two parts. First, I have to write about my eating disorder behaviors. Then I have to describe the negative consequences associated with my eating disorder. Sounds simple enough. This should be a cake walk. It's not like I haven't thought about this stuff before.

I dive right in and start writing.

Exercise 1: My Eating Disorder Behaviors   *6/22/02*

- *Excessive weighing, approx. six times a day*
- *Increased laxative use/addiction. Fleet Phospo-Soda at least twice a week*
- *Only eating once a day*
- *Consuming lowest amount of calories possible daily. Target less than 500 calories*
- *Staring in mirror and looking for something to like – focusing on midsection*
- *Bingeing on sweets and never being able to stop when full*
- *Lying about having eaten*
- *Avoided going out with friends if food was involved*

- *Collecting calorie counts on everything I eat*
- *Looking up recipes and watching food network*
- *Comparing myself to others: thinness, looks, and how much they eat*
- *Viewing my ED as a contest and endurance race–one I will win at all cost–even if the price is my life*
- *Repeating in my head: "Nothing tastes as good as thin feels"*
- *First thoughts and fear every day I woke up were: I'm not strong enough. I'm going to fall off the wagon and eat AND I'm not losing weight!*
- *Thinking I'm not sick enough to really need help because I could function and I wasn't in the hospital.*
- *Thinking if I were sick enough, my friends and family would say something*
- *Thought how much money I was saving by not eating*
- *Drinking as much water and diet soda as possible*
- *Never eating everything put in front of me – had to cut it in half*
- *Walking as much as possible and take stairs vs. elevator*

Wow, that was more things than I had thought. I scan the page and count twenty things. It just flowed out of me. When I re-read everything, I feel weird. I know I did and thought all of those things, but now it almost doesn't seem real. Yeah, I did all these things. I didn't feel good doing them. And even though it feels nice to have it all written down in one place, it doesn't feel good reading about it.

This was more than I was prepared for. I need a break. I close my notebook and set it down on the ground. It's so beautiful out today. I notice there is a small wooden gazebo in the distance, beyond the house. It would be nice to walk over there, but I can't. They said this is as far as I'm allowed. They have to be able to see me from the house.

I look straight ahead again, looking down the small hill in front of me to the little pond. It's cute, though it looks very muddy. The dark water seems pretty foul, but it's better than nothing. I think I've heard the guys refer to this as Bulimia Pond.

I love water. I could stare at it for hours. There's just something so peaceful about water. The ocean is even better with its strong, loud waves crashing on the sand and the salty air blowing through your hair. It's refreshing and cleansing at the same time. The ocean's edge is the only place I've ever truly felt at peace. It's almost as if the waves, with their violent eruption on the sand, are somehow able to expel from me—if only for an instant—the paralyzing fear that loves wreaking havoc on my soul. I love those moments and long for them to never end.

Earth to Hoyt. Hello. Time to come back to reality. Yeah, I'm not at the ocean. I'm here and I have work to do. I need to get this done today. I hate having unfinished work hanging over my head. I can't relax until the work is done. I laugh at myself when I realize I have nothing but time here to get work done.

I turn a page in my notebook and start another entry.

Exercise 2: Negative Consequences of my ED   6/22/02

1. *Health Problems caused by ED:*
   - *Always cold—felt good to be in hot humid weather*
   - *Dry and paper-thin skin. Could see my ribs and veins very well.*
   - *Poor concentration*
   - *Insomnia and obsessive thoughts day and night about food*
   - *Light-headedness and blacking out*
   - *Low energy*
   - *Chest pains and heart palpitations*
   - *Started losing hair. Got more fine hair on torso and face*
   - *Severe agitation*
   - *No sex drive*
   - *Electrolyte imbalance*
2. *Loss of Self-Respect Because of ED:*
   - *Withdrew socially. Didn't like being around people. Felt uncomfortable and like no one understood me*
   - *Lie to coworkers about eating lunch and would walk outside to avoid them at lunchtime*

- *Became mad at everyone. No one was doing anything right*
- *Would rather be at home downing laxatives than being out*

3. *Affected Relationship With Others:*
   - *I missed church because I had taken too many laxatives on Sat. night*
   - *I missed work because of laxative abuse*
   - *I didn't want to be around friends. I became more withdrawn*
   - *I became very angry and buried myself deeper and deeper so no one could touch me. I was building the brick wall higher and higher.*

4. *Affected My Spiritual Life:*
   - *As I was killing my body, I was killing my soul, believing I wasn't worthy of being loved unconditionally*
   - *Church wasn't as enjoyable and I viewed that time as time I could be taking laxatives*

5. *How I Hide ED from Others:*
   - *I would lie about having eaten*
   - *I wouldn't answer my phone or have excuses ready as to why I couldn't go out*
   - *Would wear loose-fitting clothes*

6. *What Have I Lost Because of My ED:*
   - *Faith in myself (if I ever had it) and faith in others*
   - *Hope for the future that life can be fulfilling and rewarding*

7. *Want to Accomplish:*
   - *Change my profession and have a career that I'm passionate about*
   - *Have a caring, healthy, romantic relationship*

That's a good one. A relationship. I'm twenty-five and have yet to really fall in love, let alone be in a long-term, stable relationship. I'm not even sure it can happen. But I want it to happen. I really want it to happen. *Damn it, I hate this feeling.* My gut starts to slowly drop deeper inside. I feel like I'm sinking and my mind is doing its best not to allow the tears to flow.

My notebook slides gently off my lap as I bring my legs up and hug them into my chest. The sun feels more intense and is beating down on the back of my neck. I feel the heat rising up inside me. I feel flush. My breathing slows and I just stare at the ground, trying to get lost. I don't want to be here anymore. I don't want to go down this path of loneliness and despair. I don't want to be afraid that I'm so undesirable, I'll never be with a life partner.

That smell. My nostrils flare trying to capture more of of ... that smell. I know that. It's ... Memaw? It's Memaw's house. It's the large blue hydrangea bush. It's the smell of hydrangea, which is odd, since there are none around here. In my mind, I can see that huge bush she had next to her back door, the door we always used.

I would walk up those five little steps past a huge hydrangea bush sporting the most beautiful blue flowers. And the smell of it was amazing. *She's here. She's really here.* I release my legs from my grasp and they fall back down to solid ground as I sit up as straight as I can. I close my eyes so that I can be more fully enveloped in my grandmother's sweet smell.

The smell instantly takes me back to a time of hot summers in Atlanta with my grandmother. She would cook sweet, homemade apple turnovers for me and tell me stories about Junior Squirrel who liked to play in her back yard.

Taking deeper and deeper breathes in through my nose, a warmth surrounds me. It's the warmth that can only come from a love without conditions, without rules, without boundaries. And in this case, it requires no physicality, just presence and openness. My body tingles. My mind, for the first time since I've been here, is quiet.

Moisture. My eyes. There's a break in the brick wall and, before I know it, I'm crying—or at least my version of crying. My eyes are watering. And then ... it's gone. The smell evaporates as quickly as it appeared.

I don't move, and I keep my eyes shut. I breathe. I smile at the brief glimpse of hope that I've been shown. In that rare moment, my deceased grandmother's presence has given me some peace and an inner knowing that I will be okay—that everything will be okay. My mind doesn't know how to process this. It can't. Some things can't be logically reasoned, much to my mind's annoyance. Dare I say it? I feel … good.

"Hoyt."

"Hoyt."

"Huh?" I stammer as I turn around and see Rose leaning out the door, trying to get my attention.

"You have a phone call."

"Oh, thanks." Surprised, I stand up, grab my things, and head inside to the pay phone in the hall. The receiver is propped up on the main box that is mounted on the wall. This is just odd. I don't even remember the last time I used a pay phone. I'm shocked they still have these things. But given the fact that we can't use our cell phones in this place, I'm glad the pay phone is here.

I hesitantly pick up the receiver as I sit down in the large upholstered chair below the phone. I nervously say hello.

"Jeff, hey, it's mom and dad," my parents say together into the speakerphone. I cringe.

"Oh, hey. How you are guys?"

"Good. We're good. How are you?" they ask enthusiastically.

"I'm good. Doing good," I reply automatically, not really thinking.

"So how are things there?" my mom asks.

"Umm, they're good. Everyone is nice. The other two guys here are pretty cool. They're younger than me, but we are getting along."

"Well that's good. How's the food?" my mom asks, diving right in and not asking what she really wants to know—which is whether I'm eating the food.

"It's not bad. They feed us all the time around here. We eat three meals and have three snacks a day. It's wild. You'll be glad to know I'm eating," I add with a slight laugh. I decide to reassure them, knowing they need that right now.

"That's good to hear. So how's the weather?" my dad jumps in, being ever so practical.

"It's nice. Beautiful, very sunny, and pretty humid. I'm glad I'm here in the summer. I can't imagine this place during the winter." I can almost see both my parents nodding in agreement. None of us are big winter people. After having done stints in Pennsylvania, Massachusetts, and Connecticut, we all have had our fill of harsh winters.

"So, how's the shore?" I ask, wishing I was there with them at their place in Ocean City, N.J. After fifteen moves, it's the one address and phone number my parents have had the longest. It's the place where we gather as an immediate family, and the place where I have the best memories of walking the boardwalk, lying in the sand, building sand castles, body surfing the cold waves, and stealing glances at the hot Italian guys with gorgeous tans who sound like they should be on *The Sopranos.*

"All's well here," my mom informs me. "Jessica is working today and we're heading down to the beach in a little bit. The weather is perfect. So, how are you feeling?" She suddenly shifts the conversation back to me.

"I'm good. It's a good place and I'm starting to feel a bit more settled. Oh, it's weird … I was just outside sitting and I felt Memaw. Actually, it was the hydrangea smell. It just felt like she was there. It was nice." I stop as my emotions appear again, without warning. These unexpected emotions make me feel awkward and out of sorts. I'm not used to just feeling like this.

There's a pause on the other end of the line. I feel guilty now, fearing I have said something I shouldn't have. Maybe my mom didn't want to hear that about her mother.

"That's great. I feel her a lot, too. That makes me smile," my mom says, breaking the silence.

We talk for a few more minutes and I do my best to sound as upbeat as possible. I thank them both for their support.

"Well, we'd better let you go. Hang in there. We are so proud of you," my mom exclaims.

"Thanks, mom. Love you."

"I love you, too," she adds.

"I love you, Jeff," my dad says, almost knocking me off the comfortable chair I'm sitting in. *I love you. What the hell?*

I feel totally caught off guard. This emotion directed my way from my father is so unusual, I don't know how to take it. He's *never* said he loved me. At least, I have no memory of him ever saying it. Hell, we don't even hug! It's never bothered me. In fact, it works for me. I'm not that emotional, and neither is he. *This is just too weird.* I guess it took me to get this sick before he could say it.

"Love you, too," is the best I can muster before I hang up. I'm still in disbelief. *That was just strange. I'm tired. I need a nap.*

I retreat to my room. My body is aching at what has been thrown at it this morning. It's time just to crash. I get undressed and crawl into bed for what I feel is a much-deserved nap, content with the knowledge that I will miss the morning snack.

20

"I'll be back in a minute," Kyle says. He's coughing and practically running out the door with a pack of cigarettes in his left hand, the hand that displays his smiley-face wrist band. He's so fast that he's gone before I fully comprehend what he just said.

"His parents know he smokes?" I ask J.R., who is sitting in the recliner to my right.

"Yeah, I think they do. I haven't met them, but everyone around here knows he smokes. I guess they figure that, with everything else he's trying to kick, they'll let him keep this one vice," J.R. answers matter-of-factly. It still shocks me to be in rehab with a fifteen-year-old who smokes like a chimney.

I sit on the couch, wearing my hoodie, with my journal and notebook perched on my lap. I'm not sure I like the idea of having another group therapy session. We've already had one this morning, and now it's after lunch and we are getting ready for another one. This is my first afternoon group, and I'm not sure what else we can talk about today.

So far, it's been nice hearing more from J.R. and Kyle about their experiences. Kyle has had a pretty rough go of things. This is his second time here at Rogers, and he's been to some other place in Iowa. He's been into drugs and booze, and he's vacillated between anorexia and bulimia. I can tell just from being around him these

HOYT J. PHILLIPS, III

past few days that he has a lot of nervous energy. I'm sure when that energy is not directed into healthy pursuits, it has led him down some pretty dark paths.

J.R., on the other hand, seems so calm. He's intelligent. He plays lacrosse and, from what I can tell, he is the golden child of his family. It sounds like he just got caught up in athletics and was feeling over-whelmed with life, so he just kept exercising until it took over his life and started to decimate his body.

Even though both guys seem to be so open, I don't feel ready to share that much more about myself. I'm nervous about presenting any of those assignments that I worked on over the weekend. My body shudders when I mentally picture the collage I made. *There's no way in hell I'm going to present that today.* I'm not ready to come out. No, not ready for that roller coaster.

"Hey, guys."

I'm startled out of my internal dialogue and look up to Sue walk-ing into our day room.

"Hey," J.R. and I say in unison.

"Hey, Kyle," Sue says as Kyle whirls into the room and makes his way to the other blue couch. The pungent smell of smoke trails him and slowly begins to waft throughout the room.

"Hey," he says without looking at her. He sounds like he has a frog caught in his throat.

Sue places her chair in her usual spot in front of the TV so that she is now facing the three of us. The Three Musketeers. I lower my head so no one can see the smile that is slowly creeping across my face. For some reason, the thought of how we all must look right now is making me laugh. I have a feeling it should be making me sad, but sometimes tragedy is the best comedy.

"So, how's it going this afternoon?" Sue asks.

"Fine," is my automatic response. I verbalize quickly so that I'm not the last one to talk. That way, I won't be forced to elaborate.

"Not bad," Kyle interjects.

"It's okay," is J.R.'s delayed response. He seems to have something on his mind.

"Okay. Well, why don't we get started? J.R., you had mentioned to me earlier that you would like to share an assignment," Sue says.

"Yeah," he replies.

"Okay, well, we'd all love to hear what you have to say," Sue says with a soft smile.

Instantly, my body relaxes. I'm off the hook—at least for now. If I'm lucky, J.R. will talk a long time and this one-hour group will go by without me having to do anything but sit here and listen.

"Well, I … um … had to write about some of the things that my ED gave me. Like some of the positive things it did for me and why I liked it," J.R. starts off, somewhat hesitantly. I can tell that he wants to be open, but it takes him some time to get into the groove where he feels comfortable.

Kyle is watching J.R. I glance in J.R.'s direction but then look away, feeling awkward. I don't like making eye contact when people are being so vulnerable.

Sue has a look on her face like she is hanging on J.R.'s every word. He has her total attention.

"Well, one thing that came to me was that I got a lot of attention for my ED. People noticed me and would say things. And I guess it made me feel good that everyone was more affectionate toward me when they found out what I was dealing with. I enjoyed the attention, but at the same time, that made me feel guilty, too," J.R. says. He lowers his voice as if he believes he said something bad.

Attention. Attention. My body slowly starts to sit up straighter. My mind sharpens at the truth he just spoke. *Yeah, I can relate.* It does feel nice to get attention. Who doesn't like attention? *Great, now I guess I'm going to have to really listen to what J.R. is saying.*

My body tenses in anticipation of his next sentence. *No, I don't want to hear this. Damn it, my stomach is full. I don't like this feeling. I can't believe what I ate at lunch. It was too much.* My mind is off and racing now, doing its best to keep me distracted from really hearing what J.R. is saying. My mind is trying to prevent me from connecting with someone else who understands. After a few more minutes, I wrestle back some control and focus on what J.R. is talking about.

"And being in college, as time went by, I think I also felt this overwhelming sense of responsibility. It was just too much to handle. So I think my ED diverted my attention away from all of that. I had something to focus on—or, really, to obsess about," J.R. continues.

My body pulsates with every word coming out of his mouth. I'm looking down, trying to gain control, but my body and mind are demanding that I give him my total attention. Everything he says makes total sense to me.

My mind is flashing to my apartment in Hoboken, and all I can see is the kitchen table covered in unpaid bills—bills that I can afford to pay, but for some reason just leave lying there. I feel overwhelmed at their sight. *I don't want to deal with the bills.* I don't want to deal with being a grown up and having to pay bills, living alone, cleaning, and actually going to work every day. *I hate going to work every day. I hate my job. I hate my life. It's just too much.*

Life as a grown-up feels depressing and monotonous.

Sweat is slowly starting to bead around my hair line and my pulse is speeding up. I push my back into the couch, as I've done so many times before, knowing full well that the couch won't swallow me whole and allow me to disappear. I still attempt this disappearing act. For some reason, trying the same thing over and over again while hoping for a different result is comforting. *Insanity. I know it is. I guess I'm insane.*

"Yeah, I can relate. We've all been there," Kyle says sympathetically.

I snap out of my thoughts and realize J.R. has stopped talking and Kyle is now offering his insight.

"Hoyt, what do you think?" Sue asks, making eye contact with me.

Startled, I look away. Panic shoots through my veins. I'm hoping that Kyle isn't done yet. But given the fact that Sue has just asked me a question, I guess I have no choice but to contribute something to this conversation.

"Uh, yeah, I can relate to what you said," I reply, turning to face J.R. "About feeling overwhelmed. That makes sense. I know I feel that way. Being out on my own after college has been a shock." I give him a slight smile and turn back around to face Sue, exhausted. I'm hoping that answer was good enough for her to leave me alone for a while.

"J.R., that was great. Thank you for sharing all of that," Sue says. My body slowly starts to relax now that her attention is back on someone else.

"Now Kyle, I think you want to share something as well?" she asks.

"Yeah," Kyle says, looking down at his notebook. It's a beautiful notebook that he has drawn all over. The front and back covers are completely filled with drawings.

"Okay, we're ready whenever you are," Sue says, shifting to face Kyle.

"Uhh, well, I had to write down resentments I have towards my eating disorder. I guess basically things I regret doing because of my eating disorder." As he speaks, he keeps staring down at his notebook instead of looking up at us.

The energy in the room has shifted. It feels more apprehensive and a bit heavier now. I can feel a lot of intense energy coming off of Kyle, and it's unnerving. He has so much inside of him that's just waiting to burst out. I think he does his best to keep most of it inside.

"Okay, well, here goes," he begins. "I resent my eating disorder made me lie so much. Lying to my parents about what I've done. About eating, not eating, about doing drugs. I resent my ED forced my parents to take me to Iowa for treatment and then, the first thing I did when I got out was steal a bottle of booze, just so I could get drunk. I resent my ED forced me to be here for a second time and it's costing my parents so much. I resent my ED has made me a bad example for my younger brothers," Kyle reads, almost as if in a trance.

His head stays down and his body is motionless as his lips keep moving faster and faster. His voice has almost no emotion, but his words are heartbreaking. He goes on and on. He lists behaviors known to every addict. He verbalizes the pain he has caused his family and friends, and all of this seems to be feeding the guilt and shame he is carrying.

I don't like this. This doesn't feel good. The energy permeating the room now is very heavy. The emotions bubbling up in me are suffocating. My body is more tense now than it has been this whole session because it knows what is about to come. *It's okay just sit here. All I have to do it just sit here and pretend like I'm paying attention.*

I hate seeing Kyle like this. He seems almost broken. It's just sad. I don't like it. I don't like seeing it, and I don't like how it makes me feel. I want it to stop.

"I ... ummm," Kyle coughs loudly and there it is. Tears are streaming down his face. He stammers and then stops reading. His head is still down and his back is arched. I glance in his direction but quickly look down at my lap. I'm too afraid to look around the room. I don't want to know if Sue or J.R. are crying as well.

This is too much. I hate feeling other people's pain. Slowly, I begin to feel this tingling rising up from my feet, making its way to my chest. *Oh no, this is not going to happen! I'm not going to cry. This is Kyle's shit, not mine. Run. Just run. Get the hell out of here and get outside.* My mind is doing its best to rein in the emotions that are starting to take over my body.

Moisture. My eyes. *No, you don't.* I inhale deeply and try to keep from losing it. But Kyle's pain is now firmly rooted in the room and I can't escape it. I want to stop his pain, my pain, everyone's pain. I don't want anyone of us to be in pain. It's not fair. We shouldn't have to deal with any of this. *Life shouldn't be this hard.*

Sue interjects and does what she's paid for. She keeps Kyle moving in the direction that he needs to go, which is into and through the pain. J.R. offers words of encouragement and support. All I can do is sit there, stone-faced, trying not to crack. I can't move. I don't know what else to do.

I know, deep down, that this is what I need—what we all need. We all need to be able to sit with these uncomfortable emotions and just be with them, without changing them. I don't like it, but I know I can't get better if I don't experience the pain.

Kyle trudges forward. His courage astounds me. He keeps talking, all the while wiping away the tears streaming down his face. *No, I can't do that. It's too personal.* The thought that pops into my head scares me. I shift my weight and put my right leg under my left. These guys are great, and I'm enjoying getting to know them, but I don't think I'm ready to share with them what I wrote in my journal. It's too personal and it makes me feel too vulnerable. *No. No.*

Plus, Lord knows what it would do to me, what emotions it would unleash. *What if they think it's totally stupid? What if they don't appreciate it?* I don't want to be rejected like that.

Kyle continues as I argue with myself. I know what I need to do, but I'm so scared about putting myself out there and opening up. I feel this strong need to comfort Kyle and let him, and J.R., both know how much in awe I am of them.

Silence. There's silence. Kyle stops. My heart skips a beat. Dive in. Just jump in without thinking.

"I, umm, well … if you guys don't mind, I would like to read something I wrote in my journal. I do better with writing than just talking off the cuff," I say, now fully engaged in autopilot, not feeling a damn thing. *I just hope I can get through this.*

"Oh sure, Hoyt, that would be nice," Sue says, turning to face me more directly. Kyle is still hunched over and J.R. is now looking at me. I open my journal and turn to the entry I wrote on Saturday. I read:

"I'm in awe more and more every day of J.R. and Kyle. I know I can re-late to J.R. a lot and his people-pleasing personality. We are both middle kids between two sisters. He's a really kind guy who seems to be so into his recovery

and trying to learn and be very open. I admire that so much. And then there is Kyle, who if anyone talked to for any length of time, they would have a hard time believing he's only fifteen. I can only imagine the hell he's been through, but he is so honest and definitely wise beyond his years. Both guys are so quick to offer support and insight. I think I'm still in shock with the openness and support everyone exhibits." I read with my head down, skipping over the next sentence, which mentions their lack of obvious homophobic attitudes. Even though I'm pushing myself, I'm not pushing that hard right now.

"I do find myself looking at J.R. and Kyle and just mourning for them. I wish I could take all their pain away. I kinda feel like their older brother and hate the fact they have to go through this. I do know, though, that all of us are so fortunate to be in such a wonderful place."

I end with a slight sigh and pause. My body relaxes. I feel like I just ran a marathon. I'm exhausted but exhilarated at the same time. I peek up, sheepishly, secretly hoping to be met with overwhelming approval at what I just shared.

Sue quickly dabs her eyes. *She's teary-eyed.* I feel proud. I made the therapist cry. That's pretty cool.

"Wow, thanks Hoyt. That means a lot," Kyle says, breaking the silence. Our eyes meet. I smile at him.

"Yeah, thanks," J.R. adds, smiling at me.

It feels nice. I feel connected to these guys and now hopefully they know how I feel about them. I'm not good at just saying these things. Reading it felt safer.

"Well, we got a lot done today," Sue says. "I'm proud of you guys. I think you all are doing a great job, and it's wonderful how well you all are getting along. I think this is going to be a great group." Sue sounds like a proud parent praising her kids.

We stand and do the usual closing circle of holding hands. I do my usual mouthing what I think they are saying. I still have no idea what the affirmation is, but I'm sure I will catch on eventually.

"Now I think you all have rec therapy," Sue informs us.

"Oh, cool!" Kyle exclaims.

"Hoyt, your three days are up, so you get to go. You can leave the unit," Sue says with a smile.

Really? I get to leave? I smile without thinking. I love the thought of being able to get the hell out of here for a while. Rec therapy. That sounds nice. I know that, since all three of us are anorexic, we won't be doing anything too strenuous.

The three of us get our snack. I grab an apple. I'm loving apples these days. The crunch and the sweetness. It feels safe. An apple can't have too many calories. We eat in the day room and then I follow the guys to the gym. I feel like I'm skipping school, but it feels nice.

We walk down the long driveway, past the actual hospital, and head to the gym. Both guys have been here before and seem to be looking forward to it. *So it must be a good kind of therapy.*

I meet Adam, the recreation therapist. He's nice, shorter and a bit older than I am. I'm amused at the fact that he's overweight. He has a big gut. Not that I'm judging or anything, but it's amusing, given the fact that he's a recreation therapist and we're at an eating disorder clinic. But I don't care. I'm off the unit and, after our intense group, I'm ready to just have some fun.

Adam informs us that we are going out on the lake in the pontoon boat. I'm thrilled about going out on the water. We spend the next hour just relaxing on the water. Adam drives the boat and the rest of us just relax. Adam does his best to get us to talk some. We appease him, but most of all, the three of us are just content to zone out.

We all pushed ourselves so much during group that we are due some chill time. The water is peaceful, the setting is beautiful. I'm in shock when I see what I swear is a black bear wading into the water near someone's dock in the distance. Adam laughs and informs me it's a Newfoundland. I tell him I've never seen a dog that large before. It's massive.

After rec, I go to my room for some quiet time. I want to crash and get some writing done in my journal before dinner. J.R. has decided to hang out in the day room, so I'm alone in our room. I sit up against the headboard, open my journal, and start a new entry.

Monday June 24, 2002

Well, it's been several days now. The shock is wearing off some and I'm now becoming numb. I have waves of terror and sadness.

I've been up and down with food. It's hard. I have been doing more snacks slowly. So I'm trying. The fear plays in when I think, what if I can't kick this? Or what if I relapse? The sadness plays in when I think of things changing here, like when J.R. and Kyle leave, and me having to get to know new people. I have started sleeping somewhat better. Though I still go to bed late (midnight) and get up at 6 a.m. and then nap some.

I got to meet with the dietician finally. She seems really good. I'm looking forward to learning a lot, but pretty scared of gaining weight and having to eat.

I've been doing a lot of thinking about stuff, mostly about my view of myself. I think growing up, I felt you either had to be a superhero, rich and famous, or on a deathbed in a hospital to be a worthy or an important person. I remember pretending (and still do some) that I had powers or was being praised for being able to do things that no one else could do.

I think deep down, I always felt inadequate, a lesser person, and thus not worthy, no matter what I accomplished. Then, on the flip side, I have the thought that you have to be deathly ill to warrant help, care, and compassion. This plays into some of my fantasies of wanting to die or be very sick, because then maybe I would feel worthy or deserving of love.

This really is a wild ride. It's a once-in-a-lifetime experience. I just hope I take full advantage of it. So until next time:

"You can run, you can hide, but you can't escape my love."

– Escape by Enrique Iglesias

I close my journal and decide to do my daily wrap-up, so I grab my notebook from the nightstand and turn to the back. In the fifth square on the page, I write:

Day 5: Mon. June 24:
More at peace. Glimpses of light— some hope. Bonding good but scary.

21

"Forty-eight hours since the sun stood still. It's hard to describe what I'm feeling right now partially because I don't know what I'm feeling. It doesn't feel real. . . . I had woken up that morning tired and not thrilled to be going to work. . . . in a blink of an eye the whole building shakes and there is this loud boom. . . . I pick up the phone to call Dad. When I hear his voice it's all I can do to hold it together. . . . Ambulances going by, sirens blaring. I have to keep moving. . . . I walk fighting back tears of agony thinking of all those people. . . . I run to the living room and they shout it's falling. The fucking WTC is falling to the ground! People screaming everywhere. I'm here but I'm not. I don't feel anything. I wipe my eyes. This is too much for my brain to take-in. . . . Life is slowly going back to normal. More cars on the streets, more businesses opening up. Slowly we move forward."

I close my journal and just sit there, motionless. The silence would be soothing except I know, even without looking, that Sue is crying. When I slowly raise my gaze, my fear is confirmed. Sue is lightly wiping her eyes with a tissue. This is odd. Since I'm the patient,

I'm the one who should be crying in this scenario. I was the one at Ground Zero that day.

But for some reason, I don't really feel anything, except, maybe ... wow, I feel *proud*. Yeah, proud. I just made my therapist cry with something I wrote. *Yeah, that's two times now. That's pretty cool. I made someone cry with the words that I wrote. Huh, I think I could get used to this.*

"Wow, thank you for sharing that, Hoyt," Sue sniffles.

"Sure," I say, trying not to stare at her too intently, even though I'm still in awe of the reaction I've been able to elicit.

"That's really powerful, what you read. I felt like I was reliving it with you," she says.

My body shudders. I shift my weight to my left butt cheek and look out the window. I do my best to focus on the small wooden gazebo on the lawn. *Damn, it's not working.*

My body is slowly starting to awaken from the numbness I imposed upon it to get through reading the journal entry. For the first time, I've told someone exactly what I went through. I've read my journal entry from that day to someone who is practically a perfect stranger. Even though my own mother has been asking for months to hear what I wrote, I haven't shared this with anyone until now.

I push my back firmly in the sofa, trying to control my shaking. The tiny room we are in for my private session doesn't lend itself to escape or distraction. It's just me on the sofa and Sue in front of me, with only a small table to her right and the window to my left. My mind is trying to freak out at the newfound realization that I'm not as successful as I thought I was at emotionally shutting down. Just reading what I went through that day still has enormous power to affect me. This fact scares the shit out of me.

"What's going through your mind right now, after you read that?" Sue asks, as if she's been eavesdropping on my internal dialog.

"Uh, well, I guess, uh, I guess I'm nervous. It's not easy sharing that. And I feel guilty as well. My mom has been asking for a while to hear what I wrote about that day, but I've been putting her off," I reply honestly.

"What did you feel when you were reading it aloud?"

"Honestly?" I look at her reluctantly. "I felt nothing. I just read it. I don't think it really hit me until after I finished. And now I feel sad and somewhat scared." Confiding this makes me feel even more vulnerable.

"That makes sense. It hasn't been very long," Sue says.

"Yeah, sometimes it feels just like yesterday, and then other times it feels like it was years ago," I tell her. "It's weird. I find myself referencing points in my life as either before 9/11 or after. That date serves as this odd marker in my life."

"Oh, wow. So you haven't really spoken with anyone about what happened to you that day?" There is concern in Sue's voice.

"Nope. Not really. I don't like to talk about it. For a while there, if it ever came up in conversation, I just listened. And if someone found out I was there, at first they seemed interested, but then it always ended up with them telling me what they were doing and how scared *they* were, even though they weren't at Ground Zero. I found myself getting mad. Like no one could relate unless they were there. And for the first time, I could finally relate to my father, who never talks about his time fighting in Vietnam."

"How so?"

"Well, growing up, I always wondered why he wouldn't talk about it. He never wanted to see all those Vietnam movies that came out in the eighties. Now I know why. He was there. He didn't need to relive it. And now I have no desire to see war movies anymore, either. The violence sickens me. I learned that the hard way. Shortly after 9/11, a bunch of us went to see that war movie *Blackhawk Down*. It was beautifully done, but it was way too violent. And what really bothered me was that I was watching actors about my age getting maimed and killed onscreen in violent acts. It made me to think too much about 9/11," I explain. Tension is gripping my gut.

"Yeah, I can see that. It's really good that you now have that awareness about yourself. So where are you in terms of your view on God or religion in all of this? I know we've talked some about your background, but I'm wondering how what you have been through has affected your spirituality."

"Wow, that's a really good question," I reply as I slide my right shoe off and pull my leg up under me. The room seems to become quieter, as if the universe now is waiting for my answer. My gaze darts out the window and then back to Sue. I feel pressure to verbalize some eloquent view of the world. I know I just need to start talking.

"Uh, well … I think, um, well … right before all this happened, my mom had loaned me this book from this psychic, Sylvia Browne. It was wild, because everything in the book just made sense. It was talking about her view of life after death and what happens to us and what we are here for. Basically, it helped me let go of all these draconian ideas about heaven and hell and sin and right and wrong. It all just clicked for me, and now I feel a lot more freedom around my relationship with God. I like the idea that we are all connected and that we are all doing our best. If you just focus on being open and cultivating love in your life, you can't go wrong."

Sue is watching me, nodding, so I continue. "Regarding 9/11, I think it helped me to have some peace knowing that, even though a lot of people died and even more are struggling, that we aren't alone, and that death is just a transition, not an end." I exhale, trying to collect my thoughts. "Yeah, so, I don't know. Not sure if any of that makes sense." I decide to stop now before I sound even crazier.

"No, no, that all makes sense," Sue reassures me. "It sounds like you've been able to make some peace with what has happened. It's great that everything you have been through hasn't prevented you from further exploring this part of yourself." Sue is looking at me more intently, as if she's trying to determine if I'm really taking her words to heart.

"I know I have a lot more work to do," I say. I'm trying to let her know that I don't believe for one second that I have all the answers.

During our conversation, I come to realize that I can verbalize all these great, touchy-feely ideas, but when it comes to internalizing them and applying them to my life, I'm like a fish out of water. I can talk a great game, but I'm not so adept at loving myself and trusting that my body has its own internal wisdom.

It is an uncomfortable, yet exciting, conversation. I hate admitting when I'm not good at something, but I know that's why I'm here. I have to learn a more healthy way of living.

"So, how was your first art therapy session?" Sue asks, finally changing the subject.

"Oh, it was great. It was just me, and Melissa is really cool."

"Yeah, she is great. What did you end up doing?"

"I made a collage. And well, yeah," I stammer as I look down at the floor. I'm now nervous for a whole new reason: coming out. I've done a great job of forgetting about this collage and the fact that I need to come out to the guys.

"So, are you going to share it in group?" Sue asks. We both know that is what I need to do.

"Uh, yeah, I guess," I say, laughing nervously.

"You seem uncomfortable about that."

"Yeah, I am. I, um … well, when I share it, it will be obvious that I'm gay."

"Okay, and how does that make you feel?"

"Nervous," I say, laughing. I can't stop smiling at the thought of coming out in group to these two much younger straight guys.

"Okay," Sue says.

"Yeah, I don't know. It just makes me nervous. I mean, J.R. and Kyle both are obviously straight and they're much younger than me. And with me rooming with J.R., I just don't want things to become awkward or anything. I hate having to deal with this, really. It's just something I didn't think I would have to deal with, at least not at this point in my life."

"I hear you. It's tough, I'm sure. But you do know that both J.R. and Kyle are great guys. I have every confidence that they are both going to be fine about it. I don't think it's going to be a big deal at all," Sue says. I almost buy it.

"Thanks. Yeah, I'm sure it will be fine," I reply, trying to sound like I agree with her so that we can talk about something else. The last thing I want her to do is nail me down on an exact day I'm going to do this.

The session concludes without me having to commit to revealing anything about myself before I'm ready. I'm relieved. In true Southern fashion, I ease my anxiety by noting that I can worry about such things another day.

22

"Okay, J.R. and Hoyt, I've got an assignment for you two," Sue says, smiling. My body tenses. *I don't like the way she just said that. It sounds like something I'm not going to like.* I'm still procrastinating on that autobiography assignment that, thankfully, she hasn't asked about. I don't think I want another assignment—especially not one I have to do with J.R. I'm not good working in groups. I don't like to compromise.

"You two need to break a rule," Sue announces.

"Ohhh, yeah! That's awesome," Kyle chimes in, laughing.

"Yeah, I know you can do that without any trouble, Kyle," Sue says sarcastically.

A rule. I have to break a rule. What the hell? This feels weird. My body tenses even more. I'm not good at breaking rules. I like to know what the rules are so I *don't* break them. Plus, I've only been here a week. A week. I don't think I need to be breaking any rules. I don't want to make anyone mad at me.

"Okay," J.R. quips. *Okay, just okay. He's okay with this?*

"Now, don't go off and do anything too stupid. Don't get hurt or arrested or anything. Just break a simple rule. I think this will be good for you guys. You're both so conscientious and concerned with doing the right thing. I think this assignment will allow you to step out of your comfort zone a bit," Sue says. She sounds more serious now.

"Oh, okay. So like, what do you want us to do?" I ask, wanting more clarification. I want to know the rules around this rule-breaking assignment. She's got to give me some direction.

She's laughing. "Hoyt, that's what you have to figure out," she replies.

"I think Kyle will be a good resource for you two," she says, turning to look at the youngest member of our group. Kyle immediately sits up straight with a huge grin on his face, like he's just been anointed king of the jungle.

"So think of something and do it today or tonight, and then we will talk about it at group tomorrow. Okay?" This time, Sue is looking at me, just me.

I reply, "Okay." My body is stiff as a board. My mind is racing about what we're going to do. I want to do this assignment right, but I don't know what the hell to do. Hopefully, Kyle or J.R. will have some ideas. They have been here a while and should know what to do. I'm the new kid. I'll just go along with them and hope we don't do anything too bad.

"So, let's talk about dinner tonight," Sue says, quickly changing the subject. Instantly, I feel the air of lightheartedness crash and burn. The switch in topic from breaking rules to food sends everyone's mood south. I notice Kyle out of the corner of my eye as he sinks back into the couch. J.R. turns his head so that he is staring at the floor.

I feel like there is something I'm missing. Sue just mentioned dinner, but it seems like there is something more to it. It seems like something they have all talked about before.

"We've talked about doing this, and I think tonight would be a good time. With Hoyt here, I think the group is doing very well, and I think you guys are ready for this," Sue says. She has a slight edge in her voice, as if she's informing us of something that we don't have a choice about.

"Yeah, you're right. We can do this," Kyle says as he straightens back up. His mood seems to be slowly improving.

"Yeah, it's cool. I'm game," J.R. says as he flashes Sue a halfhearted smile.

"So, pizza?" Sue asks.

"Sure," Kyle answers.

"Yeah," J.R. concurs.

"Hoyt, sorry to throw you in like this. I know you've only been here a few days, but one of the things we've talked about is ordering in dinner one night. The other guys have picked pizza. So you all just need to decide what you want and then order it. You can have dinner here in the day room tonight." Sue is casual as she informs me of this sinister plan.

All I hear is the word pizza. *Pizza. For dinner. You've got to be shitting me. I haven't had pizza in forever. This is fucked up.* I've only been here a week. I've been made to eat three shitty meals a day, three snacks, and endure countless group therapy sessions. Now you want me to eat pizza! Fat, greasy, calorie-laden pizza. Great, what's next? You want me to parade around in a Speedo?

"It's going to be good. This will be a good experience for you all in terms of eating a fear food and doing it together. You guys can provide support for each other. You can do this, and it can be fun," Sue says with a slight chirp in her voice on that last part. This is starting to sound like a pep talk. I'm not into pep. I'm into reality. And the reality is, this isn't going to be fun.

"Yeah, it's cool. Can we get a menu from someone in the front office?" Kyle asks. He seems to be fully on board.

"Yeah, they can give you one," Sue replies.

"Okay guys, time's up. Good luck tonight. Have fun breaking a rule, Hoyt and J.R. I can't wait to hear all about this tomorrow." Sue stands up, signaling us to do the same. We stand, hold hands, and do our closing ritual. Today, I don't even feign an attempt at mouthing the words of the affirmation. It's all I can do to hold it together. I feel like the next twenty-four hours are going to be anything but smooth sailing.

"Okay, I have a great idea about what you guys can do for your assignment," Kyle says enthusiastically as we all walk into the day room after lunch. I don't know how I got through lunch, but somehow I managed to eat. Now I'm feeling full and I'm not really in the mood to break any rules, let alone eat pizza in a few hours. But Kyle seems more animated than I've seen him. He's downright giddy with anticipation. I can tell he loves pushing the limits, and this rule-breaking assignment is making his creative juices overflow.

"Oh yeah, what?" J.R. asks.

"Well, you know we can't have diet soda," Kyle starts.

"Yeah, tell me about it," I groan, almost forgetting it's been more than a week since I've had any. I love that stuff. It kept me going for a long time when I was really losing weight.

"Well, in the hospital, they have vending machines. I say we go down there and stock up on all the diet soda we can. They have a lot of different kinds." Kyle sits down, leaning forward with his arms on his legs.

Diet soda. That sounds really good, actually. I wouldn't mind having some. And it would probably help me not eat as much pizza tonight. I don't know how Kyle knows the hospital has vending machines, and I'm scared to ask. We're not allowed down there. But I believe him when he says the vending machines are there.

"Awesome! That's a great idea," J.R. enthuses.

"Yeah, that sounds good to me. I haven't had any in a while," I add.

"Cool. Well, let's get our book bags and a lot of quarters, and then we can go down," Kyle says.

"Do we have to be worried about being caught or seen?" I ask. Now I feel nervous, as we get close to actually breaking a rule.

Kyle lets out a hoarse grunt. "Shit, no one around here will notice. I've done it before. It's cool," he informs me with a sly grin. I don't know if I feel better or worse now that I know he has done this before. I choose to ignore my reservations and do as I'm told. I go get my book bag and grab a roll of quarters that I have for laundry.

We meet back in the day room, and J.R. and I follow Kyle out of the room. We turn left, walk casually down the hall, and walk out the door at the end of the hall. I've never been out this door before. It dumps us into a side parking lot. We walk down a small hill, across another parking lot, and we end up at the back of the hospital.

My heart is jumping. I feel like I did when I bought Ipecac for this first time—but in a good way. I'm breaking a rule, but I'm doing this with friends. I'm not alone. It feels nice to be in this group.

"We go in here," Kyle says as he opens the door in front of us. Why it's not locked, I have no idea. Kyle goes in first, then J.R., and then me. We're inside a small room. Several feet in front of us is a doorway that heads into a hall, which leads to what I can only assume is the front admissions area.

I hate hospitals. I get a chill. I'm glad I'm not stuck in here. I've heard this is where you get sent if you get really sick or just totally stop eating. I'm glad that I passed all the medical tests before I came here and I'm able to stay at the house.

"There they are!" Kyle smiles as he points to the left of the door in front of us. I jerk my head to my left and notice two beautiful vending machines. They seem to be glowing, as if a spotlight from heaven is shining down, guiding us toward them. My heart skips a beat. I'm excited. *This is awesome. I love Diet Coke.* Feeling like an addict who is about to experience an awesome high, I walk forward and reach into my pocket to pull out the roll of quarters.

"We've got to be quiet, because if anyone is on duty over there, they will hear us," Kyle whispers as he points to the open doorway. J.R. and I nod and we all huddle up in front of the machines.

"Well, let's do it," Kyle says as he puts in quarters and presses the Diet Pepsi button. J.R. is in front of the other machine; he buys a Diet Mountain Dew. I stand there patiently awaiting my turn, hoping that no one walks through that door way.

We execute our mission in total silence. The only sounds are the quarters clanking into the vending machines and the aluminum cans plunking down. After several minutes and multiple Diet Pepsi and Diet Mountain Dew purchases, it's my turn. I take the machine J.R. was at and furiously feed in quarters to buy a Diet Coke. Then I get another one, and another one, and another one. Then I buy a Diet Mountain Dew, just for something different.

"Come on, let's go," Kyle whispers. He motions as he opens the back door and starts to leave. I turn around, zip up my book bag, and put the unused quarters back into my pocket. I'm the last one out the door.

"Damn, that was awesome!" Kyle exclaims. I can't help but laugh. The rush of getting away with something is just too much. It does feel awesome. The sun shining down on us feels like validation for a job well done as we quickly make our way back up the hill.

"Yeah, that was great," J.R. says.

"Wow, we did it," I marvel.

"So, how many did you get?" Kyle asks as we all sit down in the day room in our assigned spots. Kyle starts opening his book bag.

"Um ... I got," J.R. starts, "um, five. Three Diet Pepsis and two Diet Mountain Dews."

"Awesome. I got three Diet Pepsi's, one Diet Mountain Dew, and one Diet Cherry Coke," Kyle informs us.

"What'd you get Hoyt?" Kyle asks.

"Four Diet Cokes and one Diet Mountain Dew," I reply.

"Awesome. So we got fifteen diet sodas!" Kyle says, almost in disbelief. Fifteen diet drinks. *Damn, we're gonna have fun tonight, and I won't sleep for a week.* We all just sit there with huge smiles on our faces. It feels like we just pulled off a huge heist.

"So, you like Diet Coke best?" J.R. asks me.

"Yeah. Diet Pepsi is good, but for some reason, I like Diet Coke better," I answer.

"That's cool. So I take it we all drank a lot of this when we were active in our ED?" J.R. asks. Kyle and I both just nod in agreement. No further discussion needed. We all know the tricks of the trade, and diet soda is a basic. No calories, decent taste, and the carbonation can fill you up for hours.

"Hell, I want one now. Screw waiting for dinner," Kyle says as he pulls a Diet Pepsi from his bag. He snaps it open and takes a big gulp. J.R. and I laugh and follow his lead. I grab a Diet Coke, pop the top, smell it, and then take the biggest gulp I can without choking. Instantly, my body relaxes. It knows this feeling all too well, the feeling of fullness without calories. *I love it.*

I may have been here a week and may have started working on some of the issues that are feeding my disease, but right now this indulgence in one of my ED behaviors seems like just what I needed. I feel like I have some control back.

We each finish two sodas and put the empty cans back in our book bags. We don't want to throw them away—at least not yet. We sit back and veg out in front of the TV for a while. Then, after some time passes, Kyle looks at the clock and says, "I think we should probably order the pizza now. It's almost four and we need to go to art soon."

Damn, I forgot about dinner. I dread the thought of deciding what to order.

Kyle pulls out the menu he was able to get from the front desk. Luckily, we all seem to like the same thing, so we decide on one large pepperoni and one medium cheese pizza. I don't think any of us wants to try a pizza with everything on it. That's just too many calories.

"Okay cool. I'll call and order it," Kyle says. As he stands and starts to walk out of the room, J.R. gets up to follow him. Not wanting to be left out, I follow, too. While Kyle is at the pay phone dialing, J.R. is standing close by. I guess he wants to be supportive. I stand next to J.R.

"Hi, yeah, I'd like to order some pizzas for delivery," Kyle says into the phone. After pausing for a second, he continues. "Yeah, we'd like one large pepperoni and one medium cheese." Another pause. "Oh yeah, to Roger's Memorial Hospital—the Eating Disorder Clinic."

There's a long pause. Kyle makes a funny face. "Yeah, I'm serious. The clinic. It's cool, I promise." He sounds annoyed. There's another long pause. "Yeah, can you have it here by five? Okay cool, thanks." Kyle hangs up the phone and laughs. Loud.

"Poor guy didn't know what to do when I told him where to deliver it," Kyle says. It dawns on me why J.R. wanted to be here: he knew it was going to be interesting when Kyle had to tell the pizza place to deliver to an eating disorder clinic. The three of us have a good laugh.

"Oh, hey guys."

"Hey," we say in unison to Ray, the tech on duty. He's pretty cool. I've been around him a few times and it seems that, when he's on duty, he's assigned to us.

"Oh Hoyt, you've got mail. Here you go," Ray says. He hands me the first mail I've gotten since I've been here.

"Thanks," I say, taking two postcards from him.

"Well, we've got art. We'll meet you up there, Hoyt," Kyle says. He and J.R. walk up the stairs as I sink into the chair in front of the pay phone.

"Okay, I'll be up there in a minute," I mumble.

The first postcard has two pictures of horses on the front and says Assateague Island. I've never heard of the place. Turning it over, I read:

> *Dear Hoyt –*
>
> *Just got back from a trip with my brothers and dad. Went to a nature preserve in VA. Very nice animals etc. But the beach was my favorite . .. so much scenery Hope things are going well for you. Take care – Mark*

I can't help but smile. It was so nice of Mark to send me a postcard. He's a sweetheart. I can only imagine what scenery he was enjoying on the beach. I wish I had been there. The next postcard is a beautiful photo of a skyline and in the upper right corner it says Seattle.

Hoyt –

    Had this postcard from Seattle from a few weeks ago. It's so nice there. If I move you'll have to come visit. And I'll set you up with a Microsoft millionaire.

Later – Mark

PS – I have to stop traveling so much!

I let out a small laugh. *That's Mark, the world traveler. I don't think that guy ever unpacks a suitcase. A millionaire, that would be sweet.* I notice the postmark on both of these is just a day apart.

I feel touched that he sent me two cards. I slump further down in the chair. I'm sad. I miss everyone in N.Y. I miss my friends. I miss my life—the life I thought I hated so much. I want to be well. I want to be happy and have a life and a boyfriend. *No. I'm not going there right now.* I stand up, rush down the hall into my room, and throw the postcards on my bed. Then I head up to the art therapy room.

"Fuck, there it is," Kyle says solemnly. He stares at the two boxes sitting on the coffee table in front of him. The pizzas are here. It's dinner time, and the three of us are alone in our day room. The two boxes are closed, but the smell is undeniable. The thick smell of fresh, hot pizza is swirling around the room. It's taunting us. It's daring us just to dive in and to devour the pizza, devour all of it without thinking, without feeling. Just eat until we can't eat anyone.

My pulse is up, my body is numb, and I don't want to be here. *I'm scared.* This is a major fear food for me, and I feel like if I eat this, then I will be falling off the wagon. But I know I can't avoid this forever. I'm here so that I can have a normal relationship with food. I need to learn to eat food like this without overdoing it and feeling bad about myself. *But can I? What the hell is normal, anyway? I'm not normal. No one is!*

"We can do this," J.R. says lightly. He seems calm, almost happy. He's our resident optimist.

"Yeah, I know. Okay, here you go," Kyle says as he hands each of us a paper plate. He opens the first box and takes a slice of pepperoni. J.R. takes a slice and I follow suit. The three of us each take a bite.

If this were a movie, this would be a slow motion sequence with
the camera zooming in on all of our faces as we take our first bites.
Kyle's face would show some pleasure. He likes the taste. J.R.'s face
would show relief—because it tastes nice, but so far he is handling it
well. My face would show ... nothing. I'm numb and doing my best to
stay that way. I'm eating it and it tastes good, but I'm not happy about
it. I don't show any emotion.

Several more minutes pass in silence and several more bites are
eaten.

"So this is strange, huh?" Kyle says, laughing.

"Yeah," J.R. replies.

"How are you guys doing?" I ask, needing some feedback. I need
reassurance that I'm not the only one in hell right now.

"Okay, I guess. It's a bit rough, but it's nice having you guys here,"
Kyle says.

"Yeah, I feel the same. This would be so much tougher if you all
weren't here," J.R. says.

I feel so relieved that I can't help but smile. Misery does love company, and at least I'm in the company of two guys who know the agony
I'm going through at this moment.

"I like our group. It's really going well and I think it's awesome
how well we get along," Kyle says, out of the blue.

I'm taken aback. His unsolicited opinion makes me feel good. I
like our group. In fact, it's a downright safe feeling ... which scares
the hell out of me. I'm scared that it might change. I don't do change
well. I'm becoming attached to these guys. They feel like little brothers to me. I've always wanted a brother, and now I feel like I've got
two. I like that, but it scares me because I don't want to lose it.

We continue to eat and talk and drink our diet sodas. The talking
helps keep all of us out of our heads. We all feel like restricting, but
at the same time, we all actually do like the pizza. In fact, it's damned
good. It's a nice change from the food we have to eat on a daily basis.

After we each eat four slices, we decide we are done, so we put in
a movie to try to take our minds off what we just consumed. *Happy*

Gilmore proves to be a good distraction. The laughter is nice. About halfway through the movie, it's snack time. Ray opens the door and asks us to come and get snack. The three of us freeze and just look at each other. Thankfully, there is strength in numbers. With some encouragement, amazingly, all three of us actually eat our snacks, even though none of us wants to. We eat three apples in total silence and then quickly return to the movie.

"Here, let's put them on here," Kyle says as he pulls the coffee table closer to the blue couch where I sit. "When Sue comes, in she'll see them right away."

"Good idea," I reply. We have decided not to throw away our diet soda cans. We have to show Sue proof of the rule we broke yesterday. We carefully stack all fifteen cans on the table. The six Diet Pepsi's form the base, then the four Diet Mountain Dews, then two Diet Cokes, then another two Diet Cokes on top of that— and to cap it off, the single Diet Cherry Coke.

"Sweet!" J.R. exclaims as he stands in the middle of the room admiring our makeshift pyramid of cans. Fifteen cans. I can't believe we drank all that in one day. Can anyone say bingeing? We quickly take our spots and wait for Sue.

"Hey guys how's it ... what?" Sue stops in the doorway and lets out a loud, unexpected laugh. We can't help but join her.

"Impressive, huh?" Kyle asks.

"Oh my! You didn't! That's great!" Sue says, trying to stop laughing as she walks into the room.

"Yeah, it was Kyle's idea," J.R. informs her.

"Why am I not surprised?" Sue walks over to the table and starts silently counting the cans.

"Wow, you guys really went all out. That's a lot." She seems impressed.

"Oh, we've got to get a picture of this. Do any of you have a camera?" Sue asks.

"Yeah, I've got one," Kyle says, retrieving a camera from his book bag.

"Okay, you guys all get on the couch," Sue instructs. I sit on one side, Kyle sits on the back of the couch in the middle, and J.R. sits on the other side of him. We lean in while Sue adjusts the camera.

Here we are, the Three Anorexic Musketeers in front of fifteen cans of diet soda that none of us were approved to consume. We laugh. It feels hopeful.

23

"Yeah, Kyle usually skips this group," J.R. informs me as we walk down the hall to my first E.T. Group, otherwise known as Experiential Group Therapy. I have no idea what it means, but learning that Kyle skips it is making me nervous.

"Why?" I ask. I'm dying to know if I need to do the same.

"He doesn't get along that well with Rachel, the instructor," J.R. says. That doesn't tell me that much. I need details. I need to know what we're going to do. We already do group therapy out the wazoo. What more fun can they have in store for us?

I follow J.R. down the same hall that yesterday led us on our quest to break a rule. Before we get to the exit door, J.R. turns left and we go into a room I hadn't noticed before. The wall to my right is mostly windows and small chairs are scattered around the room.

"Hello, guys," a tall, thin woman greets us. She appears to be about my mom's age. She has a kind face, but her piercing eyes make me look away. And she is wearing a wig—I'm not sure why. Maybe she has cancer and lost her hair, although she seems healthy enough.

"Hey, Rachel. This is Hoyt," J.R. says.

"Hello, Hoyt, nice to meet you," Rachel says as she extends her hand.

"Hi, nice to meet you as well," I reply as I shake her hand.

"Kyle's not coming?" Rachel asks, sounding a bit annoyed.

"Uh, no, I think he's got class," J.R. says, doing his best to cover up for him. I have a feeling that J.R. has no clue about Kyle's actual whereabouts.

"Okay, well, I guess we can get started then," she says. "Why don't you guys take a seat."

I slump into the first chair I see. It's small. Very small. *We may be anorexic and thin, but couldn't they spring for some normal size chairs for this room? Hell, I'm practically sitting on the ground! I feel like I'm back in kindergarten.* I drop my head and do my best to stifle the nervous laughter that is struggling to break free. This is just another surreal day in rehab.

"We've only got about an hour, so let's get right to it. I think today we're going to do some psychodrama," Rachel starts off. *Some what? Psycho what?* I don't like the sounds of this.

"Oh, cool," J.R. exclaims, noting his approval.

Cool? J.R.'s reaction isn't helping my nerves. My body is now tense as I crouch in this tiny chair, bracing for what this fun little exercise is going to entail.

"Basically, Hoyt, it's some role-playing," Rachel explains. "So why don't we have you start off?"

Me? I get to start off? Oh thanks, nice way to just throw the new guy into the deep end. I freeze for a moment. J.R. is already standing. I push myself up slowly, forgetting that I don't have to worry about blacking out anymore. Now that I've been here for a week eating regularly, I don't black out every time I stand up.

"So, Hoyt how many people are in your family?" Rachel asks—demands, really. She's really direct, and those eyes are locked onto me. I feel like I'm caught in some *Star Trek* tractor beam and I can't escape.

"Huh?" I feel stunned. I'm not sure what she just asked me.

"How many people are in your immediate family?" she asks again, even faster.

"Oh, um, well, my parents, then I have two sisters and my older sister is married with two kids," I reply as fast I can. I get the feeling she's ready to get this show on the road, and I don't want to slow her down.

"Okay, well, this works better when we have more people. But I guess we can make do. Use these," she says as she walks over and starts pulling chairs closer to where I'm standing. *And I'm supposed to use them to do what, exactly?*

"This is how it works. You stay standing where you are and each chair will represent one of your family members. You tell J.R. where to put each one in relation to where you are standing. Got it?" Rachel asks, peering at me.

I have to do what? This is messed up. Chairs. My family members. "Uh, yeah, sure, okay," I mutter, lying. It's not okay. It's weird.

"Whenever you're ready," she says.

"Um, okay, well ... my mom can go here," I start off, pointing directly to my right. J.R. picks up a chair and puts it next to me. Feeling a bit more secure after this first attempt goes well, I place Amy on my left. Then I place Jessica next to mom, and then the boys and my brother-in-law are close to Amy. And, last but not least, Dad. He goes at the end of the line, after Jessica. It doesn't take long to place everyone.

"So take a look. Why is your mom right here?" Rachel asks, pointing to the chair immediately to my right.

"Not sure. We're close, I guess," I answer, hoping that is what she is looking for.

"Okay. So you would say you're the closet to her out of everyone here?"

"Yeah."

"Your dad is here?" she asks, walking to the end of the line and pointing to the last chair.

"Uh, yeah," I answer. I feel my throat start to close up, afraid of where she is going with all of this. I'm not sure I want to keep playing along.

"It's interesting that he's all the way down here. Are your parents still married?"

"Yes."

"How's their relationship?"

"Good, I guess. They've been married for more than thirty years."

"So, why is dad all the way down here?" I clench my butt to prevent myself from falling over. I feel weak. This doesn't feel good. My mind is screaming for some control. I feel like I'm being interrogated. Sweat starts to form around my hairline. I don't appreciate where she is trying to go with this. Why can't we talk about my mom? I thought moms get blamed for everything.

"I don't know. I guess I don't feel all that close to him," I answer, more honestly than I was prepared for. *Damn, she's good.* I'm almost scared not to be honest with her. Those eyes of hers can probably spot a liar a mile away.

"Let's do this. J.R., come here. You stand here. You're Hoyt's dad," Rachel says, leading J.R. to stand directly to my right as she pulls the chair away that was there. J.R. follows orders and is now standing next to me. We're almost touching. I'm facing forward, frozen. I avoid looking at him, dreading what is about to happen.

"Hoyt, turn and face him. Here's your dad is front of you. Tell me about him," she orders. She is stern. No nonsense. I turn to face J.R. We make eye contact briefly. There is kindness in his eyes. I don't like it. It feels too personal. *This is so fucked up! My dad. I don't want to be doing this.*

My mind is barreling down the highway at full speed, trying every trick in the book to gain control. My body is shutting down, going numb. It's having none of this. It knows what's in store and it's not willing to participate any longer.

The rest of the session goes by as if I'm watching it on a movie screen. I know I was there and participated, but it was all so overwhelming, it feels like I was watching someone else do this. Rachel has me "talk" to my dad, and of course, I'm more open than I want to be. I mention feeling inadequate, wanting him around more, wanting more affection, and just wanting more of a relationship with him.

Then, for shits and giggles, Rachel has J.R. and I switch roles. I get to be Dad and J.R. is me. So then I get to "talk" to myself and say everything I want to tell my "son." It's the most intense therapy session I have ever experienced. As soon as the hour is up, I get the hell out of there and run to my room. I need to be alone. I need to write.

I collapse onto my bed, shaking, and grab my journal from the nightstand, writing at lightning speed.

> *Thursday June 27, 2002*
>
> *I honestly can't even put into words what just happened. Just got out of my first Psychodrama class. It was J.R. and me. We did role play with my family and the instructor focused on Dad and our relationship. It was honestly the hardest and most emotional experience I have ever had. I have to admit, I want to run. I almost couldn't take it. It was so powerful. It makes everything so real. I'm just in shock. I don't know what to say.*
>
> *I'm really suffering. It's hard. This psychodrama has done just that to me—made me psycho! What am I running from? Those scary, unpredictable emotions is my guess. I wanted to break down and cry and just let it out, but I turned off the light inside and shut down before I had a chance. It's just so hard. Your brain does anything it can to try to get control and restrict. And of course I'm scared I'm gaining weight.*
>
> *Changing gears, I think I've calmed down about the gay thing and telling the guys. I presented my art collage on Tuesday and never used the word gay, but I don't know how the hell anyone could miss it. The guys were great about the piece. Afterwards, I crashed and shut down and skipped snack. I was freaking out about being open and then scared of getting too close and being hurt when people leave. Then the next day in group, as if by divine intervention, we talked about relationships and being hurt and loving with all of our hearts. It suddenly dawned on me that I don't have to go around and have some great discussion about being gay and announce it. I can just quietly come out and talk about myself*

matter-of-factly, like in group using "he" when talking about my love life. So I feel more peace about the whole thing.

Tonight I get to go on my first planned outing. We are going to Blockbuster and Best Buy. So we'll see what CDs I come home with

So until next time:

"Hangin' around, nothin' to do but frown ...." Rainy Days and Mondays by The Carpenters

24

Tuesday July 2, 2002

    Well, happy July! Time flies when you're having fun. Saturday, I went to my first OA (overeaters anonymous) meeting. Kyle was running it. It was interesting and made me think more. Everyone was very nice. There were more outside people than residents, and several obese people, which at first made me feel uncomfortable. It's just like in the movies. Before anyone talks, they say their name and their disease (ex. Hi, I'm Hoyt and I'm anorexic) and then everyone says Hi, Hoyt! We broke up into small groups and talked about honesty. Now if you would have asked me before this meeting if I was an honest person, I would have said yes. But this conversation made me really think, because another way of being honest in your life is being honest with yourself. I had to really think about that. The end result was, I realized I'm good at lying to myself. Lying about how I truly feel but also lying about what I want and need. That comes from hiding and stuffing emotions and being afraid of feeling. At the end of the meeting, everyone gives hugs, which was nice and always pushes me out of my comfort zone.

    The weekend and the last couple of days have been really hard. The other guys have hit emotional walls, and it's been tense. I think things are starting to kick in for me, and I hit the wall. My anorexic self has been doing everything it can to try to get some control.

The bonding with the guys is still happening and we have some pretty awesome moments. Friday night, we hung out and started kicking a ball around and made goals and played soccer in the day room. It was fun just to do something and act stupid. I also found we are more real and open up more easily in those moments. After a while of messing around, we were all sitting around and just talking. We were talking about meaningful stuff like hitting bottom and our weights and feelings about that stuff. I don't know, it just felt good and natural, and it wasn't even scripted or planned.

Then last night, all of us were talking about the real me and what does that mean and about the many different masks we all wear. It was a great philosophical question. One that I'm sure could be discussed forever. It really made me think about it. I think I've been scared of that question. It's just so much easier not to confront it, because it makes you take stock of yourself. It makes you think, where do I derive my self-worth? It scares me and saddens me, because I feel like I don't know myself. How could I, when all I do is stuff my emotions? But I'm pretty damned sure I derive my self-worth from external things. Intellectually, I know that's not good. It can get so overwhelming. I know that a huge chunk of my work here is to get in touch and get to know my real self. It just seems so damned hard.

We talked about co-dependency in group the other day. It scared me because I can relate. I feel other people's emotions so deeply and in return I attach to others too easily. The ironic thing is, because I'm so scared about opening up and being hurt, I put up an outward wall to protect myself. So people are surprised to learn that I'm so emotional. I get so scared of change, people leaving, being hurt or people disappointing

*me—which they do because of my impossibly high standards—
that I shut down and stuff my emotions and this feeds my feelings of isolation. I've been struggling with feelings of isolation
and I've been triggered recently by talking to mom and Peter.
Things seem so normal on the outside world. My friends especially act like nothing has happened and I'm okay. It makes
me angry, because I feel like no one understands the hell I'm
going through, and no, everything is not okay! On the flip
side, I don't know what I want from them or how I want them
to act. And that makes me angry.*

*Another aspect is, there are people here who do under-
stand—I'm surrounded by them—but that scares me because
I can't get too close, because that would make me vulnerable. I
would actually have to feel and be real, but part of me wants
to. I guess if none of me wanted to, then I wouldn't be here.*

*I have to work up to being more open. I go into this people-
pleasing mode and feel like if Kyle and J.R. are down and
struggling, then I can't be. I have to be positive. If nothing
else, interject a smile into the picture for God's sake, because
we know we all can't be down and struggling. You know what
would happen then? NOT A DAMNED THING WOULD
HAPPEN. Why can't I just give myself permission to feel and
be honest? So what if the other guys are down? Maybe if I was
honest with them as well about struggling, then that would be
a more honest—or in the context of food, a complex moment.
(Get it? Complex carbs are not necessarily better, but they're
longer lasting). I can't be positive all the time. It's killing me.*

*I got excited in group today when Sue said people can
experience a split from their feelings and can amazingly talk
and talk about hard stuff but not feel it. I was like, hello!
That's me! I've been that way my whole life. I feel like my
feelings are lost, locked away, and that I can talk about almost anything but not feel it. I know it's a coping mechanism.
It keeps me safe. That way, I don't have to go to those dark*

places. I can stay in my comfort zone. The messed up thing is, that's why I stay happy and positive, especially when others are not. I don't have to go there, and in some way, I'm hindering others from going there. My smile may be preventing them from being totally open and going to where they need to go.

So the theme for the past few days is being real, not putting on a defensive mask, and opening up to each other.

So to end this on a positive note, I try to think of life as a journey. I hope I will get the supplies here that I need for that journey.

25

I slide off my shoes, cross my legs under me, and open my notebook. I might as well work on another assignment, since I have
some time to kill before my appointment with the nutritionist.
I need to do something to get my mind off my body. I still don't like
how I feel after I eat. J.R. and Kyle are off doing something else, and
I have the day room to myself.

I look down at the sheet of paper Sue gave me. There are only five
questions to answer. *This shouldn't be too hard.* I turn to a clean sheet of
paper in my notebook and start writing.

1. *Do you believe that you are (or would be) a better person at a thinner
   weight? Why?*
   - *Yes – I believe I would look better and thus would be more lovable
     and acceptable.*
2. *What are some ways society supports our diet/weight preoccupation?*
   - *There is constant media attention on the topic and there are
     weight-loss fads and gimmicks being advertised everywhere you
     turn.*
   - *You get constant reinforcement for being thin. People make com-
     ments all the time when you're thin about how great it must feel
     to be thin and how nice it must be to be able to eat whatever you
     want.*

3. *List 5 things you like about yourself that have NOTHING TO DO WITH APPEARANCE OR WEIGHT.*
   - *Sense of humor*
   - *Good listener*
   - *Intelligent*
   - *Sensitive*
   - *Loyal*
4. *List 5 accomplishments in your life that have NOTHING TO DO WITH APPEARANCE OR WEIGHT.*
   - *Surviving high school and graduating*
   - *Graduating college*
   - *Getting a job in NYC*
   - *Just plain surviving life*
   - *Recognizing I needed help and allowing myself to get it*
5. *What is keeping you from letting go of your eating disorder and living your best life?*
   - *Fear – I don't know any other way.*
   - *Perfectionism – I need to look good (thin) and thus be viewed as a valuable and important person in the eyes of society.*

I hate these questions. My body is tense and my left-hand is throbbing. I can't seem to relax when I answer questions. I tense my hand and write as fast as I can, almost as if there's a time limit. I just want to get done before I have time to really take in what I'm writing. It's depressing. I know I'm scared. I know I'm a perfectionist. I want to be loved and feel important and valued. But for some reason, the only way I seem to know how to do that is by controlling how I look. It's messed up, I know that. But it's just so damned easy for me. Losing weight is just easy.

Damn it! Why the hell am I still feeling full? Screw this. I turn to the back of my notebook and go several pages in and stop on the page I'm looking for. There it is. Staring back at me are several rows of words and numbers. My heart skips a beat. It makes me nervous looking at this. I know I shouldn't have done this, but I needed to. I had to know. The night after we ate pizza for dinner, I had to know how many calories I had consumed. My mind wouldn't let it go. Based on what I had for breakfast, lunch, and snack that day, I estimated that I had eaten—before the pizza—about 1,220 calories. Not great, but not horrible. Of course, I couldn't bring myself to calculate the calories for the pizza. That would have sent me over the edge.

I just need to do some calculations. Breakfast. Yeah, my meal plan is two grains, one fruit, and two fats. I have to have that, but if I'm feeling generous, I can also add one protein and one milk (which will never happen, since I hate milk). I start writing some of the breakfast foods I've been eating and the calories counts:

2 pieces bread = 220
1 thing of peanut butter = 80
1 thing of butter = 80
1 apple or banana = 50
                    430

1 yogurt = 190
1 bread = 110
1 banana = 50
2 things peanut butter = 160
                    510

430 calories. 510 calories. Damn, that's a lot. That's too much. I don't need that much for breakfast. I used to be fine with a muffin, non-fat yogurt, and tea. Now I'm eating a fucking feast. When I see the numbers at the top of the page, I let out a small laugh. I notice that where I had scribbled this same breakdown earlier in my stay here, I had only allocated fifty calories to the butter or peanut butter. Of course, that made the calorie count a lot lower. *Boy, was I delusional then.* I'm pretty confident that my eighty-calorie allotment for those items now is close. But I would much prefer to be consuming less than 400 calories for breakfast.

"Hey."

Startled, I look up and see Kyle walking into the room.

"Oh, hey."

"Whatcha doing?"

"Oh nothing, just working on some assignments," I reply. I feel bad about lying to him, so I quickly close my notebook, trying to hide the evidence of my rebellion. I feel dirty and guilty, like I've just committed some act of betrayal.

"Fuck, I'm so tired," Kyle moans as he falls onto the other blue couch.

"Trouble sleeping?"

"Yeah, I haven't been feeling great lately," he says as he pulls out a small, blue item from his side pants pocket. Before I know it, he has turned the portable game on and the familiar sounds of Tetris have filled the dead space. Kyle doesn't go anywhere without this game. And really, who can blame him? It's pocket-sized and so damned addictive. I may have to break down and get one the next time we have a Walmart run.

"Good ol' Tetris," I comment with a slight laugh.

"Yeah, it's awesome. I just wish I could save on this so I wouldn't have to start all over every time."

"So Sue hasn't taken it away yet?" I ask, knowing that Sue hates this game. She feels that it's too distracting.

"Fuck no. I'd like to see her try. She just says that to annoy me. And I don't care what they say about it causing me to isolate and not work the program," he grunts, "We do so much fucking work, I've gotta have a break some time."

"Yeah, I hear ya. We can't do therapy twenty-four-seven." I agree. Things get intense around here. We all need some escape.

"You can say that again." We both laugh. I look up at the clock and realize I need to leave for my appointment.

"Damn, it's time for my meeting with Elizabeth." I pull my legs out from under me, slide on my shoes, and stand up slowly. I'm in no big hurry. I'm scared of what she is going to say.

"Good luck," Kyle says without looking up from his game.

"Thanks, I think I need it."

"You'll be fine. She's cool."

I walk out of the room and turn left and step into the room that's next door to our day room. It's tiny and only has room for two small chairs and a small side table. It's intimate. *Nowhere to hide.* And I can't help but wonder if anyone in the day room next door can hear what is said in here. *Whatever. It doesn't matter.* It's not like I'm going to be talking about anything all that personal anyway.

Elizabeth isn't here yet, so I sit down in the chair closest to the door. I'm early, as usual. I hate being late. My notebook is sitting in my lap, and my mind can't help but start to obsess. I obsess about my weight. I would love to know what I weigh now. Then again, I'm not sure I could handle it. I've been here almost two full weeks, and I've been eating every day. Six times a day for two weeks. My body shudders at the thought of how much weight I've gained in these two weeks.

"Hi, Hoyt," Elizabeth says as she enters the room, which makes my mind temporarily suspend its obsessing.

"Hi," I reply. She's pretty. Blonde. Probably only a few years older than I am.

"So, how are things going?" she asks.

"Fine," I reply with my standard answer, choosing not to allow myself time to truly reflect and answer in a more authentic manner. She may be nice, but I don't feel the need to really engage with her.

Once seated, she starts reading over some notes. I sit there, just staring off into space.

"Looks like you've been doing well with your meal plan," she comments. I assume the techs write about what we do and don't do, and she's catching up on my compliance.

"Yeah, it's going okay," I say. I'm not really sure if she's looking for some deep insight from me or not.

"So, you've been here about two weeks now. How are you physically feeling?"

Great, this feels like therapy. I thought I was only here to talk about food and my meal plan.

"It's okay. I feel pretty full all the time."

"Yeah, that's normal. Your body is still getting adjusted to eating regularly." She pauses. "How are your bowel movements? Are you regular?" she asks without flinching.

Am I what? She's got to be joking. We really can't be talking about this, can we? It's none of your damn business, sister. Now fully tense, I really just want to leave. *This is stupid. I don't want to talk about my bathroom habits with you.* But I'm here and I really can't leave, because I know that would be rude. So I decide I'd better give her what she wants.

"Umm, I'm good. I'm more regular than I was," I add, slightly laughing at the uncomfortable energy that has now completely consumed me. Of course, there is no need to go into the fact that it feels like I'm giving birth to bricks. If I didn't know better, I would think I've been eating concrete for the last two weeks. And don't even get me started on the gas. It's a good thing that Kyle smokes outside. Otherwise, we'd have a fire hazard around here.

"What was it like before you came here?"

"Um, well, I pretty much had stopped going. But I was using that Fleet liquid laxative, so that got stuff out. But without that, I didn't go."

"Alright. And now?"

"Well, I guess I'm going probably, I don't know, probably every couple of days or so."

"Well, that's good."

"What's normal?" I ask, suddenly curious about why she's asking. I feel slightly insecure that I'm not normal in this regard.

"Well, really, there isn't a normal. You'll hear some doctors say you need to be going at least once a day, but really, all of our bodies are different. So one person may go three times a day, and that's normal for them. But for you, it may be once every couple of days. Though I would say if it's been three days and you haven't had a movement, then that is a concern."

"Oh, okay," I mumble. I still feel so awkward talking about this.

"And just know that, since you're refeeding, it will take your body a while to adjust to food again and to rev back up to digesting and moving your food through. Now, how long did you do the Fleet?"

"Not long. Probably a few months. And it wasn't like I did it every day or anything."

"Okay, that's good. It's good that your bowels are working. I've had some clients who abused laxatives so long that it took years for them to have a normal bowel movement again. You can really do some damage. And there are some people who do so much damage that their bowels never recover."

"Wow, that's scary," I say, suddenly feeling grateful that I didn't spend years abusing myself like I know I could have.

"So, let's talk about your meal plan. You've been doing well with it, but I need to increase it. Your weight actually has stabilized," she says out of the clear blue.

Her words strike me right in the gut. My stomach sinks and I feel sick. *Increase. She has to increase my meal plan. No, you don't. We can keep it right where it is. I don't need to eat anymore. I'm okay right where things are. Please don't change anything. Please.*

"Now, don't get worried. It's okay. This happens to everyone. You're body has adjusted to this caloric intake, and we just have to bump it up a bit so that you can keep gaining weight. And it will probably have to be increased again next week."

Wait, wait a minute! It's going up right now, and then it's going up again next week? No, you can't be serious! That's fucked up! I don't need to be eating all this much food. I know I'm gaining weight. I'm sure if we just keep things where they are I'll keep gaining.

I'm frozen. I can't move. I'm sitting here like an idiot, just staring at this woman as she tells me I have to eat more food to gain more weight. But how much weight? Does this chick want me to be 200 pounds?

"What is my ideal weight?" I blurt out. I need the number. I've got to know where I'm heading.

"Well, wow, I usually don't tell patients this early in treatment. Do you really want to know?"

"Yeah," I reply, dead serious.

"Well, according to the BMI chart, based on your height and being a male, you need to be at 181 pounds for the rest of your life. And if you drop below 170 pounds, that should be taken as a warning sign."

Just kill me now why don't you! If I could disintegrate, I would. My body is totally stiff and not moving, but my mind is fucking freaking out! *181 pounds. 181 pounds. This woman has lost it. I don't want to be 181 pounds! I don't want to be 170 pounds. I know what I look like at 180, and I don't like it. I look fat. I don't like that person.*

"Now, one thing you need to know is that it takes guys a lot to gain weight. Guys plateau much sooner than girls, and we usually have to give you supplements like Ensure to get you to your goal weight. So that will happen slowly. Also, most people who have had an eating disorder will have to consume more calories than their counterparts that have never had an eating disorder. It will take more for you to maintain your weight than someone else who has never had an eating disorder." She says this as if she is reassuring me. She has to know I'm freaking out right now.

Consume more. I will have to eat more than "normal" people. I'll get to eat a lot of food. That's kind of cool. But that means I'll have to eat a lot just to stay "healthy." Damn, I don't like that. I don't want to eat a lot. I don't want to feel that much. Food makes me feel too much. *I can't think about this right now. I'm not going to think about this. It's too much.* In a sick attempt to placate myself, I realize that if I hate how I look when I get out of here, I can always lose some weight.

Elizabeth informs me that now for breakfast, I will need to eat three grains, one protein, two fats, and one fruit. For lunch I will now need to do three grains, two to four proteins, one fruit, and three fats. For dinner it will now be three grains, two to four proteins, one fruit and three fats. I hear all this, but choose not to absorb it. I can't.

I've checked out. We finish the session and I do what I do a lot these days. I run to my room to escape into sleep.

> *Thursday July 4, 2002*
>
> *Well, happy 4th! Mom and dad sent me some balloons, which was nice.*
>
> *The last couple of days have been okay. In group yesterday, I was able to slip in about being in the gay community (Sue asked me a question that set me up perfectly). And of course, Kyle was not there, but J.R. was and seemed cool. He hasn't mentioned it.*
>
> *I know I've been struggling a lot since yesterday and doing everything I can to stuff, be numb, and act happy! I'm trying not to think about what weight they want me at, but do they know how much that is? It depresses me so much! I'm scared and angry. Do they know how much better I felt when I was say 150 vs. 180? How much attention I got and how much better clothes fit! I know what I look like at 180 and I hate it! I can't go back to that person. It scares me. I won't go back. It's just too painful and I looked too FAT! Then I try to calm myself down and say that's why I'm here, to hopefully learn to accept myself and love myself no matter what I weigh. It scares me so much. I don't know if I have it in me to fight this monster. I just want to be loved and feel peace and tranquility, and not be obsessed about these things.*
>
> *At Barnes and Noble the other day, Kyle pulled out a book about EDs and opened to a story for me to read. It was a mom writing about her daughter's ED, and it hit me so hard. She was saying how her daughter was self-hating and saying she didn't deserve anything good like love, help, food, and was just hurting herself. For whatever reason, those words hit me like a ton of bricks, because I could relate. For the first time, I was admitting it to myself and being honest with myself for*

a split second. Society values the sanctity of life so much (and for good reason) but if anyone feels different or struggles with that belief, they are shunned or made to feel dirty. I felt those self-loathing feelings, but I stuffed them because the messages I got from the outside world were that you shouldn't feel that way and if you do you're a freak or bad. So I had to put on another mask and pretend everything was okay.

For whatever reason, I think I feel I'm no good, not worthy, a sinner, and need to be punished. And so starving myself was so easy because since I feel all this inside, it makes sense to starve yourself, doesn't it? The funny thing is, because I feel this, I place all of my self-worth on outside things and need constant validation. But none of the validation sinks in. Why doesn't it sink in? Because I'm no good and hate myself. So it's a vicious cycle, one that is killing me, and at times, one that I'm more than too happy to let kill me.

Standing there in the aisle with Kyle reading that story, for a split second I thought I was going to break down and sob. But being a good boy, I stuffed it in about five seconds flat. But I kept reading. When those out-of-the-blue emotional moments hit, they hit hard. Not even a good liar and mask-wearer like me can plan for and effectively combat those moments. It's my hope that, as time goes by here, it won't be second nature to stuff and go numb. That I will be able to feel and open up.

A great thought to close on was something this author said about EDs: that it was not a "life event" that causes EDs but rather the way the person views and experiences life. I really liked that. It made sense. In this world where everyone (especially Mom) wants to and needs to find causes, it's refreshing to say, it's just me. Nothing my folks did or didn't do caused this. It's how I'm wired and how I view life. I feel this has unfortunately set me up to adapt in a self-destructive way. I can honestly say under that "happy" mask there is a depressed and very hurt young man who probably has a pretty negative view of things.

Ugh, I need a break now. So until next time:

"I'm a hazard to myself ..."

– song by Pink

26

"Hoyt, do you want to read your triggers assignment?" Sue asks, looking directly at me.

"Uh, sure," I reply. I secretly want to lie and say I haven't done the assignment yet. I'm still not comfortable reading personal stuff to the group. I'd much rather listen to J.R. and Kyle. But now, resigned to my fate, I take a deep breath, sit up straight, and open my notebook to the page where I have drawn two columns—one for the triggers and one for the emotions it evokes.

I look down and start reading, determined not to feel a damned thing:

Eating food	*anger, disappointment, fear*
Enjoying food	*shame, fear, anger*
Weight/scale	*fear, pressure, anxious, determination*
Mirror/reflection	*dissatisfaction, sadness*
Phone ringing	*fear, anxious, dread, anger*
Doorbell	*fear, anxious, dread, anger*
Parties/	*fear, anxious, dread*
social settings	
Parents	*anger*
Beautiful people/	*sadness*
models in magazines	

Hearing from exes	*anger*
Work	*anxious, sadness*
Paying bills	*anxious, sadness*
High school	*anger, sadness*
Confrontation	*fear, anxious*
Bars/alcohol	*sadness, dissatisfaction*
Overweight people	*fear*
Very thin people	*sadness, anger*
Clothes/t-shirts/	*sadness, shame, determination*
shorts	
Pictures of me	*sadness, shame*
Physical intimacy	*shame, fear, sadness*

I gasp for air. I've read all of that as fast as possible. *Thank God it's over. That actually wasn't so bad. I'm good, I didn't feel anything. It was just like reading the weather report. Cool.* I'm not looking up, though. I don't want to see a reaction from Sue or from the other guys.

"Thank you, Hoyt," Sue says softly. I still refuse to look up. I close my notebook and turn it over in a feeble attempt to signal that I'm done with this and don't care to discuss it any further. I should know better. Sue doesn't play by my rules.

"Those were a lot of triggers. They were good. How did you feel reading them aloud?" she asks. I briefly look up and catch her gaze, but then I look away, breaking our connection before I lob out my standard retort: "Fine, it was fine."

"You mentioned something about bars and alcohol, I think. Can you tell us more about that?" Sue seems to ask innocently, although she knows I've stopped drinking. *Ugh, I don't want to tell you more about that, Sue. In fact I don't want to talk about this anymore. Wasn't I good enough just to have read this?*

"Umm, well, I stopped drinking last February after a rough night, and thankfully haven't started again. I think I used booze to numb out what I was feeling. Drinking helped loosen me up when I was out and allowed me to be more open and friendly. But I know I felt more depressed when I drank. It clouded things and made me actually feel more isolated. To be honest, my drinking just made me feel sad. I didn't like how I felt when I drank a lot. So now the thoughts of doing it again make me sad. So hopefully I won't go back to it," I explain.

I feel I've been too honest. J.R. and Kyle are sitting on either side of me in their respective spots, focused on what I'm saying. I have their undivided attention. I shudder. I hate being the center of attention. I feel totally exposed, naked. I don't like it. It's like I've just handed everyone in this room the key to unlock my soul and to peer inside, unfiltered. *Here I am, warts and all.* Shifting my weight to my left, I pull my right leg up under me.

"That makes sense. That's very healthy, and it's wonderful you have that insight," Sue reassures me. "Your parents—are they a pretty strong emotional trigger for you?"

Sue is going for the gold. She's good. She starts out somewhat slow and now she's going right for it. The one item on my list that, if I was smart, I would not have mentioned.

"Uh, yeah, I guess." I'm not giving this up too easily. My body is now more tense, if that's even possible.

"What comes up when I mention your parents?"

"I don't know. I feel uncomfortable. Mad, I guess. That's what I wrote down anyway," I blurt out, without thinking. Agitation slowly starts to rise up from the floor beneath me.

"Okay," Sue says. "How would you describe your childhood?"

"Fine, I guess. It was normal, nothing too exciting. I can't really complain. We moved a fair amount."

"What was that like?"

"Fine, I guess. I don't know. It's not like I had much of a choice," I reply sharply. I'm starting to get annoyed. *Where are we going with this, Sue?*

"What do you remember about moving?"

"Well I was born in Atlanta and then when I was a toddler when we moved to Connecticut. I don't remember living there. Then after Connecticut, I remember living in Texas when I was really young.

Then we moved to Georgia for a year, that's where I went to kindergarten. That was fun because we lived in the same town as an aunt and uncle. Then we moved to Pennsylvania for eight years, and that was nice. That's where I feel like I grew up. Then in the middle of freshman year in high school, we moved to Nashville, which was total culture shock. I hated most of it. Then, two weeks after high school graduation, we moved to North Carolina. Then two weeks after I graduated from college, I moved to New Jersey to work in Manhattan."

I feel awkward right now like all eyes are on me. I just want to get this over with so I continue on. "It was hard. I don't feel like I can ever answer the question of where I'm from. I don't relate to that. I've never lived anywhere longer than eight years. But at the same time, it just seems like something we do in our family. Almost like it's in my blood."

Silence. There's a long pause. No one is saying anything. My body is pissed off. I don't feel well. I'm tense and doing my best to hold it together. I don't like tripping down Memory Lane. It's not fun. It's the past, and there is nothing I can do about it.

"That sounds difficult. Moving can be rough on a young person. How did your family deal with it?" Sue asks.

"Deal with it? We didn't. We just did it. It's not like we had a choice. We just moved."

"How did you feel about that?"

"I don't know. I guess I didn't feel anything. I mean, it was tough, I guess, but I never stopped to think about it really. I didn't have a choice. I don't feel like I have roots anywhere. None of my friends have known me for more than three years. I don't have any childhood friends. I've lost touch with everyone I've ever known. I think I've tended to burn bridges. Once I moved, it was just easier to move on and not look back."

"I can imagine that's painful. Moving is really like a death. People tend to experience the stages of grief when they have a major life move," Sue informs me.

"Damn, it's funny you said that. I never heard that until my mom mentioned that to me, not too long ago. It really pissed me off. I had never heard that, and no one had ever told me that. I wish they had. I wish someone had told me that what I was feeling, or trying not to feel, was normal. I think all these years I've been mourning and I never knew it. I just stuffed it. And I was really good at that."

I exhale, doing my best to expel the rage that is starting to build up inside me. I don't want it in me anymore. I don't want to be angry, but damn it, I am! I'm pissed that I had to move, that I can't be one of those people who identifies as being *from* somewhere. I'm not someone who can say they've had the same best friend since the first grade. I want all that, but I don't have it. And I never will. This is so fucked up! Why didn't we ever talk about this before? Why didn't mom and dad ever mention this to us when we were kids?

Well, Sue, you got your wish. I'm feeling all that anger towards my parents really strongly right now. In fact, if I wasn't so tired from eating all the damn time, it would feel great to go break something, or maybe punch a wall. The sad part is, I know it's not my parents' fault. I know that this anger is really about life, but it's so easy to direct it toward them.

Suddenly, my mind flashes to the small envelope sitting on my nightstand in my room. It's addressed to me in my mom's handwriting. I got it yesterday, but I still haven't had the courage to open it. It's thick, and I'm scared to know what's inside. I'm pissed about being scared to read it. I know I just need to suck it up, put on my big boy pants and read it. It can't be that bad.

I'm grateful when the rest of group turns toward other topics and J.R. and Kyle take over talking more. I spend the rest of the time obsessing about finally reading that letter. I don't want to read it because I'm afraid of what I might feel—or not feel. But I know I need to. If I want an open, real, adult relationship with my parents, I need to act like an adult.

This is probably not the best thing to be doing right after lunch, but I know if I don't do it now, I won't do it today. So I sit on my bed with my legs stretched out in front of me, the small envelope on my lap. I take a deep breath and carefully run my finger along the back flap. It opens easily and without tearing. I pull out the thin, folded sheets of paper. *Damn, there are a lot. Thirteen.* There are thirteen sheets of paper. Thankfully she has only written on the front side, and these are small sheets. Here goes:

Tuesday, June 25, 2002

Dear Jeff,

I wrote you yesterday but still have not mailed it – surprise, surprise I hope you are fine. You are on my mind a lot. I hope you still feel that you are where you need to be and that you can see your time there at Rogers will be very beneficial.

I rented and watched the video "28 Days" with Sandra Bullock. Now I'm very curious as to how Rogers is that times ten. Maybe we can talk about it.

Also, wanted to let you know that I talked to Dr. Lauder at your church today. I had called her a while ago after I listened to her sermon on tape, to tell her how much it meant to me, but we never connected and I left a message. She kept leaving me messages, so finally today I called and talked to her. She knew who was on the line for her (her secretary told her) and when she came on, she said, "How's Hoyt?" – no hello, etc. As it turns out, she said Peter had spoken to her this past Sunday, and I guess he mentioned you to her. She is very concerned and said to tell you they are praying for you. She said she is anxious to meet you and she thought Peter is the nicest young man. She said their church is full of young people just like you and Peter and she hopes you both join the church soon. She also referred to Peter as your partner and I told her that he is a best friend but not a partner, and she said, "Oh." Anyway, thought you'd be interested in this and wanted to write it out while I could remember it. Dr. Lauder also told me that she was so glad I had called because she wanted Peter's phone number and didn't know it. So I gave it to her and then called Peter to tell him what I had done. Left him a message on his cell. Hope this does not feel to you as if I'm too into your business. I'm so happy you have found Marble Collegiate.

You'll be interested to know that I told Wendy Henderson that you are gay. It rolled off my tongue and she just said "I did not know that" and asked a few questions and moved on. They are straight-laced Catholic but with a very non-judgmental attitude.

Wednesday, June 26, 2002
Hi!

Hope you are having a good day. How's J.R.? Also how's the fifteen-year-old boy? Don't know his name. It's hot and humid here today.

I rented and watched "Moulin Rouge" and liked it a lot. I can see it as a Broadway play. What do you think?

How's your routine? And how's the food? Hope you are feeling good.

Will write more later. Take good care of yourself.
Love you,
Mom

Thursday, June 27, 2002
Congratulations!

You have completed your first week!
Love,
Mom, Dad and Jessica

Friday, June 28, 2002

Jeff,

Hope your day is good today. I'm wondering, do you stay really busy during the week with more free time on the weekends?

Sandy Stokes called and she's very concerned about you and asked lots of questions. Said to tell you they are thinking about you. Claire also called and is very concerned. Curt and Ricky have called Dad and Carol B. has called. All are concerned and said to tell you hello. Curt has a friend whose son had anorexia and recovered.

Jeff I want to remind you how much we love you and are here for you. If and when you want us to come there for anything or any reason, we will come. It makes us very sad to think of the pain and suffering you have endured. We know a better day is coming and please don't ever hesitate to let us know how we can facilitate your recovery. Your health and well-being is our top priority. You are the only son we are privileged to have, and you are precious to us. We would do anything for you. And that includes facing our mistakes in parenting you. We are obviously flawed with feet of clay, but we love you with our whole hearts and if there are things you need to confront us about or discuss with us, please give yourself permission without hesitation. You can count on our love and support forever. And please don't feel (as Amy has said at times she does) that you can't say critical things to us after all we've done for you. Anything we've done for you we did because we love you—no strings attached—and what we want more than anything besides your recovery is to have a healthy, open, honest relationship with you. Whatever that means and whatever that takes. And I hope that in all of this we each will discover more about who we really are and just be who we are.

I hope you feel our love and affirmation. I apologize that I was so slow in evolving with the gay issue. At the time, you were always so kind to me and told me to take my time and do it my own way. Now I look back and it makes me sad that I took so long. It was so based on fear and ignorance. As hard as it has been to see you so sick, I have not been as fearful as before. I truly do believe that you will recover and your experience at Rogers will, of course, become a part of who are you. I am so convinced that, as our hearts and lives are broken open, we expand and our capacity to feel and experience life expands. It is a tough principle, but I trust it and know it is true.

Guess I got on a soap box, but I feel I can never emphasize enough how much we love you and cherish you as our son. Jeff, if you spent the rest of your life doing everything you could think of to make us miserable, it would be fine because the first twenty-five years of your life have brought us more joy, happiness, pride, laughter, adventure, anxiety, hope, love, mischief, etc. etc. than we could've ever imagined. Our lives would have been very different if we had not had you, and I would not have wanted to miss one thing nor one moment with you.

I will never forget when you were born and they immediately put you in my arms. You were the most beautiful baby in the world. With your big blue eyes and your blond, peach-fuzz hair. Your first year of life was idyllic—tranquil—a parents' dream baby. Then you realized you had your own will and, of course, you exercised it, and the fun began. I could remind you of all the poisonous things you drank, the tantrums you threw, the sand you threw at your Sunday School teacher, splattering green paint on the light grey car, jumping off the roof of a friend's house, etc. etc. I ask you, what mother would've wanted to miss any of those events? What we often don't talk about are all of the everyday mundane joys that spontaneously happened in between those events. I have so many precious memories of family meals, bath times, lying down together at bedtime and reading stories. I still know "Green Eggs and

Ham" by heart. I look back and know that parenting was a huge task and responsibility and none of us by ourselves are really capable of doing it perfectly. I also have learned that being the parent of adult children—you and Amy—is just as daunting. We never know if we are saying or doing the right thing, that's most beneficial to you. So we try our best to be real, be who we are, use as much common sense as we can think of and then we hope and pray (knowing all the while we could've done it or said it better or not at all) that love and grace will cover all of the mistakes of commission and omission. With good communication in place, I believe that love and grace will just about do it.

I heard recently that some friends come into our lives for a reason, some for a season and some forever. And that each is okay. I might remind you of the card I sent you in college—I'm forever—so you'll never completely be rid of your problems.

Hope this rambling letter from my heart to yours makes sense. You could always use the paper to make one of those paper chains like Sandra Bullock did in "28 Days."

Take good care of yourself. With lots of love and hugs,

Mom

Oh, that's good. Believe me, if I knew how to make those paper chains, I would. One thing mom can do is ramble.

I neatly fold up the sheets and place the letter back into the envelope. Then I just sit and stare out the window on the other side of the room. I read it. I understood everything she wrote, but I don't really feel anything.

Silence. *I love the silence. Shit, there it is.* Yeah, I'm not totally numb. I'm pissed. *Okay there, I admit it! I'm mad. I'm mad at my mom and mad at what she just wrote me. And I'm mad I'm mad. I shouldn't be mad.* She just wrote me a nice, albeit long, letter about how much she loves me. I should be happy about that. I know some people never get a letter like this from their parents. But no, I'm not happy, not me. I'm mad.

And I know I need to respond to her letter, and that scares the shit out of me. I don't want to have to be honest. I'm scared of hurting her, but I know if I'm not, I can never have the relationship I want with her and I will never be able to let go of this anger.

I open the nightstand drawer and pull out my journal. I don't know what is going to come out, but I know I need to just write. I open to a fresh page.

Friday, July 5, 2002

Mom's letter was nice and thought-provoking. It took me a day to build up the courage to read it. I think one thing that jumps out is her apologizing for taking so long with the gay issue. I'm angry with her for not being honest with me and for saying everything was okay when it wasn't. I knew she was struggling, but she would wear her happy mask. That hurts. Who the hell does she think she was kidding? And yes, I am hurt and mad that it took her so long. I needed both of my parents at that time in my life, and they weren't there. Of course, the flip side is, I didn't know I needed them then. But I did, and I guess I wish they had known it and had reached out. Dad, on the other hand, just shut down—business as usual—nothing wrong. If I can't change it, then I won't talk about it. That pisses me off as well. He's my dad, the adult in the situation. Is it too much to ask him to step up to the emotional plate and reach out?

The other point in the letter that struck a nerve was when she said something about parenting being so hard and hoping you say and do the right thing but knowing afterwards you could have done it better or not at all, and praying grace and love will cover the mistakes. This enrages me because it showed how she obsesses! My deal is, just be my parents, do what you think is best, learn from those decisions, and move on! Talk about it and be open, but don't obsess and be like, well, I should have or would have. It goes back to her being indecisive and second guessing so much. I guess I just feel like I needed a parent who was strong and just did it and knew that it was done out of love and that, in and of itself, that made it okay. Part of this is so raw because mom kept asking me if I felt I was making the right decision and if I felt I was where I needed to be—i.e. at Rogers. It made me so mad because I feel I'm the sick one. If anything, I need you to be strong and let me know that yes, I am doing the right thing, and not to use me as a sounding board to work out your own obsessions and insecurities.

So my main feelings with my folks that I have been stuffing have been hurt, anger, and confusion. The confusion comes in when they give lip service to wanting an open, honest, and direct relationship with me, but them not practicing that. I figure I might use the next few pages as a rough draft letter to them. So here goes:

Dear Mom and Dad,

Well, it's been two weeks now, and all I have to say is this is one incredible journey. As hard as all this is, I do know deep down what an incredible blessing and gift I have been given to be here at Rogers and work on myself in such a caring and supportive environment. Every day I get more insight into myself and this disorder that I have too readily taken on as my own. Every weekday we have group therapy, just us guys, with our counselor, Sue.

Shit! I slam my journal shut and throw it on the nightstand. I can't do this right now. I don't want to do this. It's too much. I'm tired. I stretch out fully on the bed, throw the covers over me, and bury my head into my pillow. I just need to escape for a while. I'll think about the fucking letter tomorrow.

27

Tuesday, July 9, 2002

To me, there is nothing better than that spiritual connection with a person or group of people. It's so pure. It's what I imagine perfect love or heaven to be like. I think souls can resonate and connect with each other. I truly feel it and honestly, when it happens, I wish I could freeze time and keep experiencing it. For me, it's my heroin, my drug. It's a spiritual orgasm. I think part of the depression and mask-wearing comes in because it does have to end. I hate that fall-out and coming out of it. I hate having to face reality again and not knowing with whom or where I'll make that connection again. Like a drug addict, I want to live in that "high" all the time! It's difficult when you know how wonderful it can be, but this world is so dense and emotionally numb that it makes it hard for those connections to occur.

This brings up the point of wanting to freeze time and not wanting to grow up. When I look back, I get sad because my whole life, I couldn't wait to grow up, get older, and be with more mature people. I never felt totally comfortable with kids my own age until college. I knew there must be something better. I was so numb for so long and just in survival mode. So now, looking back, I mourn that young man. I think I'm angry because I feel my childhood was taken away by fear. Fear that I had to conform and just survive. Fear of not being loved and of people finding out my secret. I couldn't wait to get on my own, but now I feel like I wished it all away. I didn't stop to enjoy being young, dumb, and having no responsibilities. I did love college and found my place and started to come into my own. But after college, I didn't like this adult game I was expected to play. No one prepared me for it being so hard, and what were the rules? How do I play, and is it supposed to hurt this much?

It also made it harder to see my family changing and growing older. Amy was having kids and lived in the same town as Mom and Dad for a while. That made me feel so left out because I was the only one not there. Jessica was driving, dating, and starting to look at colleges. And mom and dad were just aging. It really scared me to think, how will things be now? What are our roles? I think I'm really a sappy family guy. I love my family and love those times we are all together. That people connection again. Part of me wants that 1950's idea of a family where we all live on the same block for the rest of our lives and go to each other's homes for Sunday dinner. It saddens me because I know that can't happen, because life is forever changing. Also, part of me knows I'd get restless and everyone would drive me nuts sometimes.

Even though I don't want to admit it, I guess I don't do well with change. I have these ideas of how my family should be and how life should be. Since it's all just so unattainable, I shut down. Because, well, if life can't be like that, then it's hopeless. What's the point?

So somehow I have to come to terms with knowing life can be full of connections with people and I can define what role

I want to play in life and with my family. That feeling from childhood of complete security with no real responsibilities can be a drug as well, something that we don't want to totally let go of.

Well enough rambling for now. Until next time:

"Forever young, I want to be forever young . . ."

28

Wednesday, July 10, 2002

Group today was wild. After about ten minutes of silence, I thought I would throw out the body image subject. It seemed benign enough to me. Well, it turned me on my ear! It really hit me. The more and more the other guys talked, the more I was feeling. I can look at myself and say, yeah, I'm thin and don't look that healthy, but I feel totally different. I feel fat and I don't like what I see. Looking back, my whole life I have spent in front of mirrors obsessing about my looks and that "image" staring back at me. I know throughout the years, people probably thought I was vain or stuck up, but the opposite is true. Truth be told, I can now say I was and still am desperately searching for something to like about myself.

Do you know what it's like to stare at your image and instantly see what's wrong and what needs to change? I know now that, because of my self-hatred, confusion, and fear, I was projecting all of that outwardly toward my body. In my mind, I needed to find that lovable quality on the outside. Because I could control my body, in a tragic attempt, I was trying to mold it to what I felt would make me lovable. The funny thing is it's an unfillable void. It doesn't matter how fat, thin, or ripped I became, nothing filled that void. That little boy was still staring back at me in the mirror and he was always the same: scared, hurt, and just plain confused.

The other scary aspect is that food doesn't fill the void, either. As I ate more, the void was still there. So I swung to the other extreme—starving. That didn't fill the void, but you know what it did—it numbed me so well and preoccupied my mind and body so much that I didn't have room to feel the void or feel anything else, for that matter.

So I ask myself, when does the pain stop? I don't know and that scares the shit out of me. I'm so consumed with the need to be thin and stay that way.

I can look back now and see how I have dealt with this my whole life. There were clear red flags, and no one ever said anything about them. I have some anger about that. I never liked wearing shorts. Hello, that's weird, especially when you're in Orlando in 95+ degree heat and wearing jeans! I've always struggled and felt totally awkward swimming with my shirt off, even though I've never been overweight. And of course, I could spend hours in front of the mirror checking myself and having to put every freakin' hair in place. I would yell at my reflection and hit my head, saying I hate myself and wished everyone was bald.

Do you know what it's like to go through life always worrying about how you look and feeling the need to rush to a mirror to "fix" yourself? Then giving the mirror the power to ruin your day based solely on what it decides to project back at you? I've never known anything else. No one ever told me it wasn't healthy or that there was a happier way to live. I just thought I was a freak for it. It's a lonely way to live, and that feeds the isolation.

It's funny we all know people who are just magnets because of their loving, energetic personalities. They just attract others to them. It's not based on their looks. It's based on the fact that they truly love themselves and are accepting of who they are. They glow, and people pick up on that and want to be around that. So intellectually, I know that is the best place to be. The hard part is emotionally making that leap.

I'm sitting here in my room and just looked out the window to see one of the residents out on the back porch hugging her kids good-bye. It was surreal to watch. Here I am inside, catching a glimpse of this very emotional, private moment in the noon-day sun. She hugs her son, then her daughter, and then talks to them some. Then hugs her daughter again, and it turns into a long embrace where she just keeps stroking her daughter's hair. Then the son comes back over and, after a moment, they all are hugging. I can only imagine the heart-ache that family is going through. What it must be like for a mother to say good-bye to her kids until who knows when. And for the kids to see their mom go back to a place to live that's not home. If this disease wasn't disgusting in my eyes before, it is now. It just goes to show that we are not alone. Even if we think we are self-reliant and going through stuff all by ourselves it does affect other people.

29

Wednesday, July 17, 2002

Well, today is five months sober.

I'm realizing more and more, every day, how proper acting and looking I have to be. It's so ingrained. Like I can't start a new book until I finish the one I'm reading. I can only sleep in a bed; I dare not fall asleep on the sofa or in a chair. I have to finish every movie I start, and I can't fall asleep during it. I have to finish every journal entry in one sitting—I can't work on it throughout the day. I have to look nice with perfect hair all the time and can't totally cut loose and act like a kid. When I start something, I have to finish it, no questions asked. I'm not good at giving myself permission to let go and just walk away, even if I know walking away would be the healthy choice (i.e. my job). My job has been killing me for three years, but because of my beliefs and outside pressure, I have stayed. There is probably some anger at mom and dad because they put so much emphasis on the money and me needing another job before I could leave this one (even though I was drinking myself to death).

It's amazing to think of the rules and confines we attach to ourselves. We don't even realize how much more fulfilling and freeing life would be if we just allowed ourselves to be ourselves—no rules applied!

I guess, overall, I'm still in the anger stage of mourning my ED. So I guess the next step is to look forward to the bargaining stage. That should be interesting!

30

Friday, July 19, 2002

Sue told me this morning in group that I seemed genuinely happy and upbeat. I got to thinking that I am. This is what doing hard work and gaining hope feels like. It is a different feeling from that "happy" mask I wear a lot, trying to convince myself and the world that I am happy. It just dawned on me that there is a difference. This genuine happiness feels a hell of a lot better and requires no effort to sustain.

I guess now I have recognized the difference. If I don't feel happy but I say that I am, then I need to step back and see what I am truly feeling. I swear, as I get more into therapy and learn more, there is more pressure to change and to be healthy. I also realize how much more work there is to be done. I'm just praying that I'll have the courage to keep doing the hard work and to continue it when I leave here.

I know I came in here thinking I could do three months here and leave healed. That's such faulty thinking. This place just stabilizes us and provides us with the tools to start our recovery. So I have to get it through my thick head that this is a journey, one where I need to be open and learn along the way. I guess it's slowly becoming more real to this black-and-white mind of mine that there is no beginning or end, just a journey in which change and love are my only two constant companions.

31

I can do this. It's no big deal, and it's about time I eat a truly compliant meal.

I peel off the top of the butter packet and stick in my knife. For the first time, I remove all the butter from the packet and spread it across my toast. Funny, it covers the entire piece of toast. Up until now, for every breakfast, I have only partially opened the packet and taken a small amount of butter. I've never completely used the entire packet of butter, which means I have never completely consumed all the fats I should be eating. I'm sure I haven't been fooling anyone. But it's time I start being more honest, even though I feel no need to announce this little moment of truth to anyone.

Calm down. It's not like it's that many more calories. I'm doing my best to be rational, but all the while, anxiety is gripping my gut. I know this isn't going to make or break me, but I'm nervous. It's stupid. I know and I'll get over it. I eat. I eat all the toast, the banana, the yogurt, and both packets of butter.

Breakfast is pretty quiet, and as soon as I'm done, I leave. I don't feel like hanging out and talking. Plus, I've got to psych myself up for group this morning. Sue wants me to read the letter I'm going to mail to Mom and Dad. I wrote the letter more than two weeks ago, and I still can't man up enough to mail it. So Sue, in her infinite wisdom, has suggested that I read it aloud in group. I'm guessing this gesture might provide the support I need to get off my ass and just mail the damned thing. I'm not convinced. But I know Sue won't let me flake out on this one. So I need just a few more minutes alone this morning to steel up my nerve.

Grabbing my journal, I head out of my room and down the hall. As I pass the bathroom, the thought arises that I need to check myself out in the mirror. I know this game all too well. I'm nervous, so my first inclination is to camp out in front of the mirror, obsessing. I just know, deep down, that I don't look good or I have something on my face or that my hair is every which way but Tuesday. My mind is yelling at me to go into the bathroom, just for a second. I don't. I don't know why, but for some reason, I keep walking.

As I plop down in my spot in the day room, I'm thankful that I'm alone. I was the first one out of breakfast, so hopefully I will have several minutes of solitude. I open my journal and turn to the entry where I wrote the letter. Hell, I still haven't even written it out on loose leaf paper yet. Scanning it, I get tense. I'm still not keen on reading journal entries to anyone. It's so private. But I guess I need to do this. As I close my journal, I decide I will just wing it. I don't have to rehearse it now. Off-the-cuff is better anyway.

I start fiddling with my metal watch, the one I got as a twenty-first birthday present. I unclasp it. It creates a small circle. It doesn't fully open up; the two straps stay connected with a metal link. My right hand starts to slide the watch up my left wrist. It passes my forearm, my elbow and keeps going. Before I know it the watch is resting at the base of my shoulder. It slid up my entire arm without any trouble. *That's weird. I guess I am pretty thin.* Or this just further highlights the pathetic fact that I don't have an ounce of muscle on me.

I quickly slide the watch down and off my wrist. Gazing at the watch, I'm surprised at the small size of the wrist opening. I know I have small wrists—so small, in fact, that my forefinger and thumb can easily wrap around each wrist and touch. My entire arm can fit through this small opening. That's cool on some level. For some reason, that makes me happy and scared at the same time. I know it won't be that way for long. I'm eating a lot more now; my meal plan has already been increased two times since I've been here.

I slide the watch back on my left wrist and scold myself. I don't need to be thinking about things like this. I need to be focused on getting well and being okay with gaining weight. If only it were that easy.

"Hey, Hoyt."

I glance up and am surprised to see Steve walking through the door.

"Oh hey, Steve," I mutter. I'm not sure what he is doing in here, since group is starting in a few minutes. I hope to God he's not planning on staying. Just then, he crosses the room and grabs a chair and sits down. *No, he can't be! Please, any day but today.*

I don't feel like coming out to Steve today. As hard as I try, I can't warm up to this guy. The voice, the huge muscles—I'm just not that comfortable around him. If there were a magazine for hetero guys, he would be their poster child, posing with his German shepherd and pet boa constrictor. I mean, come on, the guy has a pet boa constrictor for crying out loud! The only boa I'm familiar with is the fluffy kind used by drag queens. What the hell do we have in common?

"I'm gonna be in group with you guys today, if that's okay," he says—as if I have a say in the matter. I would love to tell him no.

"Uh, sure," I mumble. I look down, trying my best not to freak out. Then Sue walks in and breaks the tension I've created in the room. Kyle and J.R. follow a few moments later. After everyone has taken their usual positions, I start staring at the clock. *Only ninety minutes to go. Fun.*

We check-in, and then I'm on.

"Hoyt, you want to read your letter now?" Sue asks.

I knew this was coming, but my stomach lurches up to my throat as if I have just jumped out of a perfectly good airplane. I take a deep breath and do my best to hide my fear.

"Yeah, sure," I reply. "I got a letter from my mom about two weeks ago, and I wrote a reply. I haven't mailed it yet. Been kinda scared to, I guess. Sue thought it would be good if I read it. So here it is."

In newscaster mode, I look down and pretend I'm just reading a teleprompter.

> *Dear Mom and Dad,*
>
> *Well, it's been two weeks now, and all I have to say is this is one incredible journey. As hard as all this is, I do know deep down what an incredible blessing and gift I have been given to be here at Rogers and work on myself in such a caring and supportive environment. Every day, I get more insight into myself and this disorder that I have too readily taken on as my own.*
>
> *Every weekday, we have group therapy, just us guys, with our counselor Sue. Before I came here, I had all the misconceptions and fears about group therapy that I think most of us have, most likely gleaned from years of TV-watching. Thankfully, though, none of those myths and fears are true. To sit in a room with other guys who are able to talk about their struggles, thoughts, fears, and feelings is truly a remarkable experience that I would not trade for all the tea in China!*
>
> *Having an ED and being so deep within its clutches made me feel so isolated and lonely—like no one understood me or what was going on inside me, because how could they? I didn't even understand it. So group therapy with these guys has helped me to see that I'm not alone and that, no matter how different our backgrounds, amazingly enough, we are all struggling with a lot of the same fears. I'm amazed every session how much I progress by just hearing the struggles and thoughts of the other guys. I truly gain more insight into myself by sitting in those sessions.*
>
> *You might be wondering right now just what insight am I gaining. Well, the biggie has been that I stuff*

everything—from feelings, fears, hurts, and emotions to my sexuality—being gay, my true self. You name it and I stuff it. I've been doing it for years, and it's so ingrained that I don't even realize I'm doing it. I have to be the ultimate people-pleaser and optimist, and so I wear masks for the outside world that everything is fine. I run from my true feelings. I make myself go numb because I'm scared. Scared of what? Well, that's what I'm still exploring. But unfortunately, this coping mechanism leads me down a path of self-destruction directed toward my body.

It's been great to be surrounded by other guys who are the same way. We all wear masks, stuff our feelings, and say everything is fine. So my journey here will include getting in touch with those feelings and allowing myself to feel them and know it's okay to feel them and be honest with myself.

Now I know you both are probably thinking, what caused this, and is there something I did wrong? I want you to hear this and hear it well, because it's true: there is nothing that either of you did (nothing anyone did, for that matter) that caused this! I read somewhere that it's not a life event that causes an ED but the person's relationship with and view of life. If I was to be honest, my life view is probably not too good. Sure, I've been able to cope most of my life by wearing masks, but it finally caught up with me.

Now this doesn't mean that I don't have any feelings toward you guys. Of course I do, but I have stuffed them for so long that it's going to take some time to get them out. I do know that there is probably a lot of hurt and anger—about what, who knows? But the important thing is, I have to start allowing myself to feel these feelings, because it was killing me slowly to keep everything inside. My hope is that, in the end, we all will have a healthier and open relationship.

How do we get there? Well, it probably means that Mom, you might have to come to terms with the way you obsess about issues and decisions and use us as a sounding board to try to dissect every issue. And it means me being honest that it hurts me and angers me. And Dad, it probably means you taking small steps to allow yourself to feel more and be more open and not stuff everything, and me being honest that, in the past, that was hurtful and angered me.

I'm saying all of this not asking for an apology or any explanation, but just so I can say it and get it out of me. It's so healing just to let it out and allow myself to feel. I know you both have been the best parents that you knew how to be and have done everything out of unconditional love for me. So I don't blame either of you for anything. But at the same time, it doesn't negate my feelings. I hope to gain the tools to work through my feelings in a healthy way.

I hope this has made some sense and was not too painful to read. I find more and more, every day, just how freeing, important, and difficult honesty can be. I first have to learn how to be honest with myself before I can be honest with others.

Thank you both so much for all of your support, love, encouragement, and overall strength throughout my life— but especially now. In return, I encourage you both to write during this time. Write whatever comes to mind, thoughts, feelings, actions, etc. You'll be surprised just what might come out and the insights you'll gain. Writing in my journal has been more of a blessing than I could have ever believed possible.

Okay, I'm really going to end this now. I look forward to more letters and talks, and hopefully I'll be seeing ya'll soon.

Thank you again.

Love always,

Jeff

Damn, I'm glad that's over with. I just keep staring at the page. I don't want to look up. *That's weird.* I actually wasn't totally numb reading that. In fact, it felt somewhat good reading it. It's funny. I was afraid it was too harsh, but now reading it aloud, it seems downright lightweight. *Hell, I could have been more real! But it's a good start.*

"Thanks, Hoyt. That was great," Sue assures me. Her voice snaps me out of my head.

"Yeah, thanks for reading that," J.R. adds.

"Sure," I mumble, looking at J.R.

"Yeah, Hoyt, that was cool. That takes a lot of courage to do that," Kyle says with sincerity.

"Wow, Hoyt, that's awesome."

Up until this point, I haven't been able to bring myself to look at Steve. He now knows that I'm gay. And for some reason, I feel awkward. I hate this feeling. It's how I always feel around overly masculine straight guys. It's like I'm allowing myself to feel like I'm less than I am, just because I like guys. It's so messed up.

"You know, Hoyt, that was really well written. I think you should mail it. And you know, there is nothing wrong with you just because you're gay," Steve informs me with a kindness that is startlingly.

"Yeah. Thanks, Steve," I reply. When I look up at him and meet his gaze, I see that it's intense and heartfelt.

Wow, what the hell? That felt really good, what he just said. Here is this straight, jock stereotype sitting in front of me, validating me. A straight guy! Suddenly, it dawns on me. Very funny. I get it, God. I needed this, and even though I've judged and kept my distance from Steve, he's a pretty cool guy.

"So?" Sue leans forward in her chair, looking at me.

"So what?" I ask, smiling back at her.

"When are you going to mail it?"

"Good question. I need to write it out, and I think I may add some more stuff. This has actually helped me feel more comfortable with what I've said," I explain.

"Okay, sounds good. I think it will go over just fine. Your parents love you very much," Sue says.

"Yeah, I know," I reply. But I still can't shake the fear that this letter may not go over so well.

The rest of the group flies by, and I find that I grudgingly enjoy having Steve present.

32

"I, uh, finished this interesting book the other day, and there was this quote in here that I think is really powerful," I say as I open the book, *Assuming the Position* by Rick Whitaker. "It's a book written by this guy who used to be a hustler. You mind if I read this?"

"No of course not," Sue says. "Go ahead."

Opening to page 166, I read the quote: "I was addicted to the experience of being taken away from myself."

"I don't know, for some reason that really struck me," I say. It's like a light bulb went off. That's what I've been doing with my ED."

"Wow, that's a great quote. I'm going to have to write that down," Sue says as she picks up her pen. "Now what was that again?"

"I was addicted to the experience of being taken away from myself," I repeat. "He talks about how the addiction brings you back to a familiar condition. You know how you're going to feel and what to expect, and that feels safe. I can totally relate. I hated what I was doing to myself, but I kept doing it."

"That's a really powerful quote and a great insight, Hoyt," Sue says.

"Thanks. And it's scary, but after reading this, I could see how I was doing this in other areas of my life as well."

"How so?" Sue asks.

"Well, you know, I stopped drinking in February. I know I used booze to check out. It numbed me and helped me to interact with people more easily—or so I thought. And even after countless hangovers and making a fool of myself, I would keep drinking. And now I see why. It was because I knew what to expect."

"I can see that. Anything else?"

"Uh, yeah. I, um ..." I stammer as anxiety prevents me from speaking coherently. Part of me is yelling at myself to shut up, but the other part is saying, out with it. I need to open up. Sue isn't going to judge me. This is my private session with her, so if I'm going to share this, now is the time. Shifting my weight to my right, I look down.

"Well, I think I've used sex the same way," I say, quietly waiting for some kind of reaction. Nothing. She doesn't say anything. Since I don't get the reaction I was expecting, I decide to just go for it.

"I can see that it was just another mechanism I used to try to escape from myself. It numbed me. The messed up thing is it's easier for me to sleep with a guy I don't know well than with a guy I care about it. And I think it comes down to being vulnerable. Sex with a guy I don't care about, and who doesn't care about me, is easy. I know I won't get hurt, because I'm not opening up. But making love with a guy I really care about is terrifying. Doing that means I'm being more real and there's a chance I could get hurt. A stranger can't hurt me but a boyfriend can." I abruptly stop and lean back into the sofa. I can't believe what I'm saying. I've never talked about this with anyone. I don't talk about my sex life, not with my friends, not with therapists, not anyone. It's just too fucking personal and I ... I feel vulnerable right now. But I have opened this door, and now I can't seem to stop.

"It's been hard to see this until now, but my ED helped me to avoid all of this. I know I've felt a lot of shame concerning sex and being gay, and it was overwhelming. So the sicker I got with my ED, the less I felt, and obviously, the less sexual I was. I had no libido. And so, as my ED took over, my life became dull. It just flat-lined. Everything was this dreary grey, and that felt safe. That was nice. It felt like a break from all these overwhelming experiences that I had to deal with."

Damn, I can't shut-up about this. As I push my back harder into the sofa, my mind orders me to shut up before I say anything else absurd. *Yeah, like the fact that my libido just came roaring back, unannounced, the other night.* I clench my jaw at the vulgar sound of the phrase in my head: wet dream. *Ugh, I've never liked that term.* Dropping that thought, I just sit there, looking down at the floor.

"Thank you, Hoyt, for sharing that. I know that wasn't easy. Any thoughts on where your relationship with sex comes from?" Sue asks innocently.

Shit, that's a good question. "Wow, that's tough. I think, well, um, I think probably how I grew up had something to do with it. I mean, in our family, we didn't talk about any of that. It just wasn't discussed. So for me, it was this taboo, dirty, subject that you weren't supposed to talk about. So I got no education on anything other than what they told us in school, which was jack shit. And I grew up in a very conservative, evangelical Christian church. It was drilled into us that we had to marry a Christian and we had to be a virgin until we got married. Then, add on my little secret about being gay and all the fear and shame that I carried around regarding that—it's no wonder I have a screwed-up relationship with sex. Luckily, I'm healthy and have never gotten anything," I finish, laughing slightly.

My body feels like a live wire. Energy is pulsing through every vein. This isn't exactly the type of conversation I was expecting to have today, but I know it's good for me. I need this.

"And yeah, there's, uh … yeah, probably another thing as well," I blurt out. *Shit! Where the hell did that come from? No, no, I'm not going there. If I'm lucky Sue didn't catch that last little part.*

"What's that?" she asks.

Great! Now I have to tell her. "Well, when I was eighteen, there was this time. I mean, well I, uh … met this guy. It was December and I answered this personal ad in this alternative paper. I can't remember all the details, but I ended up going over to his house. I think he was about eight or nine years older than me. We talked for a very long time and then one thing lead to another and we ended up in his bedroom. It was my first time and I was a willing participant up to a certain point," I explain, glancing up at Sue. Her eyes are locked onto me. She's intently listening to what's about to come next, but I'm not sure I want to tell her. My body is stiff as a board.

"Well, after a few minutes, I said no. I just, it just … well, I said no and asked him to stop. He said he wanted to finish. He leaned over me, pinned my arms down, and did his thing. I was scared, and I left as soon as I could."

I exhale, feeling nothing. I don't feel anything. I just told Sue one of my darkest secrets, and it's like I just told her what I ate for breakfast. There's a long pause. She's just looking at me with sympathy written all across her face.

"Hoyt, I'm so sorry that happened to you," Sue says.

"Thanks. It's fine. It's weird, though. It wasn't violent or anything. I mean, I really don't even consider it rape, since I was into it up to a certain point. And maybe since I didn't say stop really forcefully. I don't know," I trail off, trying to make sense of what I'm saying. I can't. I've never been able to make sense of this event.

"Oh, and get this. This guy was a plumber, and he owned his own company. When I got home that night, I noticed his company's magnet on the fridge. Needless to say, I threw it in the trash," I say, smirking at the sick irony. I'm still grateful that guy never showed up at my parents' house for any plumbing problem.

"Are you mad?"

"Huh?"

"Are you mad?" Sue asks again.

"I don't know. I mean, well, no. I'm not really anything. I don't feel anything about what happened. I know it happened, but I don't really know how to make sense of it. I mean, maybe I've used booze, sex, my ED, and Lord knows what else, as a way to control my body and any situation I find myself in. I don't know. But I do know that what happened definitely fed into the shame I was already feeling about myself," I explain.

I don't really want to talk about this anymore, yet I surprise myself by talking more than I ever have about this subject. Sue listens patiently. She's very open and understanding. But nothing gets solved. I don't get cured, although I'm struck by how much lighter I feel. Strangely enough, I'm starting to realize how just talking about things diffuses the power they have over your life. Even though we didn't solve anything, I feel better for the rest of the day. And it feels nice that someone knows the darker side of my personality and doesn't hate me or think I'm a horrible person. Maybe what I've done and what I've been through isn't so shameful.

33

"Oh, Hoyt, you're family's upstairs," Rose says, casually leaning into the day room. *Shit! They're here already? Damn, I was expecting them later.*

"Oh, cool. Thanks," I reply, as calmly as possible. Of course, they show up right after lunch when I'm not feeling the best. *Deep breaths. Deep breaths.* It's been five weeks since I've seen them. My body is tense as I force myself up off the sofa and out of the room. I go up the stairs to the front lobby.

As I round the corner of the stairwell, I spot Amy. She is leaning forward and reading a plaque on the wall next to the sofa. My dad is standing awkwardly close to the front door, almost as if he's ready in case he needs to make a quick exit.

"Hey." I smile as Amy turns around.

"Hey you!" she exclaims with a slight Southern accent, clearly masking the fact that she was born in Boston. She hugs me. It feels nice, but then I quickly begin to feel uncomfortable. The physical contact causes me to notice the physicality of my body. This sense of myself is still somewhat new.

"You look great," she says as I step back from our hug.

"Thanks, I feel good," I honestly add. "Hey, Dad."

"Hey, Jeff. How's it going?"

"Good. Thanks for coming." We just stand there making small talk. I take comfort in the fact that our dynamic hasn't changed.

"So how were your flights?" I ask.

"Oh, fine. I had to change in Chicago," Amy says.

"Mine was good. I got a direct out of Philly," my dad states.

"Cool. Well, thanks for coming."

"No problem. I wouldn't miss it. But the boys were pretty upset with me when they found out I was coming to see you," Amy says, smiling.

"Oh, how are they doing?" I have a sinking feeling in my gut, wishing I could see my nephews.

"Oh, they're fine. Wild as ever. They were all doing wrestling moves on our bed the other day and Brooks ended up cracking Craig's front tooth."

"Oh, Lord, that's wild. I can't believe Craig does those moves with them. They'd kill me if they did that stuff with me."

"Yeah, they would, because you're so skinny," Amy comments.

I smile at the fact that, even though I'm in this place, my older sister can still dish out a healthy dose of reality. I can always trust Amy to tell me the truth.

"So, ya'll want to see the unit?" I ask.

"Sure," they answer in unison.

"Cool, follow me. It's just down these stairs." We walk down the stairs, bypassing the elevator.

I show them the day room and introduce them to Kyle and J.R. They then get to see my room and the large bathroom I use—which impresses Amy. Then we walk around outside. It's the first time I walk all the way down the driveway to the main entrance sign. Amy wants a picture, so we pose on either side of the sign announcing Rogers Memorial Hospital. I can't help but laugh at the strangeness of this act. I can understand wanting to commemorate the hospital of one's birth, but to commemorate the hospital of one's rehab seems a bit odd. But Amy loves pictures, and she's the oldest, so I do what I'm told.

After showing them around and pointing out the main hospital, which houses the vending machines that I raided on my first week here, we all pile into their rented Honda and exit the grounds.

"So, where do you want to go?" Amy asks.

"Oh, gosh. I'm not sure. We've got some time to kill before the movie. So why don't we do some shopping?"

"Awesome. You know I'm always up for that," Amy says cheerily.

"Where to, then?" my dad asks.

"There's a shopping area with a Target close by. Go to the end of drive and turn left," I say. After several minutes, I have successfully directed us to the shopping center.

"There's a parking spot, Dad," I point out. My dad pulls in and I laugh.

"What's so funny?" he asks.

"Ya'll remember that movie with Michael Keaton called *The Dream Team*? The one where they are in a mental institution and all travel around in a white van?" I ask.

"Oh, yeah," Amy replies.

"Well, it's like that at Rogers. When we go out, we travel in this white van and park in a handicap parking space—because you know anorexics can't walk a parking lot," I add sarcastically.

"That's wild," Amy says.

"So this is my first outing that I haven't parked in a handicapped space."

We make our way into Target and just start walking around the store. I'm not totally feeling the desire to shop for clothes, but Amy encourages me to at least pick out a few things to try on, since dad is buying. It's weird being the center of attention. Both Amy and my dad keep asking me what I want. If I was up to it, I think I could milk this entire situation. After some more prodding, I pick out a hoodie and a long-sleeve t-shirt. I skip the pants and shorts, because they still make me too nervous to try on. Plus, I know I will gain more weight, so anything I buy now won't fit much longer.

Once inside the dressing room, I freeze. I'm faced, for the first time in weeks, with a full- length mirror staring back at me. I take a couple steps closer and then stop and stare. *Huh, there I am. All of me.* Turning to my right, I gaze at my profile. *Yeah, I still look pretty thin.* My pulse increases and I breathe more heavily at the invasive thought that I might not look this thin much longer. *Okay, I know I can do this without obsessing.* I'll just try on the hoodie first. That way, I don't have to take off any other pieces of clothing. Plus, Lord knows I need another hoodie. The grey one I've been wearing nonstop since I got here needs a break.

With the new hoodie on, I turn to face the mirror. I smile half-heartedly. It fits and feels soft. *Yeah, this works.* I exhale. *That wasn't so hard.* I slip out of the hoodie and hang it on a hook to my left.

Next up is the long-sleeve t-shirt. I was surprised to find one of these, given that it's the middle of summer and hot as hell outside. I don't wear regular, short-sleeve t-shirts anymore since I'm cold all the time. I face the mirror and just stand there looking at my torso, which is covered in the grey, long-sleeve t-shirt that I'm wearing. Dread is now fully encompassing my body and mind. I'm terrified about what I'm going to see, very clearly for the first time, when I take off this shirt. My mind is off and racing.

I can't help but think about my last conversation with my nutritionist.

"So, how are you feeling about me increasing your meal plan?" Elizabeth asked. There was softness in her voice.

Totally pissed, but not wanting to upset her, I lied. "It's cool."

"You're doing really well. Like I said before, guys plateau pretty quickly. It just takes more for you to gain weight."

"Yeah, okay," I mumbled.

"You have any questions or concerns?" she asked.

"Actually, yeah. What did I weigh when I came here?" I blurted it out, surprising myself. I wanted to know, but I didn't. I shifted my weight in my chair in dreaded anticipation. I was so scared that she would be honest, and just as scared that she wouldn't tell me.

HOYT J. PHILLIPS, III

"Well, are you sure you want to know?"

"Yeah, please."

"Okay, you were at 126 pounds."

The number just fell out of her mouth and landed on the floor like dead weight. A heavy, dead weight. *One hundred twenty-six pounds! You've got to be shitting me. I was at 120 like two weeks before I got here.* I felt like a total failure.

Elizabeth broke the silence. "I wouldn't worry about that. You were very sick when you got here. And you told me that, before you got here, you had been eating a fair amount for about a week."

"Yeah, I spent a week with my parents at the beach before my mom brought me here. I know I ate more regularly that week," I said, trying to console myself, trying not to feel like a total loser. It was screwed up, and I knew I shouldn't care what I weighed when I got there. But I did. I had thought it had been a lot lower than that.

I remembered looking in the little bathroom mirror, right after my talk with Elizabeth.

Shit. I knew it! I leaned forward over the sink and peered into the tiny mirror. By looking down, I could see the upper part of my naked torso. Now that I knew what I weighed when I came here, I had to see for myself what I looked like now. I was not happy with the results. I couldn't move. *I knew it, they're filling in! My ribs are almost not visible anymore. Great! Lucky me.*

Ouch! My head jerks, snapping me out of my sadistic trip down memory lane. Exhaling, I dive right in and, without much thought, pull my shirt up over my head. I toss it to my right and look up into the mirror. And start laughing. Laughter spills out of my mouth and into the air. I can't help it.

The first thing I noticed isn't my ribs, chest, or waist. It was my fucking hair! *Yeah, it doesn't look the best right now. But I just pulled a shirt over my head, so it's messed up. Oh God, it's nice to know some things don't change. Okay, focus. Yeah, my ribs are filling in more.* Overall, it's not as bad as I was expecting. My ribs aren't totally invisible yet. I can still see some of my lower ribs. *And if I … yeah, there they are.* If I inhale deeply, my entire rib cage exposes itself.

I don't want to give into this visual masturbation too much longer, so I reach down grab the t-shirt and put it on. After deciding it fits and feels good, I slip it off and quickly put on my own shirt. My pulse is still racing and I feel light-headed. *I don't want to be in here any longer.* This has been enough excitement for one day, and I don't feel the need to shop anymore.

After checking out, the three of us make our way to the movie theatre. We see *Austin Powers 3.* Amy and I thoroughly enjoy the spectacle and get most of the jokes. My dad, on the other hand, sits through most of the movie with a confused look on his face. Surprisingly, I am able to focus on the movie, even though I know what is waiting in store afterwards: my first meal in a restaurant, outside of Rogers. The thought is doing its best to freak me out.

After the movie, we go to the Water Street Brewery for dinner. It was recommended by Sue. We sit on the back patio overlooking a cute little pond where ducks are swimming around. I sit down and immediately start eyeing the menu.

"Wow, they have a lot. It looks great," Amy enthuses.

"Uh, yeah. I've heard this place it good," I reply. I'm trying to be casual, not looking up, but my stomach is tense and my mind is screaming at me not to choose anything bad. I have to eat something that is good for me. *Ugh, I'm hungry. Really hungry. Chicken sandwich. I can do that. That's not so bad.*

After what seems like an eternity, the waiter finally takes our orders. I have to pick a side with my sandwich, so I order the homemade chips. I try to ignore the guilt that overtakes me after ordering. I do my best to make eye contact with Amy and Dad and engage in conversation.

"So, how's school going?" I ask Amy.

"Oh, it's good. You know, you have great veins. I would love to practice drawing blood on you," she says, laughing.

"Uh, yeah, don't think that's going to happen. That's why you have Craig," I say. I laugh along, but I place my arms under the table and out of her view.

"So, when do you graduate?" I ask. I know she has told me before, but I can't remember.

"My LPN ceremony will be in December, but I'm going to keep going to get my RN."

"Cool. So, Dad, how's the shore been?" I ask, turning to my father. He's been pretty quiet.

"Good. The weather has been really hot and humid. Jessica's been working a lot on the boardwalk at night," he says.

"Have you and mom gone into New York lately?" Amy asks.

"No, you know I don't like to do that. Even though your mom has been bugging me about it."

After more small talk, our food arrives. A large plate with a chicken sandwich and homemade chips is set in front of me. I lower my head, take a deep breath, and just eat, trying not to think about what I am doing. It tastes good, but I don't stop too often or for too long to really notice. I just want to get through this experience with as little damage as possible.

Then it's over. Looking at my mostly empty plate, I sigh. I feel neither happy nor overly upset. I ate. I ate some stuff that I consider bad, but it didn't kill me, and I'm still thin.

"Oh, could we see a dessert menu?" Amy asks as the waiter is leaning over, clearing the table. My heart skips a beat. *Dessert? Damn, I wasn't prepared for that. I wasn't even thinking about the possibility of dessert. Thanks Amy!*

"Oh, sure," the waiter replies.

"We can get something," she says smiling at me. I know what she is doing, and I don't like it. She wants to push me to eat more. I sit there, frozen, and I start to feel pissed off now. Not only did I just eat a lot—for me—but now I'm being faced with the temptation of dessert. And I just know that I'm going to fail and eat more.

"You know you look so much better. People don't stare at you anymore," Amy blurts out. *Great, another sign that I'm changing.* I'm not so sure it's a change for the better.

"Okay," is all I can muster.

"Here you go," the waiter announces as he hands each of us a menu. My eyes go into overdrive again as I scan the options. My pulse is racing and my mind is screaming at me not to give in. *Cheesecake! Damn it, I can't resist cheesecake. I'm gay, and I love the Golden Girls. It's a given that I'm getting the cheesecake.* After a couple of minutes, the waiter takes our order. Amy and I get dessert and my dad gets a glass of wine.

"Excuse me, I'm going to run to the bathroom," Amy informs us. She leaves, and it's now just Dad and me. Alone in silence. This is our usual routine when it's just the two of us. It drives my mom crazy. She can't understand how two people can just sit in silence. I love it.

"So, how are you doing?" my dad asks, catching me off guard.

"I'm good. Doing much better," I reply.

"How do you like Rogers? You think it's helping?" He seems apprehensive, almost as if he needs reassurance.

"Uh, yeah, I do. It's a good place. I like everyone and I'm learning a lot." He seems to like this answer.

"You think you've had this all your life?" he asks.

Now I'm starting to feel uncomfortable at the serious tone this conversation has taken. I pause trying to collect my thoughts. "I think it's always been there, and 9/11 just magnified it. If 9/11 hadn't happened, I think I might still be in New York just doing my thing and being thin, and maybe where I am now would have taken ten more years to manifest," I explain nervously.

This is probably the most personal conversation my father and I have had in I don't know how long. My mind doesn't quite know what to make of it. After a few additional questions, I steer the conversation to more benign topics. I don't feel like having a therapy session at a restaurant. Amy comes back and dessert arrives. I eat the entire piece of cheesecake. The entire piece!

We sit around and talk some more after eating. I go in and out of beating myself up internally. Finally, we return to Rogers. We walk around some more and then say good-bye. It was a nice visit, but I was ready for it to be over. It was a lot of stimulation and challenges for one day. And deep down, I just know I failed. I'm afraid of what that means for my chances for when I get out of this place.

The next day, I need to write.

> *Sunday, July 28, 2002*
>   *Yesterday it was great seeing both Dad and Amy. It felt good. I'm just really struggling now because of that cheesecake. I skipped the nightly snack and the one this morning. The power of my ED never ceases to amaze me. I had a dream last night about throwing my food away and not eating breakfast. All the while, in my head—in the dream—I was thinking, you ate that cheesecake. You can't eat for a while now!*
>   *I'm beating myself up so hard over this. Why? What does the cheesecake represent? I think I'm scared that I have no control. It was surreal with Amy and Dad visiting me like that, without any other family. It was also odd with them driving me around and that being my first outing without Rogers staff. I think my mind was looking for something to obsess about so it didn't have to feel those feelings. It was weird and uncomfortable, but at the same time, it was safe. I knew I could come back here and get back on track, and I liked that. That scares me, because I know I won't always have this place. I don't want to get too attached or institutionalized (like that old man from "Shawshank Redemption"). I'm afraid I won't be able to live normally in the real world.*
>   *Also making things somewhat worse is the fact that Dad was so nice. I'm more scared now to mail that letter. How can I say those things after having such a nice visit? I know I'm looking for an excuse, and I just need to do it. I know I can*

never hope to have a good relationship with my parents if I'm not honest.

Things are getting harder. I'm having to start letting go, and my ED doesn't like that. It wants control! I have to keep reminding myself that I am worthy of recovery.

34

I need to do this. I open my notebook and turn to a clean page. Glancing up, I watch as a small bird flies from one tree to another. I love sitting outside and just zoning out. But today, I need to get this assignment done. Sue gave it to me several days ago, and I've been putting if off. It's Sunday, and there's nothing else to do right now, so I'm going to just bang this out.

I have to write a letter to my younger self and then write a letter from my younger self to my adult self. Younger self. That sounds easier. I'll start with that one first.

> *Dear Jeff,*
>
> *"I'm starting with the boy in the mirror. I'm asking him to make a change." These altered lyrics from the Michael Jackson song take on a new meaning for me as I gain more insight into myself. It's funny as I look back. I've been through a hell of a lot. But you know the one constant that has always been there is you. No matter where I went or how bad or good I was feeling, I knew I could always find a mirror and there you'd be, staring back at me.*
>
> *Some of my earliest memories of our time together were when I realized I could urinate my name on the bathroom mirror in Texas. I was so excited that I could actually point*

and shoot wherever I wanted it to go. Then, of course, as I got older, we got into clothes and hair having to look and feel just right. You were always there to critique. Then I got into middle school and from then on, it wasn't just hair and clothes but my body and what it looked like clothed and un-clothed. Boy, did we ever spend some hours poring over what needed to be improved.

I realize, Jeff, as I was growing up and changing, you never changed because I never asked you to. You always looked the same and provided the same insight, which became more critical and even more important to me as time went on.

So I'm sitting here wondering what it is I see in you. The first thing that comes to mind is insecurity/inadequacy. You are the embodiment of all the years of feeling like the odd man out. You are great at projecting from the mirror everything that I should be insecure about and everything that makes me unlovable. You are the perpetual little boy who is desperately seeking outside approval and affection. The only way you know how to get that is through appearance. You don't know any other way. You are seeking others, but in reality, you want to be the one who is sought after and taken care of.

You are hurt and confused. It feels like you are alone and have to learn to fend for yourself. So you learned early on how much appearance could get you and how far it could take you. You remember those times being young with the platinum blond curls and blue eyes and strangers saying how cute and angelic you were. You remember the times teachers gave you higher grades just because they liked you, even though you knew you really didn't deserve them. You remember the times as a young teen getting so much attention when you dropped just a few pounds. Then, of course, there was losing weight after college and getting so much attention for it. People, even family, said how good you looked, how good clothes looked on you and how it must feel so good to be thin. These events naturally reinforced your importance and made you all the more determined to keep me in line. Unfortunately, it has become more and more self-destructive. Now I can't keep looking at you and function.

I have never truly looked at myself and allowed you to change. It felt safer for me to keep you right where you are. Life is ever so changing that I needed you to remain constant— something that I knew I could always count on. It made my emotional world simpler. I was being a perfectionist. You were giving me good, honest critiques—or so I thought. So in my mind, if I lived up to your standards, then everything would be right in the world, because then I would be lovable. But you know what? The inherent problem is, I can't seem to ever live up to your standards. So as time goes by, I spend more and more time looking at you and all I see is a bigger and bigger void.

I'm tired of fighting a war against the mirror every day. I can't keep carrying around all my childhood pain. I need to mourn my childhood—what it was and what it wasn't—and then let it go. If I don't, I'm afraid the only one who will be left standing will be you.

I love you and you'll always be a part of me, but you aren't my whole. You are a small puzzle piece that makes up the mosaic of my life. So be on notice: it's time to take your place in my past, because it's time I start looking at the "man in the mirror" instead of the boy.

Love,

Hoyt

Ouch. Dropping my pen, I rub my left palm. I don't know why I grip the pen so hard when I write. It's like I'm hanging onto the pen for dear life. My knees hurt. Looking down, I realize I'm shaking slightly. My knees are bumping against each other. I move my feet apart and take a deep breath. I need to calm down. Emotional crap always causes me to shake. I feel like a lightning rod sometimes, as if all the emotional energy is just coming right at me and my body is trying its best to diffuse it. *This was good. I needed to write that.*

I feel proud of myself at what I got out on the page. I lean my head back, close my eyes, and just enjoy the warmth of the sun.

Now Part Two, the letter from young me to adult me. Adult sounds so grown up. I'm not sure I'm one of those yet.

Dear Hoyt,

"The greatest thing you'll ever learn is just to love and be loved in return." This line from "Moulin Rouge" pretty much sums up life. So simple, yet so true. Every time I see you on the other side of that mirror, I see a shell of a person. Someone who is hurting, lost, and confused. A young man who's trying to hold it together and doesn't feel loved or worthy of love. You keep staring in that mirror in the hope of making sense out of life. You think something will magically click inside of you and fill that void. Life to you seems so overwhelming at times, and so you shut down. You have put so many rules, demands, and expectations on yourself. It's no wonder you feel confused and smothered by life.

Life really is simple, and you just need to let go and real-ize that. Break free from those rules and have fun. Be more childlike. The faith and wisdom of a child—that's the key to happiness. You remember us getting that tattoo six years ago? Pooh serves as a constant reminder of the childlike faith we all are born with but eventually lose. You're able to look at Brooks and Kellen and see how they love unconditionally and with-out inhibitions. You love hearing their laughter that radiates pure joy.

You just have to allow yourself to listen and do what you know to be true. I'm inside of you, not in a mirror—that's just a reflection made by man. The true you is inside and can't be reproduced in any earthly reflection. Your true self resonates,

*it's holy, and it was made by your Creator. People sense it, and
that's what they love about you—not what you think you see
in that mirror.*

*We are in this together. We know what really matters. We
know what path to take. You just have to allow yourself to
take it. And along the way, if you need a reminder, just roll
up your sleeve and look at your arm.*
Love always,
Jeff

I lay my pen down inside my notebook and gently rub my upper right
arm, where the tattoo of Winnie the Pooh holding a cross hides beneath the hoodie I'm wearing. I can't help but smile as I think back
to my freshman year in college when, on a total whim, I decided to
get inked. It's a pretty boring story. I can't even say I was drunk at the
time. It was a beautiful spring day and I had driven my friend, Mary
Rose, to the parlor so she could get a tattoo. When she chickened-out
at the last minute, I decided not to waste the trip there, so I got one.

The artist didn't have a drawing of Tigger, so I chose Pooh, and I
put a cross in his hand. It seemed appropriate at the time, given the
fact that I was still in my holy-roller phase and attending Campus
Crusade for Christ. Now, I'm not so sure I like it. But I know what
I just wrote is true. I need to let go. Life isn't that hard. I just have
to learn to roll with the punches more. I need to be more childlike.
Lord knows I could use more levity in my life.

"Hey, Hoyt. Whatcha doing?"

"Oh, hey Kyle. Nothing, just finishing up some writing."

Kyle has walked out on to the patio. "Cool. You up for some UNO?"

"Always," I answer, smiling. I push myself out of the small chair
I'm in and walk over to the table on the patio. Kyle starts dealing and
we play. He wins the first game and deals again. We play and talk
about nothing in particular. It feels nice. It's one of those beautiful,
peaceful days when, if I allow myself, I'm able to enjoy the moment
and briefly feel normal and healthy.

35

Thursday, August 1, 2002

    So the theme for the day was shame. I don't think at this juncture I can fully appreciate or realize the power of shame in my life. Adam, the rec therapist, gave me a sheet about the seven healing medicines (laughter, tears, touching, sweating, screaming, talking, shivering) and it says, "The source of all addictions is untamed energy meeting internal obstacles. We must not try to manage the addiction; we must clear the obstructions." It dawned on me that shame is a huge obstruction. It prevents our true energy force from realizing its potential. It becomes our shield/mask, and we use it to "protect" ourselves. We also beat ourselves up with it and don't let anyone in.

    I've allowed my ED to tell me that I can become more lovable by doing certain things. All this does is feed the shame, the shame that's the great pretender. The shame that masks itself so deep within me that I don't even realize it's there, and that it's the driving force of my life. It's the faceless driver of my existence. When you don't know who's in the driver's seat, you only set yourself up for a head-on collision with life.

    I use shame too easily to prevent me from living life. It's time to start letting it go. I can't ever expect to be happy and truly live life if I'm obsessed with beating myself up.

On another note, my meeting with Elizabeth yesterday went well. She told me my weight, 136 pounds. Surprisingly, I didn't freak. Part of that scares me, because maybe that means I'm starting to let go. My ED says, oh no, you can't let go, then you won't care how you look and you'll eat, eat, and eat some more, and then you'll be unlovable. But my healthy side knows that it's nice to let go of that crap and focus on more interesting things.

Elizabeth also put me on blinds for a week, which means a tech will be picking out all of my food at every meal. I know it's good for me, but damn, I get so anxious before meals. Dinner last night and breakfast this morning went okay. The food wasn't all that bad, but it was stuff I normally wouldn't have chosen for myself. There is also a weight lifted from my shoulders in that I don't have to look at all the exchanges and obsess about what I'll allow myself to eat and what will fulfill me. Of course, I know the trap is that no food can fulfill me emotionally. So it will be interesting to see what this all brings up.

36

"So, did you mail that letter to you parents yet?" Kyle asks.

"I actually did, last Monday. My mom has already called me about it, and of course, it was fine. She was very nice about it. So go figure—I was scared for nothing."

"That's awesome," Kyle exclaims.

"Yeah. Now I'm just dreading family therapy," I add with a laugh.

"Ahh, it's not that bad."

"Tickets, please."

I hand my ticket to the kid at the theatre door.

"*Signs* is playing in Theater Three, to your left."

"Thanks." I walk forward and wait for Kyle and J.R.

"You guys gonna get anything?" J.R. asks.

"No," Kyle and I say in unison, laughing. Considering we are a bunch of recovering anorexics, there is no need to ask if we are going to get any of the calorie laden snacks from the concession stand.

"Yeah, me either," J.R. replies, "though I think some of the girls are going to." J.R. motions over to the line that is forming in front of the concession stand. I notice a couple of the women we came with standing in line. I can't help but smile and be happy that they are allowing themselves a treat. Then again, they're probably only going to get a Diet Coke, since that's one thing we are not allowed to have.

This is my first co-ed outing. Rose, the tech, agreed to take the three of us guys and four of the adult women to the movies. It's nice to get out on a Saturday night. It makes me feel almost normal. Of course, not totally normal, because we did after all arrive in the big white van and parked in the handicap spot.

"I'm gonna go to the bathroom before we go sit down," I inform the guys. After paying $8 for a movie, I'll be damned if I'm going to miss any of it because I have to pee.

When I exit the stall, I'm startled by the large, plate glass mirror facing me. It's the second large mirror I've been faced with recently— but this one isn't full length, like the one at Target. I still can't get comfortable seeing myself so clearly reflected. After staring for an unhealthy amount of time, I'm interrupted by another man entering the bathroom. I can't help but think that, in some sick way, I've enjoyed not being tempted this way during the past six weeks. It's amazing how much time I can spend in front of a mirror just obsessing. Bondage is a word that comes to mind, and not in a fun way. I smile at the thought of how much time I could save by not having mirrors around. Noting the impractical nature of that sentiment, I dry my hands and leave.

The eight of us all sit in a row in the middle of the theatre. As we choose our seats, I can't help but laugh to myself as I imagine how we all must look. Here we are, a motley crew of seven patients ranging in age from fifteen to fifty, and one chaperone. We must look like some messed-up Von Trapp family—minus the singing talent.

"Did you see the *Sixth Sense* by this guy?" I ask J.R. who is sitting to my left.

"Yeah, it was good," he replies.

"That movie was awesome," Kyle comments as he walks in front of me and sits down to J.R.'s left, leaving a faint smell of smoke in his wake.

"I hope this one will be as good," I say.

We don't have to wait long to find out. The theatre goes dark and I settle into the seat the best I can. I realize that, because of my lack of an ass, the position I settle on now will only be comfortable for about ten minutes.

After what seems like a slew of never-ending previews, the feature starts. I'm enjoying the movie, and more particularly the beauty of Joaquin Phoenix, when suddenly Kyle stands up and makes his way out of the row. He mumbles something about needing to go to the bathroom and take another smoke break. Annoyed at the interruption, I glance at my watch and see it's only been twenty minutes since the movie started. I choose to ignore his odd behavior. I readjust my position and then turn my focus back to the screen.

Glancing back at my watch, I notice it's been about fifteen minutes since Kyle left. Now I'm worried that something isn't quite right. I shift my position again, trying to distract myself, but it doesn't work. All I can think about now is where is Kyle and what in the hell is he doing. It doesn't even take ten minutes to pee and smoke a cigarette.

Heat slowly starts to radiate from my body. I unzip my hoodie in an attempt to cool off. I'm not the chaperone or staff person here, so it's not my job to keep up with him. Leaning slightly forward, I glance to the end of the row where Rose is sitting. She seems fully engrossed in the movie and oblivious to the fact that Kyle is still gone.

With anger now welling up inside, I want to lean over and yell at Rose to get off her ass and go find Kyle. She's the staff person on duty and she needs to keep up with everyone. But I talk myself down, afraid of interrupting anyone's enjoyment of the movie. I sit back and turn my attention towards the screen. I get lost for a few minutes in the story and, just like magic, I hear Kyle making his way back down the row. I push my arms against the armrest to shift my body upwards as he passes. Again, the faint smell of smoke lingers in his path. I can't tell if it's fresh smoke from a newly smoked cigarette or not.

Kyle sits down. I exhale in relief and then look at my watch again. About twenty-two minutes. *That kid was "peeing" for twenty-two minutes—my ass! Whatever. I don't care.* He's back, and I'm going to enjoy the rest of this movie.

Walmart. There's a Walmart across the street. My mind flashes on the large, blue sign that I noticed across the street as our van pulled into the theater parking lot. *Shit.* All I can think about now is that Kyle had more than enough time to run across the street and get whatever he wanted.

Kyle and I have talked, on more than one occasion, about his past drug use. I've learned that it's popular to abuse over-the-counter drugs now. He likes Coricidin, I think. Something about taking it in very large doses makes you feel high. *Shit, shit, shit. Can't I just enjoy the aliens and Joaquin Phoenix?* I don't want to think about Kyle having gotten some OTC meds to abuse tonight.

The movie ends and everyone seems to be in agreement that it was pretty good. Not as good as *Sixth Sense,* but good. Of course, now I'm obsessing about what little adventure Kyle went on and what trouble he got into.

I hate confrontation. Part of me doesn't want to know, but part of me is afraid for him. I'm quiet on the ride back and I'm pissed. I seem to be the only one who is concerned about Kyle's little AWOL stunt during the movie. I can't believe it. No one has mentioned it to him, not even Rose.

"Thanks for taking us Rose," I say as I'm exiting the van.

"No problem," she replies.

"Ugh, I guess we have to get snack now," J.R. comments as we are walking back into the unit.

"Yeah, I guess so." The three of us guys head downstairs. Kyle is behind me, and I hear rattling coming from his pants. *What the hell! Shit, now I know he has something.* Trying my best to sound as disinterested as possible, I probe.

"Kyle, what's in your pants?" I ask with a slight laugh, secretly hoping he has a very convincing answer.

"Oh, just quarters and shit," he says without skipping a beat and without making eye contact. Instantly, my body tenses. The little fucker is lying to me. Damn it, I don't know what to do.

"Hey, did you go to Walmart when you were gone so long during the movie?" I blurt out, shocking myself at the directness of the question.

"Uh, no," Kyle replies quickly. By this point, we are down on the unit and making our way to the snack area.

"I'm tired I'm going to bed," Kyle mumbles. He keeps walking down the hall with his right hand firmly placed against his thigh, doing his best to silence whatever drug he thinks is going to take away the pain he is in here to face.

"Um, did you notice how long Kyle was gone tonight during the movie?" I ask J.R. as we sit down to eat snack in our day room.

"Yeah, it was kind of long," J.R. replies.

"And you heard that rattling coming from his pants?"

"Yeah," J.R. says with a slight grimace on his face.

"I'm pissed. I can't help but think he did something like go to Walmart across the street."

"Yeah it sounds like something's up," J.R. comments, but there is a slight hesitation in his voice, as if he doesn't really want to talk about this.

"I don't know what to do. I mean, if we confront him and it is something bad, then he could get kicked out of here. But if we confront him and it's nothing, then he could get really pissed off," I exclaim. I feel exhausted.

"It's tough. I don't know," J.R. says, not helping one bit. I'm getting the feeling he's not as upset about this as I am.

"I just hate confrontation," I say.

"Yeah, me too," J.R. agrees.

Suddenly I realize that here we are, two passive people, trying to decide what to do regarding another resident who in all likelihood may be relapsing with his drug use. This is so messed up. We are not the two to be handling this situation. We're both too nice and trusting.

After a few more minutes of getting nowhere, I decide to go to bed.

Damn it! This isn't fair. I don't want to do this. I'm not sure I can do this. I'm pacing the floor in my bedroom and I'm mad—no, I'm thoroughly pissed off. I still can't get Kyle off my mind. What he did the previous night is haunting me. I haven't been able to look at him all morning. I still fear the confrontation that I know needs to happen, so I'm doing what I do best: isolating in my room and trying to talk myself out of it.

I shouldn't have to confront him on this. The staff should be talking to him. I mean, come on, I wasn't the only person who saw what he did last night. I can't be the only one who thought it was odd. I don't want to do this. What if he hates me afterwards? What if he didn't do anything? I don't want to make waves. Shit, shit, shit! I hate this!

I look up and make a final plea. God, I need a sign—anything that lets me know that I need to confront him about this. I stop in front of my bed and just fall onto the mattress and let my head flop onto my pillow. I breathe heavily and stare up at the ceiling, waiting for that sign. It could be anything, really. Just a little sign to let me know that I'm on the right track. And if there's no sign, then I won't say a thing. That will be just fine by me.

Minutes pass, seconds maybe, I don't know. I just lie there. My mind turns to my gut and the wrenching feeling I've had there ever since the movie. My gut knows that something just isn't right, and that something needs to get out.

Oh, funny. That's funny, God. Is that my sign? My gut. I guess this is what they call "gut" instinct. I can practically see the light bulb going off over my head. My body is the sign. It's pointing me in the direction that I need to go. And the irony is that if I hadn't been eating and getting well, I wouldn't be feeling this right now.

I sit up and swing my feet onto the floor. *Great, now I don't have an out. I have the sign I asked for, so now I have to do this. Ugh, I hate confrontation.*

I run through my mind what I'm going to do. I have to walk into the day room, then ask Kyle and J.R. to stay and everyone else to leave.

Then I get to accuse—no, ask—Kyle what happened last night. If he doesn't come clean, then I get to tell him what I think happened.

I can do this. Kyle can do this. It's going to be okay. He'll thank me for this. Suddenly, it dawns on me. *It's unfair for me to ask Kyle to come clean if I'm not willing to do the same.* I need to show good faith and open up to him about something I haven't shared. Maybe if I do that, he'll be more willing to be honest.

Not wanting to drag this out any longer, I grab my journal—I know just what passage I need to read—and leave my room. As I pass the bathroom, I make a hard left, deciding I need a few more moments to collect myself. I pee, wash my hands, and then just stare into the tiny mirror. I'm startled at my reflection. For the first time, looking back at me, I see strength. The overwhelming fear and disgust that usually occupies the mirror has, for the moment, been replaced by strength. I smile and take a deep breath. *It's going to be okay.*

As I enter the room, my heart is about to leap out of my chest. I stop and am relieved to see that it's only Kyle and J.R., so I don't have to ask anyone to leave.

"Um, guys, I need to talk," I stammer as I close the door and sit down. The guys don't say anything, so I continue.

"I just need to read this and then talk about something," I say. I flip open my journal and start: "*I need to be honest and open up. I need to come clean about the sit-ups I do every other morning. Why do I do them? Because it's a routine, something I need to do in order to prove to myself that I have the dedication and power to do it. It helps me feel in control. At first, it didn't bother me to do them. It felt good. Now, though—and this really pisses me off—I feel some guilt and shame that I do them in secret. I need to talk about it. I need to stop if I ever hope to get well. I guess I'm progressing, because now I realize that if I don't stop, recovery will forever be an elusive concept to me.*"

"So now you both know," I say as I close my journal and slowly look up, hoping to be met with a gaze of sympathy.

"Wow," J.R. says.

"Thanks for sharing," Kyle adds.

"It feels good to be honest. And I'm stopping. I didn't do them this morning, and it felt good. Though the main reason I just said this was because of you, Kyle." I turn and look at him, trying my best to hide the fact that every muscle in my body is now shaking uncontrollably. I shake when I get really nervous. I try to breathe slowly and methodically as I go for it.

"I need to be honest with you. I'm really upset. Mad, actually. And I'm scared. Ever since last night, I can't get out of my head what happened. You were gone for more than twenty minutes from the movie. Then, when you came back, you were rattling louder than a baby toy. All night and morning, I've been doing my best to explain it away. I hate confrontation, so I didn't want to say anything. But I can't shake this feeling that something happened."

Kyle is staring at me blankly. I continue. "Kyle, we've talked about your past drug abuse. Part of me wants to ignore all of this, because that would be easier. But I know we all are here for a reason. When I was sick and my friends and coworkers didn't say anything as I got sicker, that hurt. It hurt that they couldn't get beyond their own fear and insecurity and just say something. I don't want to be that person to you. You deserve a real friend. I don't want you to look back and think that we didn't care enough to confront you. So I'm asking you for the truth. What happened last night?"

There is a long pause. A deafening pause. All I can hear is my heartbeat, which is finally starting to slow down, just a bit.

"I'll be right back," Kyle says quietly as he jumps up and leaves the room.

"What the hell!" I exclaim as I look at J.R.

"I don't know," he says, shrugging his shoulders.

"Here," Kyle says. As he walks back into the room, he hands me a bottle. I take it and look down. Benadryl. It's a bottle of allergy pills.

"What's this?" I ask.

"It's what I stole last night at Walmart," Kyle says without any emotion.

"So what the hell happened?" I ask, confused.

Kyle sounds exhausted. "When I left the movies, I ran across the street to Walmart and stole that bottle of pills."

"What do these do for you? They're just allergy pills. Don't they make you sleepy?" I ask naively.

"If you take a lot at once, it makes you feel high. It's euphoric. I took twenty last night before bed."

"What? Twenty! I, I … I don't know what to say," I exclaim. He meets my gaze and then quickly breaks it. "How long has this been going on?"

"For several weeks. Actually, I haven't been clean for more than two to three days at a time since I've been here," he admits, somewhat deflated.

"Kyle, I'm scared for you. I don't want to go to breakfast one morning and be told that you never woke up," I say. My voice breaks at the thought of this kid killing himself with over-the-counter pills, something I didn't even know was possible until now.

"I know. It's fucked up," Kyle says, slumping backwards. I notice out of the corner of my eye that J.R. is just sitting on the other couch, motionless, with a look of disbelief on his face.

"I have to admit, I feel totally out of my league," I tell Kyle. "Since drugs haven't been my thing, I don't know what to do. You're really good at holding things close, and obviously I'm not smart enough to be able to call you on your bullshit all the time."

"It's cool. Thanks, though, for doing this. I appreciate it," Kyle says, looking at me.

"It's cool, but you know, I'm wondering if this is a good place for you. Do you even want to be here?" I feel annoyed as I fully realize that this kid hasn't been sober most of the time we've interacted.

"No, yeah, I do. I mean, I like it here, and you guys are awesome. I need to be here. I just need to work the program," he says, almost pleading.

"Well, I want you here," I say. "But I'm just worried."

"It's cool," he says.

"Now, to be honest, it's great that we are having this talk. But you know Rogers needs to know. I don't feel comfortable just keeping this among us. I think you need to tell the staff. And if you can't, then I will. I can't keep quiet about this. It's too important, and your health is at risk," I say, as firmly as I can. Now that I feel more at peace about how this is going, my body has finally stopped shaking. The energy in the room, while not happy, feels more healthy and headed in a positive direction.

"Okay, I understand. I'll do it," Kyle replies without looking up.

"Great," I say with a slight sigh.

"J.R., you okay?" Kyle asks, looking up.

"Uh, yeah. I'm just shocked," J.R. says hesitantly.

Neither Kyle nor I are buying this. J.R. has been totally silent this whole time. I can sense something is brewing inside of him, but I know you can't push J.R. He has to think about it for a while before he's ready to talk. Hopefully, whatever this triggered, he'll be able to open up about it.

"No offense, but I feel better," I laugh as I stand to stretch. My body is starting to ache after being released from the tension that has gripped it for the last twelve hours.

"I understand. Hey, hug?" Kyle asks sheepishly as he stands up.

"Sure." I walk over to him and we wrap our arms around each other. I can't help but smile at how uncomfortable this makes me. Here I am, a gay guy, significantly older than this kid, and we're hugging after having had an impromptu intervention. Jerry Falwell would be so proud.

"Okay, you can do this," I tell Kyle as I step back from our embrace.

"Yeah, thanks," he says as he turns around and picks up his notebook.

"Good luck," J.R. adds as Kyle walks out of the day room and towards the staff station.

My heart skips a beat. I am hoping, pleading, that the outcome will be good and that they won't kick him out. I don't think I could handle knowing that my personal triumph came at the expense of breaking up our group.

The next day, after having time to process what happened, I write.

Monday, August 5, 2002

All three of us guys talked for a while and I personally felt a huge weight lifted from my shoulders. I had just pushed myself further emotionally than ever before, and I had a peace that whatever happened to Kyle, I knew it was the best thing for him. By giving him the chance to come clean with the staff and face the consequences, hopefully in time he would come to know he was choosing life. We don't learn jack shit when times are easy and people let us get away with our same old bullshit.

All of this was a catalyst for J.R. It upset him enough that he was feeling uncomfortable. Anger was actually making itself known to him, and he wasn't able to run anymore.

So at check-in that night, Steve was asking a lot of hard questions, and eventually the whole Kyle situation came up. Steve kept pushing J.R. to discuss it and, like a light switch, J.R. connected with his emotions. He broke down and let it all out. He wasn't just crying, he was wailing. He was healing himself. It was so powerful to witness. I honestly haven't ever heard wailing like that before. It was almost eerie.

So the check-in proceeded to be about two hours long and then we moved into the room where we have experiential therapy with Rachel. J.R. hit the hell out of all the pads in the room. Then after that, I suggested we go outside and yell. So once outside, J.R. takes one look down the hill and starts running towards Bulimia Pond, the affectionate name we residents have dubbed the tiny pond on the property. He jumps in, clothes and all (no shoes though). Then Kyle joins him! It was wild. I was hesitant, but after a moment, I took off my pants and joined them. The water felt and smelled disgusting. I didn't want to think about what empties into it. But it didn't matter, we were all intoxicating ourselves with J.R.'s newfound freedom—his breakthrough. We needed the release after such a tense day.

So I was able to cut loose and yell and scream. We all hugged and pictures were taken. Afterwards, we all went inside, cleaned up, and then starting running through the unit yelling "I'm free!"

I told J.R. that, by facing his fear of letting out his emotions, especially anger, and dealing with it, he got everything his ED said it would give him but never produced: peace, confidence, love, and feeling connected. At one point, Kyle said he had never felt so connected. We all shared a huge peak experience.

I realized today that my biggest fears—rejection and confrontation—had to be faced and dealt with if I ever expect to get better. Having to confront Kyle was really me having to confront myself. I learned that I could express my feelings and be honest, and since it was coming from a place of love, it was okay. Neither of us fell apart and in fact, it made us stronger. It gave me a huge amount of confidence. Most of all, the day gave me hope. Hope that I can get better and start using these tools every day.

I learned that by doing this, it strengthens a relationship and makes it more real. I'll take real over perfection any day. But what I think J.R. learned is that by being real, he found the so-called perfection he was trying to create. You just have to let go and accept it.

J.R. said it finally hit him and he accepted reality that he had screwed up. He was trying to be perfect and ended up not so. But by facing reality, accepting it, and letting go, he found everything he had been looking for.

So in true fashion around here, I turned this back on me. Do I accept reality? Probably not. I still feel like I have to be the best and not make mistakes. I don't want to admit I'm human because, by doing so, that would make me vulnerable and I would have to open up. I know I need to accept myself and know that I'm okay.

This also gets at the gay issue. I use that as a brick wall of shame to keep others out. The guys and everyone else here don't have an issue with it. Hell, Kyle gave me a huge gift by being thankful I cared enough to confront him and then asked for a hug. Me—this fifteen-year-old hetero kid asked me for a hug. It made me uncomfortable, but at the same time, I was screaming for it.

For some reason, I make me being gay an issue. When other people are cool with it and think nothing of hugging me, then why should I not accept myself? I need to face reality. There is nothing wrong with being gay. It has no moral judgment on me as a person. The fact that I can love is what makes me a worthy person. If someone treated me as badly as I treat myself, I would kill them.

I know that part of the shame regarding physical contact is that gay men are viewed as pedophiles and sexual deviants. So I've internalized that and allowed it to prevent me from fully enjoying and experiencing intimacy with guys, gay or straight. That's a fear I have to face because only by facing it and challenging it will I ever hope to get what I thought I could get by running away.

37

"It's weird. My right eye is bugging me. It's been hurting the last few days and now I can't wear my contacts. It feels like there is this line or scratch across it," I tell the nurse.

"How long has this been going on?"

"Oh, about two or three days I guess."

"Okay, blink for me."

I take off my glasses and do as I'm told.

"Again," she instructs.

I do it again. I feel my body starting to tense. I don't like the expression on her face. It looks too serious. She seems to be thinking awfully hard about something. I had just wanted to see the nurse in the hope that she could give me some eye drops. I figure this is just some allergy thing. And truth be told, I'm more pissed off at the fact that I have to wear my glasses. I don't see as well with them on, and in true anorexic style, I hate how I *look* in them. Vanity is such a bitch.

"Smile real big for me," she says. I comply.

"Okay, now blink each eye separately." I blink my left eye fairly easily but it takes some work to blink my right eye. *Ugh, that's a pain.* I was in middle school before I was able to master this little skill.

A long, uncomfortable pause follows. Here I am, sitting in the nurse's office on the third floor. I've never been here before. Judy, the nurse, is nice. She seems to be about my mom's age. But right now, her mind seems to be going about a million miles a second.

"Uh, Hoyt, I think we need to take you to the ER," she says suddenly. *The emergency room? For a dry eye? What?*

"I'm concerned," she says. "Your eyes are not blinking in unison. I would feel better having a doctor check you out, okay?" She sounds like she is trying to convince herself that it's no big deal.

I don't like this one bit. I don't see why I have to go to the ER. Maybe my eyes are just tired. I didn't know they had to blink at exactly the same time.

"Okay," I mumble, not sure what to say. I guess I don't have much of an option. If the nurse says I have to go to the hospital, I have to go. Hell, if nothing else, it will kill a few hours and I'll get out of this place for a while.

A short time later, I'm standing at the hospital counter. "Yes I have insurance," I answer as I pull out my wallet and hand the nurse behind the counter my insurance card.

"Thanks, I'll be right back," she says. I'm impressed at the cleanliness of this place. For some reason, I always expect emergency rooms to be these dingy, dark, dirty places. Everything here is so white and bright. It's downright cheery. Though it's weird that there is almost no one in this place.

"Here you go," the nurse says, handing the card back to me. "We got a call from Judy filling us in. I can take you back and the doctor will see you in a few minutes."

"Oh, really? Okay, so should my ride just wait on me?" I ask, somewhat surprised. I didn't think anything ever happened fast in an ER. I figured I would be here at least a couple of hours. Then again, this is a tiny town, and it sounds like nurse Judy called in a favor.

"Oh, I'm sure it won't take long," the nurse says.

I walk over to where Steve has taken a seat in the waiting room. "Hey Steve, they're taking me back now and they said it won't be long. So if you want, you can wait."

"Oh, cool. I'll be here," he says, looking up from the magazine he's reading.

The nurse is waiting for me by the door. "This way," she says. I follow her through a large door and down the hall. Again, everything back here is so bright and clean. This must be a new facility. We walk down the hall and then turn left into an exam room.

It's a generic-looking room. I sit down on what looks like a gurney. The nurse takes my blood pressure, temperature, and pulse, which at this point is probably through the roof. I feel fine, but I'm nervous as hell. I don't like being in hospitals, no matter how bright and clean.

"Okay, well the doctor should be here in just a few minutes," she says as she leaves the room.

I try to relax my posture. I hate sitting up straight. *Great, now what?* I look around and start counting. One, two, three light fixtures in the ceiling. Two, four, six, eight, ten, twelve nail heads in the kick plate at the bottom of the door. Two, four, six, eight doors across the bottom of the counter. Numbers. I love counting, especially when I'm nervous.

"Hello."

I'm startled at the opening of the door and the sight of a very attractive, younger looking doctor entering the room. *Damn it, just my luck. The first hot guy I've seen in weeks and here I am looking like crap.*

"Oh, hi," I reply, trying not to stare. He's about five-foot-ten with short brown hair, a beard, and a gorgeous physique. *Okay, don't stare, don't stare, don't stare. Just act natural.*

"I'm Dr. Johns," he says as he walks toward me. *Ah, he's straight. The walk gives it away every time.*

"Hi, nice to meet you. I'm Hoyt."

"So what's the problem today?"

"Well, several days ago, I noticed my right eye was hurting. It feels like there's a scratch or something. So I haven't been able to wear my contacts."

"Okay, look up for me," he says as he leans in with the lighted scope. He shines the light directly into my right eye. I hold my breath.

I don't want to breathe on him nor smell him. I don't like being this close. He pulls on my lower right eye lid.

"Look down, please." He then pulls on my upper right eye lid. I take a small breath in through my nose.

"Blink for me," he instructs after he places the scope on the counter. I look at him and blink several times.

"Now smile," he says. I smile, feeling somewhat like a trick pony.

"Can you feel this?" he asks as he places his fingers on my right cheek and moves them up and down. Now in a different setting, this would demand a sarcastic, flirty retort. But since this guy is a raging hetero and I'm not feeling all that flirty, I just answer honestly.

"Yeah, I can, but it feels kind of weird."

"Do you have any tingling feeling or numbness on this side of your face?"

"Actually, I think I have had some tingling. And when you pressed against my face, it felt odd."

He steps back and now has the same expression on his face that Nurse Judy was sporting earlier. *I wonder if this is something they learn in school.* He's deep in thought. I just sit still trying not to feel too awkward. I mean, this can't be *that* bad. It's not like I feel sick or anything. It's probably just some weird allergy thing. I mean I'm in the Middle of Nowhere, Wisconsin. I'm sure I'm being exposed to some odd new environmental stuff that my body isn't accustomed to.

"Have you ever heard of Bell's Palsy?" Dr. Johns asks.

"Uh, no."

"I think that's what this is. It's a paralysis of the cranial nerve. Basically, what happens is the nerve on the side of the head that controls the facial motor functions swells and gets paralyzed. In effect, it slows down or stops the movement on one side of your face," he informs me.

Paralyzed? But my face does move. "What causes it?" I ask. *And how in the hell did something like this happen to me?*

"We don't know. We think it's viral, but we're not exactly sure. And we're not really certain how you get it."

"How long does it last?" I ask, not sure I want to know the answer.

"That varies. For some people, it's only a few weeks, but for others it can be longer. From what I can tell, you seem to have a mild case. Your eyes aren't blinking together, but it seems you still have a fair amount of movement in your face. And when you sleep at night, your right eye is not closing all the way. That is why you are waking up with that scratched feeling. It's basically a dry spot. So what you'll need to do at night is close your eye all the way and then place a piece of gauze over your eye and tape it down."

"Okay. Is there anything else I can do for this?" I ask, pleading for some light at the end of the tunnel. I don't feel so well right now. I want concrete answers. I want to be told that this isn't all that bad, that it will go away fast and that it won't come back!

"I'll write you a prescription for a steroid that should help with the swelling of the nerve. Just take it until it's all gone," he says.

"Okay, anything else?"

"No, that's about it. It will just have to run its course," he says without any emotion.

Run its course. Oh, that's a great line. Thanks, doctor. This guy may look hot but he could take a lesson on bedside manners. It wouldn't hurt to offer a little more reassurance.

After getting the prescription, I meet Steve out in the waiting room and we head back to Rogers. *Bell's Palsy. Bell's Palsy. It's just a weird name. I don't like it.*

When I woke up this morning I thought I had a dry eye, and now this. In a flash I've got some weird aliment that I have never heard of before. And viral. It's viral. My body shudders at the thought. I can't help it, the word viral makes my skin crawl. All I can think about is AIDS. That's viral and for my entire life, every time I've ever had sex, that is the one thing I think about. Even though I'm always careful, I can't help but be a hypochondriac when it comes to that.

It just seems like "the virus" has cast this dark cloud over my life or I've allowed it to do as much. I've grown up as a gay man in the age of AIDS and, honestly, it hasn't been fun—especially given my nature to worry. I have this automatic aversion to anything dealing with viruses. The word itself just feels dirty. And now, ironies of all ironies, the one word I've been doing my best to run from has caught up with me. *And* they don't know exactly what it is or how you get it.

As soon as we get back, I'm told that I need to see Judy again. Feeling like shit, I slump down in the chair in her office.

"How are you doing?" she asks.

"I'm okay," is the best I can muster.

"So what did they say?"

This surprises me. I figured they would have called her. It's nice to know I have some privacy.

"Oh, it's Bell's Palsy, which I've never heard of," I inform her.

"Oh, wow. Bell's Palsy. That's interesting. I've never had a patient with that before," she says with a bit of excitement in her voice. *Well, here you go honey, I'm your first. Lucky me.*

"I have to admit, I'm relieved. When I first saw you today, I was afraid you'd had a stroke," she says.

A stroke? Damn I had never considered that. That's nuts.

Before I know it, Judy has pulled out this massive medical book and is thumbing through the pages. She stops on a certain page and then proceeds to read to me all about this dumb aliment. I learn that it's caused by the inflammation of the cranial nerve. It comes on suddenly and people recover spontaneously. She also informs me that this is thought to be brought on and exacerbated by stress.

Now I'm stressed at the thought that I have to remain calm if I hope to get better. Given where I am and what I am dealing with, I figure it's a losing battle.

Judy also throws in the tidbit that she's only heard of this affecting older people, which makes me feel so much better. Not only do I have some weird virus affecting my face, but now I'm a freak because this usually only happens to the geriatric set. I don't remember this ever being the subject of a *Golden Girls* episode, and those gals talked about everything.

Our session finally ends with Judy taking my prescription and telling me I can start taking the medication tonight after dinner. I thank her for her help and leave.

After dinner that night, I inform the guys of what happened. In true form, they are very supportive, although Kyle can't contain his curiosity. He asks me to blink for him. I humor him, and he affirms what everyone else has been saying all day—that my eyes don't blink at the same time. Choosing not to deal with my feelings of anger and shame, I skip the evening snack and hit the sack early. I start my new nightly routine of placing a square piece of gauze over my right eye and securing it in place with a large piece of surgical tape. Before I fall asleep, I note that at day fifty-one in here, things have just gotten much more intense.

38

"Have you had an MRI before?" the tech asks. Susan seems nice, probably about my age. She's pretty.

"Uh, yeah. It was several years ago," I reply, remembering back to when I was in college. I had been grinding my teeth at night and the orthodontist ordered one. That scan didn't find anything, but it was wild being shoved into a huge metal tube.

"Okay, so you know you'll be on a bed which will then go into a long chamber. Are you claustrophobic?" she asks.

"No, it doesn't bother me."

"Oh, good. Well, here is a gown. You can stay in here and change. I need you to take off your shirt and pants. You can leave on your underwear. And take off your watch and anything else that is metal. You can put your things in one of the cubbies. Okay?"

"Sure."

"When you're done, just open this door, and I'll walk you into the room," she says, closing the door behind her.

I just stand there, frozen. I'm in this small, sterile room with a wooden bench in front of me and to my left are some cubby holes. On the bench is the hospital gown I have to wear. A chill runs through me. It's cold in here, or maybe it's just me. I'm nervous. This is the second time in four days I've been in this place, Oconomowoc Memorial Hospital. On Friday, I was here for them to tell me I have Bell's Palsy.

Now it's Tuesday and I'm not sure I want to hear what they have to say this time around.

The last few days feel like a blur. I slept most of the weekend away, but when I was awake, I started noticing this odd sensation in my head. A few times over the weekend, this shock or zapping feeling went streaking through my head. It didn't hurt, but it felt like my brain was being shocked with electricity, like I was licking a nine volt battery. In an odd way, it was also like someone was playing Ping-Pong with my brain, which caused me to feel off balance. Today the shocking sensation has become more frequent, and I know it's not a good thing.

I can't fucking believe this. Over the last few days, the right side of my face has become more numb and harder to move. And now this. I'm about to be squeezed into some tiny metal tube and have pictures taken of my head. And for what? For them to tell me something else is messed up with me?

Screw this. I allow the chill in the air to fully penetrate my body until I'm numb inside and out. I quickly undress and, after three tries, I'm able to secure the hospital gown around my thin frame.

"Okay, so I'm going to place this frame over your head to hold everything in place," Susan explains as I'm lying on the bed that will be moving me into the MRI machine. She lowers a white plastic dome that holds the upper part of my head in place. My mind suddenly flashes to *Silence of the Lambs* and Anthony Hopkins with his face mask. I hope I look better than that.

"Okay, so as you probably remember, it is very loud when the machine is taking the pictures. So I'll give you some ear plugs. You'll hear a series of loud clicks followed by silence. I ask that you try to hold as still as possible. Now we can communicate, so if you need to stop or get out, just let me know. Okay?"

"Okay, sure."

"This should only take about thirty minutes. Now sometimes, once we start taking pictures, we need to get more contrast. And if that happens, we will bring you out and insert an IV that will put contrast into your system. All this does is help provide better pictures. The solution that is put in you is not dangerous," she informs me. "Do you have any questions?" "No," I reply. *Let's just get this over with.* I place the ear plugs in each ear, after which the bed slowly glides into position. My entire body is practically inside the machine. It's white, small, and almost comforting. I like cozy spaces, although the fact that I'm pretty much pinned down makes me a little bit nervous. I couldn't really get out of this thing on my own if I wanted to. I start taking deep breaths to slow down my pulse.

"Hoyt, we're going to get started. Are you okay?" the voice of God thunders from inside the tube. *Damn, that's loud. And freaky.*

"Yeah, I'm ready," I reply, though I'm not totally sure she can hear me.

"Here we go."

CLICK, CLICK, CLICK, CLICK, CLICK is all I hear, in a slightly muffled tone. The clicks are encircling my head and vibrating slightly. I close my eyes and pretend I'm in a sci-fi movie with a young Harrison Ford, á la *Stars Wars. Damn, he's hot.*

Oh, how I wish I really was in some movie. A movie where these last eleven months would have been from the imagination of some brilliant script-writer and not the reality I've been living. ZAP, ZAP, ZAP. The pulsing in my head doesn't let me forget why I'm here.

My mind wanders from the thoughts of aliens visiting Earth—like in the movie *Signs*—to what I'm going to do when I finally leave Rogers. Then I wonder if I will ever feel like visiting Ground Zero, especially given the fact that the first anniversary will be here soon.

In the beginning, the loud clicks startle me and wrench my attention back to where I am. But after several minutes, the clicks start to lull my body and mind into an almost trance-like state. The sound and vibrations from this enormous machine are having the same effect that the listing and humming of a train have on me. It's soothing.

"Okay, Hoyt, we need to add some contrast," Susan announces.

Contrast, okay. I can deal with that. Needles really don't bother me, though they probably wouldn't do this whole contrast mess if they knew there was nothing more to see.

Before I'm ready, the bed is slowly moving out of the tube and Susan is standing over me. She quickly and quietly inserts a needle into the crease of my left arm. My veins are so prominent that a blind person could stick me without any trouble. Within a matter of minutes, I'm back in my cocoon, relaxing to the sounds swirling around my head.

After I do a little more day-dreaming, it dawns on me: something is wrong. I've been in this machine for much longer than thirty minutes. They now are pumping me full of some type of dye to get better pictures. They found something. *Huh, they found something. In my head.*

There's something in my head, but for some reason, this doesn't freak me out. My pulse isn't racing and I don't feel numb. I feel calm. Dare I say, almost peaceful. Maybe this is what acceptance feels like. I've been through so much hell this year that there isn't much more that can surprise me.

"Hoyt, we need to take you down the hall to get a CT scan. There's a, um, a spot we need to get a better look at," Susan says somberly. She's taken the needle out of my arm and helped me off the table. *A spot. Huh. Okay, I can deal with that.* I'm not surprised.

She walks me down the hall and into an expansive room. In the middle of the room is this large, open circle that looks like a big, white doughnut. There is a bed in the center of the circle. This must be the CT machine. At least it's open and not a closed-off tube. This will be a new experience for me.

Susan introduces me to Joe, the tech, who will be taking over. Susan leaves and Joe instructs me to lie down on the bed. This whole routine is a lot easier and faster than the MRI. I lie still while something inside the doughnut rotates around and takes more pictures of my head, hopefully getting a closer look at the spot. After several minutes at the computer, Joe looks up hesitantly.

"Hoyt, I need to take you down the hall to the ER. One of the doctors there needs to talk to you," Joe says quietly.

Then there is silence. Dead silence. My body stiffens and my pulse speeds up. *ER. I have to go to the ER, again? A doctor. A doctor has to talk to me.* I'm not stupid, I know this isn't good news. I suddenly feel cold, very cold. I'm alone. I don't know any of these people, and no one is here with me.

I'm sitting on top of a gurney covered in that cheap, loud paper they cover everything with in hospitals. My legs are hanging off the end, and I'm fully dressed. How the hell did I get in here? One minute I was with Joe, and now I'm here sitting on this damned gurney. None of this feels real. I guess this is what they call disassociating. My body is stiff as a board and I'm just waiting—waiting for whatever bad news is destined to come my way.

This area I'm in is tiny. There is a small counter to my left and cabinets above the counter. A small, beige phone is mounted on the wall above the counter top. To my right and in front of me are white curtains suspended from tracks mounted on the ceiling. I'm not even in a private room. I can hear talking next to me on the other side of the curtain. *Great, there goes any hope of privacy.*

I'm cold. I slouch and rub my arms. *I can do this. It can't be that bad. They did an MRI with contrast and they did a CT scan. Even if it's a tumor, they can operate on those things. It's no big deal.*

ZAP. ZAP. ZAP. Three quick pulses shoot through my head. *Ugh, they're getting more frequent.* I guess I should be thankful it doesn't hurt.

"Uh, Mr. Phillips?" I hear as I look up to see a tall, thin, middle-aged man in a white lab coat opening up the curtain in front of me. He takes one small step into the room. The curtain falls and rests against his left shoulder.

"Yes, that's me," I reply, looking up and feeling awkward.

"Hi, I'm Dr. Milburn, the attending ER doctor here," he informs me.

"Hi," I answer. I suddenly realize this guy is almost whispering and not even completely in the room. In fact, he seems to be scared to walk any closer. I closely examine his face and it dawns on me that he's white. No, he's pale. In fact, this guy doesn't have any color in his face at all. He looks sick, or as if he's just seen ghost.

"We've been looking at your scans and well, we, um … it looks like you have a um … brain aneurysm," His voice is almost inaudible, and he's not looking at me. He's staring at the floor. ZAP. ZAP. ZAP. *Aneurysm. Aneurysm. This thing racing through my head is an aneurysm!*

"I've got a call in to the on-call neurosurgeon for a consult. As soon as he has a chance to take a look, we'll know what we need to do. We may need to operate today," the doctor drones on, barely looking my way.

I'm in a Peanuts cartoon. I'm listening to the teacher in that cartoon that just sounds like muffled moaning. The room, overly bright and white, seems to have become ten times brighter. I feel light-headed and now I'm instantly hot. It's burning up in here. *Aneurysm. Surgery.* Those are the only two words I really hear from this obviously terrified doctor. I'm sure he hasn't had to tell many twenty-five year olds that they may have to have emergency brain surgery. He leaves. I think he says something about coming back in a few minutes.

It's bright. Damn, it's bright in here. My chest is heaving up and down and my body is pulsing with energy. I'm shaking. I'm hot. I'm alone. I'm completely and utterly alone. No one is here with me. I was dropped off and told to call Rogers when I'm ready to leave. My parents are half-way across the country. I'm alone. I want my parents. God, please I don't want to die alone.

Any second now, this guy could come back in here and wheel me into surgery—a surgery I may not wake up from. Can they do that? I'm just twenty-five. Don't they have to get my parents' permission? *No, no, no, no, no! I can't do this. I can't die alone. I can't die in the middle of nowhere. Mom, damn it, I need you!* Tears slowly start to stream down my face.

Alone. I hate this feeling. It feels like … I'm back there. My mind went there first and now my body is reacting … the screams, the smoke, the building shaking, walking up the West Side Highway while I hear fire trucks speeding past. Even though I was in a city of millions that day, I was alone. I wasn't with my family. I felt like I was in a place that was going to kill me and I would have never had the chance to say good-bye. I would have died alone. And damn it, here I am again!

This feeling, the utter terror of being alone, is what most of us spend our whole lives running from. It feels like a black hole, a soul-sucking black hole from which I can't escape. The phone. Snapping my head to the left, I see the small beige phone mounted on the wall above the counter. *Mom. All I want to do is hear my mom's voice.*

I feel like I did when I was three and skinned my knee falling off my bike, and the only thing that could make me feel better was crawling onto my mom's lap, feeling her arms caress me and hearing her sweet voice tell me softly that everything would be okay. But she can't do that for me now. I'm an adult. I don't want to be, but I guess I am. And I'm alone, and I can't call her to hear her voice. It's long distance, which I'm sure this phone won't let me dial.

Deep breaths. Taking deep breaths, I slowly start to calm down. ZAP. ZAP. ZAP. I lean back and lie down on the gurney. Staring up at the ceiling, I'm distracted by the voices next door to me, which are more discernible now. A smile slowly creeps across my face. It's a husband and wife talking to a doctor. The guy hasn't taken a shit in several days and he's in pain. *Lucky bastard. That ain't nothin'.* He should hang around a bunch of anorexics. We don't shit for weeks sometimes, and when we finally do, the smell could strip the chrome off a trailer hitch.

ZAP. ZAP. ZAP. *Screw it, I want to sit up.* My mind does a great job of scaring me by noting the fact that this thing inside of me could burst and kill me. I remember the story Mom told me about the little girl she knew growing up who dropped dead one day running to the school bus. The girl had died from a burst aneurysm. And now I've got one, and it could kill me, right here, at any moment.

After what feels like an eternity, Dr. Milburn comes back and informs me that the neurosurgeon doesn't think I need immediate surgery. This news, for some reason, doesn't calm me as much as I wish it would. I'm given the anti-seizure medication Tegretol and the number of the neurosurgeon. I'm to call his office the next day to schedule an appointment.

Once I'm back at Rogers, everyone is shocked and supportive. I get asked the very stupid question: "Am I scared?" I figure that, if I say, "No I look forward to dropping dead or having my head cracked open," it will sound too sarcastic. So I just mutter "Yeah" and leave the room.

I'm going crazy with the thoughts that, at any minute, the next ZAP could bring with it total and permanent darkness. I decide I need to call home. I'm dying to hear my mom's voice, but at the same time, I'm afraid I'm going to break down and cry. Plus, I don't want to worry her.

"Hello," I hear on the other end of the phone, tensing at the sound of my dad's voice.

"Oh, hi Dad, it's Jeff," I quickly reply.

"Hey, how are you?"

"Oh, I'm good. How are you?" The words just come out of my mouth without me thinking. I don't know how to tell him. I want to talk to Mom.

"Fine," he replies.

"How's Mom?"

"She's fine. She and Amy are out at the boardwalk," he says. I slump into the chair and do my best to hide my disappointment.

"Cool. How's the beach?" I ask, wishing I was there with them.

"It's nice. It's been warm. Amy and the kids are having a good time. They are here for a few more days."

"Nice," I say. "Uh, dad, there's something I need to tell you. I, um, just got back from the hospital. I had to have an MRI done. They found something. I've been having this zapping feeling in my head. They found an aneurysm." I blurt everything out, not able to keep my secret any longer. I'm met with silence. Usually, this works for us, but right now it's not working. I can't stand the silence, so I keep talking.

"I've got to call the neurosurgeon tomorrow to schedule an appointment. They gave me some medication to help," I say, hoping this will help lessen the shock.

"I'm not going to tell your mother," he says. My mind freezes in disbelief at what I've just heard. *You're not going to tell Mom? That's all you can say to me?*

"Uh, okay," I mumble back.

"Are you okay? How do you feel?"

"I'm fine. It's okay. I'll talk to the surgeon tomorrow. It's cool," I tell him. But I feel so deflated that I get him off the phone as quickly as possible and retreat to my room.

He's not going to tell my mom. The first thing he can think to say to me is that he's not going to tell mom. *That's great, Dad, thanks for your concern.* My whole fucking life, he's been so over-protective of Mom, and now this. I'm the sick one, and he's still more concerned with Mom.

Defeated and exhausted, I write my daily wrap-up before escaping into sleep:

> *Day 55: Tues. August 13:*
> *Just diagnosed with brain aneurysm! Scared, hurt. Called home and Dad was a jerk! Want answers!*

39

"Here, take this," Kyle says as he slides his smiley face wrist band off and hands it to me.

"Oh wow, thanks," I say, caught off guard. I don't think I've seen Kyle take this off once since I've been here.

"Oh, and here, you might need this today as well," Kyle says as he hands me his little blue Tetris game, which hasn't left his side since he bought it.

"Thanks, yeah, this will definitely help pass the time. Seriously, thanks. I'll give these back to you later today," I tell him, genuinely touched by his generosity. I'm glad that the Rogers staff decided he could stay after the incident with the pills. I don't want to think how different things would have been without him around.

"It's cool. I just, ugh, I don't know why bad things have to happen to good people," he moans, looking away from me. He seems upset. It's sweet, but it makes me feel uncomfortable, like I have to comfort him, when I really don't feel like I have it in me.

"Hey, it's going to be okay. It is what it is," I say with a smile, trying to keep things light. I'm on autopilot right now. I can't stop to feel too long or else I may lose it. I just need to get through today and see what the doctor says. Just one step at a time.

"Mr. Phillips, we're ready to take you back now," a soft voice announces from behind me.

"Oh, okay. I'll be right there," I reply, turning around to face the nurse. She's standing in the doorway, waiting to take me back for my cerebral angiogram.

"Well, this is it. I guess I need to go back. Thanks for coming with me this morning," I say to Sue, J.R., and Kyle. I'm doing my best not to make eye contact with any of them. Luckily, I'm taller than all three of them, so it's pretty easy to just talk over their heads. J.R. and Kyle insisted on accompanying me this morning to Waukesha Memorial Hospital. Sue offered to be the chauffeur. It's nice they want to support me this way, but I also feel awkward. I'm not the most adept at receiving support. It's so much easier to give it than take it. Right now, I just want to get this good-bye over with before it sinks in that I might really be sick.

"Good luck. We're thinking about you and will see you later today," Sue says as she gives me a big hug.

"Yeah, good luck. I'm sure it will go fine. We'll see you later," J.R. says as he hugs me.

"Stay strong," is all that Kyle can manage as he hugs me. He still seems upset.

"Thanks, guys. I appreciate it. It's gonna be fine. I'll see ya'll soon," I say. Then I turn around and walk to the doorway with the waiting nurse. I briefly turn back and slightly raise my right hand in a half-hearted wave.

"Follow me," the nurse orders. We walk down a generic hospital hallway and make a left turn into a room with a gurney, a small table, and—to my pleasant surprise—solid walls on either side. At least I'll have some privacy in here.

"I'm Nora, by the way," the nurse says matter-of-factly. She seems focused on what she has to get done. I like that. I'm not really in the mood for small talk.

"Hey, I'm Hoyt," I reply, not extending my hand.

"Okay, so you're scheduled to go back at about eleven for the angiogram. You've got some time. I need you to put on a gown and take everything off, underwear included." Nora says this as if she's reading a script she's recited a thousand times.

I knew this was coming, but my heart sinks anyway. My mind flashes every image I've ever seen of naked butts hanging out of hospital gowns.

"You can put your stuff in this plastic bag," she says. "I'll leave and give you a few minutes to change." As she exits, she grabs a white curtain and closes it, blocking off the front of the room.

I take a deep breath and find my body is surprisingly calm. I know all of this hasn't yet sunk in. I'm just going through the motions. *Get naked. Put on gown. Lay on gurney. Get procedure done, whatever it is. Listen to doctor. Get well. It won't be that bad. Just keep moving.*

After stripping down and successfully securing my gown—in only two tries this time—I climb onto the gurney. I feel like I need more privacy, so I slip under the thin sheet and blanket. This gown is paper thin and it's chilly in here. Plus, I feel naked wearing this ridiculous thing. I'm a person with significant body issues and I'm in a place that affords little privacy. The irony is not lost on me.

I sit up as straight as possible, trying my best to look normal and healthy. I adjust my glasses, wishing there was a mirror in here. *I know I must look like a hot mess right now.* My hair has to be all out of sorts, since I just undressed. And I hate how I look in my glasses. *And my face, ugh!* I shudder at the thought of how I'm looking these days.

Ever since being diagnosed with Bell's Palsy, my face has gotten worse. I have limited movement on the right side of my face now. I can still blink my right eye, but other than that, it's not pretty. The right side of my mouth droops slightly, forcing me to chew my food on my left side. It feels like someone is pushing the right side of my face in and down. I feel a constant pulling downward. It's exhausting and makes me feel like I need to constantly prop my face up. I would rather be dealing with more than one aneurysm than Bell's Palsy. At least the zapping doesn't hurt.

"All set," Nora says as she enters the room, flinging open the curtain.

"Uh, yeah," I mutter.

"Okay, let me take some vitals real quick," she says. She records my pulse, temperature, and blood pressure.

"So you're at Rogers?" Nora asks out of the blue. Caught off-guard, my body tenses.

"Uh, yeah," I reply, hoping that this line of questioning doesn't go any further.

"That's a good place. Yeah, I've had bulimia in the past. It's pretty much in check now, but I find at stressful times it can come back." She says this calmly as she is reaching down and attaching some clip to my finger. I just stare straight in front of me in disbelief. I can't imagine why this woman feels the need to tell me something so personal. It feels too intimate and strange. *I don't know you.*

"Are you here alone?" she asks. I'm glad she has changed the subject.

"Um, no, my mom should be here soon. She's flying in this morning. I think her plane landed a few minutes ago," I say. I'm grateful I was spared having to tell my mom what's going on with me. My dad finally came to his senses and told her.

The clock on the wall to my right reads 10:12. My mom's plane should have landed at 9:35, so she should be here soon. My body relaxes a bit at this thought. *I won't be alone today.* It's nice but it feels scary at the same time. *Shit, I can't ever win.* Nothing right now feels all that comforting. I'm nervous. I haven't seen Mom in almost two months, and now the reason for our reunion is a medical emergency. *Fun times.*

Nora leaves me to take care of other business. I'm alone, for now, in this outpatient room. It's quiet and cold. I pick up the Tetris game and turn off the sound before I start playing. The silence in the room is nice. It gives my mind the room it needs to obsess without distraction.

Time passes too slowly. I keep looking up at the clock in nervous anticipation. I don't know what I'm more anxious waiting for, my mom's appearance or this procedure. I see 10:15, 10:19, 10:21, 10:29.

"Hey you," I hear as I look up and see my mom, dressed beautifully, standing in front of me. It's 10:32.

"Hey!" I smile big and my heart skips a beat. I can't stop smiling. My mom is here! She's finally here. I feel safer somehow. She walks in and puts her purse down on the floor and comes over to the right side of the gurney. I lean forward and we hug. She squeezes me harder than I can remember her ever having done before. I exhale to accommodate the embrace.

"You look great!" she enthuses.

"Yeah, right. I'm wearing a nasty hospital gown," I say, laughing. I watch my mom, who is sitting in a chair next to the gurney, just staring at me. Her penetrating gaze makes me feel even more naked. I tug on the blanket and pull it up further over my waist.

"How was your flight?" I ask, trying to keep things light.

"Oh, it was fine. Smooth and on time."

"Cool."

"How are you feeling?" She's not trying to keep things light.

"I'm fine. Can you tell?" I turn toward her and take off my glasses and blink. She leans in and stares even more intently.

"Oh yeah, I can tell. Can you feel it? Does it hurt?"

"Nah. It's just really annoying. I can totally feel gravity pulling on my face. It's weird."

"And your head?"

"Oh that. Yeah, it's fine. It really doesn't hurt. It's just this zapping that shoots throughout my head. It's fast."

She grimaces. "How often does it happen?"

"Last weekend, it was only happening about two or three times the whole day. Now it's happening about every five seconds."

We keep talking. The conversation feels normal and neither of us gets emotional. I tell her everything that has happened during the last few days. Then I fill her in on the drama that went down surrounding Kyle and the pills. It feels good to just talk, face to face. Time passes quickly.

"Hello." A woman with wiry, jet black hair is standing in the entrance. "Mrs. Phillips?"

"Yes, hi," my mom replies, standing up.

"Hi, I'm Dr. Spillman."

"Hi, doctor. I'm Hoyt's mom."

"Nice to meet you. And you're Hoyt?" the doctor, quick on the uptake, asks.

"Yes, nice to meet you," I reply, trying not to laugh at the awkwardness slowly creeping up my body.

"Well, I just wanted to stop by and introduce myself and go over what we'll be doing today," she says.

"Okay," my mom says.

"I'll be doing the angiogram, and then Dr. Burns will be going over the results with you all and what the next steps will need to be. So Hoyt, basically, what we will be doing is opening a small artery in your groin and threading a tiny catheter up to your brain. Once there, we'll release dye through the catheter and then take x-rays. These x-rays will help us get a better look at your blood vessels to see what's going on."

I just sit there feeling totally awkward and doing my best to pay attention. This feels way too technical. And I'm not loving the words groin and artery being in the same sentence.

"This isn't painful. We will give you a small dose of a sedative to relax you and then just numb the area where we will insert the catheter. It won't take very long," she says. "Now, I noticed that you're pretty thin. Usually, after this procedure, I like to use this small plug-like device to close up the incision. But I'm not sure you have enough body mass in your thigh for that. I'll just have to play it by ear. If I can't do that, then the only other option is to have you come back here and lie on your back until your body forms a clot. That usually takes several hours. So do you have any questions?"

"Will we know the results of what you find today?" my mom asks.

"Oh yes. Dr. Burns will go over everything with you right after I'm done with the procedure."

"Okay, good," my mom says.

I stay quiet. I don't want to know any more than I absolutely have to. Dr. Spillman leaves and my mom and I continue talking. Before long, I'm wheeled out of the room and the gurney is stopped in a hallway. I lie flat on my back and stare up at the blurry ceiling. My glasses had to be left in the room with my mom. Now I feel naked and I can barely see. I feel way too vulnerable.

"Hoyt?" I hear a sweet voice ask.

"Yes, that's me," I reply, lifting my head slightly.

"Hi, I'm Barbie. I'll be the nurse with you today during the angiogram," Barbie says as she leans over the gurney. My eyes slowly begin to focus. I'm able to make out a helmet of hair-sprayed blond hair, heavy foundation, dark eyeliner, and pale pink lipstick, all on the face of what appears to be a sweet, late fifty-ish looking ... Barbie. *I've got my very own Barbie looking after me.*

I turn my head towards the wall so she can't see the smile creeping across my face. If I'm lucky, there will be a hot Ken waiting for me in the operating room.

"We're gonna get up and I'll walk you into the room here," Barbie explains as she motions to the door that is right behind my head. I sit up and hop off the gurney with my right hand firmly planted against my backside, holding my gown closed. I follow Barbie into the room and am met with bright lights and a shot of cold air. *They must use this room as a meat locker.* Several other people are milling around and take no notice of my entrance.

"Right over here, Hoyt," she says, pointing to a small table. I climb up on the padded table, managing not to flash anyone in the room. Once I'm on my back, I notice bright lights shining down on me. It feels like I'm on one of those medical examiner slabs that I see on *Law & Order*—except I'm not dead. At least, not yet.

"Extend your right arm, please," I hear as I look to my right and see a woman pulling out an extension from the table beneath me. It forms a T and I lay my right arm on it as she straps it down. She attaches a small clip onto my middle finger and then easily inserts an IV in my arm. I feel a flush after the nurse inserts a needle into the IV. I feel gooood.

"Hi, Hoyt, I'm Max." I see this head hovering right in front of my face. He's a nice-looking, fair-skinned man with red hair.

"Hi," I reply, somewhat annoyed that's he's so damned close to my face. I guess they have been told I'm almost blind without my glasses.

"I'm going to prep you now. We need to open the artery in your groin, so I need to shave the area," he says, quickly retreating from my line of sight. *Shave. Did he say shave?* I feel my buzz instantly disappear and quickly glance down toward my feet to see Max opening a plastic bag and pulling out what I assume is a razor. *You've got to be shitting me.*

Cold air. My penis is cold. Max has pulled my gown up and over to my left. *Oh, there we go. Hello everyone! Nice to meet you all.* Yes, I'm naked, in a meat locker, with a bunch of strangers. And now some guy that I can't even see is going to shave my crotch. A straight man is shaving my crotch. This is so not hot. *This can't be happening, this can't be happening. Ohhh.*

I feel a slight tugging on the right side of my groin, and I can't deny what's going on down there. Max has started shaving. *Do they teach this in nursing school?* No one seems to have noticed the intimate moment Max and I are sharing. I'm grateful for the lack of fanfare that my initiation into exhibitionism has elicited, and I do my best not to think about how all this must look.

Before long, I'm shaved and a local anesthetic has been applied to my groin. Dr. Spillman is now in the room, ready to start.

"Okay, Hoyt, we're ready. I'm inserting the catheter now. You won't feel anything," she says. I hear the sound of metal rubbing against metal. It produces that spine-tingling feeling, as if I was scraping my fingernail along the edge of a quarter. I hate it. She is inserting metal in my groin and threading it up to my brain. *This is freaky! And I don't feel a thing.*

Several more minutes pass and then I hear it again. No, I feel it. The friction of the catheter. I feel it ... behind my ear! It passes behind my ear, and then nothing. I don't feel anything or hear anything. I'm still. I'm scared to move, for fear that any jerk on my part will cause the catheter to veer off course and wreak havoc in my body.

I'm doing my best not to think that I now have several feet of metal wire running through my body and into my brain. I stare up at the ceiling. Barbie unexpectedly leans over and pats my head with a wet wash cloth. I hadn't noticed I was sweating.

"Hoyt. we're there. Now what's going to happen is, we are going to inject the dye. You will feel some slight pressure. Then we'll ask you to remain very still while we take the x-ray. Okay?" Dr. Spillman asks.

"Okay," I reply, suddenly feeling very nervous at the thought of anything being injected into my brain.

Whoa, what's that? Barbie is sliding this massive, white, round instrument over my head. It must be suspended from the ceiling! It's huge, larger than my head, larger than this table I'm on. And it's right above my head. Right above, maybe ten inches, if that. *God, I hope this thing is bolted in tight. I'll be decapitated if it falls.*

"Everyone out," I hear someone say. The room empties faster than a pint of ice cream during my last binge. I lift my head slightly and see everyone walk behind a wall at the other end of the room. There is a large, plate glass window that everyone is now staring at me through. *Great, here I am, the lab rat strapped to a table with wires hanging out of my crotch, about to be injected with dye and lit up like a glow stick.*

"Okay Hoyt, we're injecting it now. Hold still, please," Dr. Spillman instructs me.

Warmth. Warmth floods my head. Thick, slow-moving warmth envelopes my brain. It's awesome and so much better than the cold griping my chest and groin. It's the total opposite of the brain freeze from drinking a Slurpee too fast. I hear zapping, not in my brain. This time it's coming from above my head, from the massive machine hanging over my head with its rays penetrating my brain. It's the familiar sounds of an x-ray machine.

Then it's over and everyone is back in the room. The doctor maneuvers the catheter some more and again, everyone exits. Again,

I'm overcome with warmth. This goes on for a while longer. By about the third time, the warmth is accompanied with pressure. Significant pressure in the back of my head. It feels like the dye is pooling at the back of my head. It doesn't feel good, and I'm ready for this experiment to be over with.

"Okay, that's it. We're all done," Dr. Spillman announces as I hear the sound of the catheter snaking its way out of my body. It takes a while for her to pull all of the metal out of me.

Ahhh, ohhh God. Pain. My groin is screaming. Tugging. There is this tugging on my groin. *Oh my God, this kills!* My chest heaves up and my back arches. I now feel the sweat rolling down my hairline. *Damn it, this hurts.*

"Oh God, oh God, oh God ... it hurts," I moan.

"Just hold on," I hear the doctor tell me. *You hold on, bitch! This hurts. Oh great, here we go . . . ugggg.* My head jerks up along with my stomach. My mouth opens and nothing happens. It's just a dry heave. Nothing comes up. Now I know why they tell you not to eat before the procedure. I'd be puking right now if I could.

"It's okay Hoyt, just hold on," Barbie coos to me as she wipes my faces with a wonderfully cool, wet cloth. *Ahh, that feels nice*—but I can't savor the moment. My groin screams back at me. This crazy-ass doctor is trying to sew me up, and the local anesthetic has worn off! I can feel every pull and every inch of the sutures she is trying to place in my groin. And I feel them not holding. This isn't working. *Oh God, please stop!*

"You okay?"

"Yeah, I'm fine," I shoot back. My body is aching and now I'm lying flat on the gurney, back in the room where I started. I have a small sandbag draped across my right thigh to help with the clotting process. My mom is sitting beside me, looking worried. I don't feel like talking. I'm pissed. Not only did I get to feel stitches ripping out of my groin, but now, because they didn't take, I get to lie flat on my back for five hours while my body naturally clots the incision. What the hell am I going to do for five hours? On my back, no less, with my mother in the room!

I eventually calm down and my mom and I do what we do best. We talk. And we talk. Time goes by quickly again. I'm grateful when Nora brings a large plate of fresh fruit. Starving, I inhale everything. It tastes incredible, and eating on my back isn't as difficult as I would have imagined. After a couple of hours, Nora cranks my bed up several degrees. I'm told that every hour or so, my bed can be raised a couple of degrees.

"Umm, Mom, I need some privacy. I've got to go," I sheepishly tell her, glancing at the small, plastic jug that is on the table next to my gurney.

"Oh, okay. Sure. Here you go," she says as she hands me the jug. She leaves and closes the curtain. Sliding the sandbag off my thigh, I pull down the sheets and lift up my gown. *Huh, Max did a nice job.* It's pretty smooth, at least on the right side.

The jug is long and at the end it bends upwards. This looks simple enough. I place it between my legs, place my penis inside the opening and then look up. Thinking about a waterfall helps me relax enough to pee. It's flowing and then ... warmth. Damn it, I'm not supposed to feel anything. I clench and stop the stream. Shit! Looking down I notice I have slipped out of the jug and have managed to piss myself. I place my penis back in the jug and finish my business.

I'm not wet enough to tell anyone. Plus, I don't want some nurse changing me. I'll be fine. I place the cap on the jug and yell for my mom to come back. She sets the jug on the table and we continue talking while I try my best to shift my weight around on the bed so I don't feel the wet spot.

"Hello there." I look up to see a thin, fifty-ish looking man wearing a white lab coat and dark glasses.

"Hello," my mom and I say together.

"I'm Dr. Burns," he announces.

"Hi, nice to meet you," my mom says as she stands.

"So, how are you doing?" he asks, making eye contact but not stepping any closer. He is still standing at the front, by the curtain.

"I'm fine, thanks," I reply. He's a textbook photo of a nerd. He just looks geeky, but like a smart geek. I doubt just anyone can become a neurosurgeon.

"Sorry it's taken me so long. I had to review all the x-rays," he says. Checking the clock on the wall, I notice I've been here about six hours. It doesn't feel like it's been that long.

"So I've reviewed everything, and the angiogram really hasn't told me much more," he says. "The purpose of this was to get a look at what's causing the seizures. As you know, we thought at first that it was an aneurysm. But the angiogram isn't showing that. If it was an active aneurysm, the dye would have flowed into it and that would have shown up on the film." He's talking pretty quickly, almost as if he's nervous.

"So it could be a plugged aneurysm, meaning it's been clotted off—and that's a good thing," he continues. "Or it could be a tumor. But the odd thing is the location. This is at a fork in the blood vessel," he says as he holds up his left hand, making a peace sign.

"Whatever this is, it's right here," he says as he points to the bottom of the V his fore finger and middle finger are forming.

"This is where most aneurysms form. They are basically a bulge in the blood vessel. So it's an unusual place for a tumor. But it could also be some remnants of an infection," he says. Now he's looking up to his right, almost as if he's searching for ideas. This guy now seems to be brainstorming what possibilities are inside my head. He's talking faster and faster with each new theory. My mom is standing, frozen. All I can do is lie in this bed and listen to him. This doesn't seem real.

"Yeah, and so you need to have surgery. You really need to do it in within the next two weeks. And what we would do is be prepared for whatever it is. So if it's a tumor, we would remove that. If it's an aneurysm, we may remove it, or we may apply like a clip to it and just leave it. One tricky thing is, when you operate on the brain, you don't have much time. You have to get in and get out. So one option would be to cool your body temperature. We could lower it with ice," he spits out. *Ice. You want to put me on ice? I'm cold now. I can't imagine what lying in ice is going to feel like. You're nuts.*

This guy is basically standing in the corner of the room, just spouting off. He's having a conversation with himself as my mom and I just stare at him. This guy is weird. He's talking, but he doesn't really seem to care if we're listening or not.

"Yeah, so that's it—and like I said, you need to have this done soon. I wouldn't wait. And there is the possibility that you could stroke and need some rehab after the surgery. So yeah. So, it's your decision. You want to have it done here?" he asks, looking right at me.

"No. I want it done in North Carolina," I demand. My body is totally stiff and my mind has been racing since I heard the words "stroke" and "rehab". I've been in rehab the past two months. This rehab I can handle—but rehab because of a stroke would be screwed up. I can't do that. I don't want to think about that. I just know that, if I have to have my head spilt open, I want it done at home where I can be taken care of by people I know. *Wisconsin, you've been great, but you're not home.*

"Okay, I understand. But one thing is, you can't fly back. If this is an aneurysm, any change in cabin pressure could cause it to burst and you'll die." He says this as if he's telling me the weather. *Die. Die? I could die from this?* My chest rises and falls quickly three times. I do my best to catch myself, but it's too late. My eyes well up almost instantly. *Die. No, no, this can't be happening.* Until now this was just some sort of weird dream or exercise. No one mentioned death. But now it's not so dreamlike. *Die. I could die.*

My mom and Dr. Burns leave the room, close the curtain, and talk in the hallway. I'm not sure if they leave because they can tell I'm upset or not. I quickly regain my composure and do my best to try to hear what is being said. I can't. They must have walked down the hall. After several long minutes, my mom returns. She's calm, but I can tell she's shaken.

The next few hours pass slowly. We talk some more, but this time it's more serious. She has to make plans tomorrow to get a one-way rental car, and I have to face the fact that I will be leaving Rogers sooner than I had planned.

Around six that night, I'm wheeled out of the hospital. I'm not allowed to walk out, which is fine by me. I'm terrified that, at any moment, the clot that has formed in my groin is going to break free and I will start gushing blood from my crotch. Of course, it didn't help that Nora told me that if I start bleeding, I have to get to the ER immediately. The thoughts of bleeding to death from my crotch is just … embarrassing.

We ride back to Rogers mostly in silence, both of us lost in our thoughts. My mom tells me she will be by tomorrow in the afternoon so that we can make arrangements for me to leave. We set a tentative plan to leave early Saturday morning. I walk back into the unit stiff-legged, trying my best not to move my right side. I don't want to upset the clot.

I eat the nightly snack, since I barely ate all day. After watching a movie with the guys, both Kyle and J.R. head to bed. I stay back in the day room. Knowing that tomorrow will be pretty tough, I open up my notebook and start writing. After finishing, I do my daily wrap-up:

> *Day 57: Thurs. August 15:*
>
> *Well, leaving soon—have to have surgery! Numb and totally scared!*

40

It's so peaceful. I'm sitting on a bench looking out over Bulimia Pond. Just a few days ago, Kyle, J.R., and I were ceremoniously splashing around in the water. I can't help but wonder what I'm going to miss.

A week ago, my life was trucking along normally. Now I feel like I've been shot out of a canon and am hurtling back toward earth, and I'm afraid there isn't anything below to break my fall. My face feels like it's falling off, my head is still zapping every few seconds, my equilibrium is shot—and now I have to leave this place in the morning so that I can go back to North Carolina to have brain surgery. And no matter what anyone says, that surgery might find something that will change the rest of my life or even end it.

Leaning back, I exhale and readjust my butt on the bench, which is so damned hard that I have to lean to my left and put most of my weight on my left butt cheek. *I don't want to leave. It's so beautiful here and I feel safe.*

Kyle and J.R. have been great. They feel like the brothers that I always wanted. This is so fucked up. I don't like this feeling. I hate this feeling! I've been running away from feeling this way my whole life. Not being in control is scary. I don't know what's going to happen. And now for the first time in months, my body is calling the shots. I don't have any say in the matter.

For as long as I can remember, I've been trying to dominate my environment and my body. When life finally became too much, I shut down and started sadistically dominating my body. I was starving it, but at least I was the one doing it. I had the control. Now I have no control. I can't change this and I have to surrender to it.

As I shift my weight to my right butt cheek, I can't help but wonder if this is some sick, cosmic joke. Is my body now having its revenge for the hell I've put it through?

"Hey."

I sit up straight and turn to my left, hearing the one voice that can instantly ease my mind.

"Hey, Mom."

"How are you?" She walks around and sits on the bench next to me.

"I'm hanging in there." I try to add a slight laugh.

"How's your groin?"

"Fine," I reply, not elaborating. I don't feel that comfortable talking with my mother about that area of my body. Thankfully, the incision area seems to have healed quickly. I'm not walking around as stiffly today, although I had some trippy dreams last night about blood gushing from various body parts.

"Well, I talked to Rogers and let them know that you're leaving today," she says.

"Okay, thanks." I stare straight in front of me. This day is just too beautiful for something so dark to be happening to me. It should be storming, or at least cloudy. Then again, 9/11 was a gorgeous day as well. It just doesn't make sense. Life is going on as if nothing bad is happening. I don't like it.

"So what's the plan?" I ask, needing to know what to expect.

"Well, I've gotten a new, one-way rental car. It's nice. It's a Buick SUV. I called your dad and got directions back home," she says. "So we'll leave first thing in the morning. It's going to be a trek, but I think we can do it in one day."

"Okay," is all I can manage to say.

"I was able to get Dr. Howard on the phone. You know, she's my gynecologist. She went to Harvard, so I figured she would know the best surgeon. She gave me a name and number at Duke. I have a call into them. We should be able to get you in there." Leave it to my mom to find the best surgeon in the state.

"I guess I'll pack my things. Should I go back to the hotel with you tonight?" As I ask, I turn to my right and face my mom, but it startles me, so I look down. My mind isn't prepared to make eye contact. It feels too intense and personal right now. The energy between us is calm but restrained. Lurking just beneath the surface, I know there is a reservoir of pain and fear just waiting to burst forth. Neither of us is willing to release it. We have to keep moving. We have to make it home. We can't afford to get lost in emotions right now.

"Yeah, that would be best, since we have to leave so early tomorrow," she says.

I look up and stare at her face. My face tingles and my glasses feel heavy. My mom, with her soft features and unshakable love for me, is just staring back at me. Her eyes penetrate my soul and I'm gone. The wall that has been holding me together crumbles. My body quivers, my gut lurches upwards, and tears instantly fill my eyes. I feel like my three-year-old self who just skinned his knee falling off his bike, running into the arms of the only person who can comfort me.

"It's okay, Jeff. It's going to be okay," she says softly, leaning toward me as I unconsciously fall into her. Her arms instinctively wrap around me and she slowly rocks me back and forth. Tears are now falling down both of my cheeks. I try not to make a sound and do my best to catch my breath. For the first time in days, I'm not holding back and I'm not putting on a brave front.

"It's okay. It's going to be okay," she says over and over again. She's reassuring both of us at this point.

"I'm good. I'm okay. Thanks," I say after several moments. I sit up and break away from her embrace. The release felt good, but now I need to get it together. I sit up and turn back around so I'm facing forward again. Then I look down at my watch and notice I don't have long before my last group.

"I think I'm gonna go pack before group. That way, after group I'll be ready to leave," I tell her. This will give me some much-needed time alone before I have to say good-bye to everyone.

"Okay, I'll be here,' she says. We hug and I leave.

Well, that's it. As I look over my suitcase, I'm surprised at how easy it was to pack. But since this wasn't a vacation, I'm leaving with pretty much the same amount of stuff that I arrived here with. *Okay, I can do this. It's not good-bye, it's just so long for now.*

I head out the door and walk down the hall to the day room. The emotional release with Mom earlier has given me the room to revert back to autopilot mode. I'm not feeling much right now, and that is fine by me.

Group goes well. The conversation is not centered on me the whole time, which I appreciate. I now know why some people keep their illness to themselves. That feeling of being treated with kid gloves is infuriating. And the feeling that life has suddenly changed and you're living in a *Twilight Zone* episode is unnerving. My mind keeps scrambling for something unchanging to focus on, but it can't find it. Everything seems to be changing around me.

All I want to do is go back to before I was sick, to when everything was normal and I wasn't the recipient of sympathetic glances or reassuring axioms.

I wander in and out of most of the conversation. I have an amazing ability to be there but not, to disassociate and not enjoy the moment. Of course, I'm not sure I really want to enjoy most moments these days. The dread of what could be coming next keeps me from truly engaging. But I'm not sure this is a bad thing. Survival right now is paramount. I can't afford to fall apart.

Before long, group is almost over, and I realize I need to say good-bye. I knew I wouldn't be able to do this coherently on the fly, so I stayed up the night before writing what I need to say.

"Uhh, Sue, if you don't mind … I, uhh, hate good-byes, but I've written something I'd like to read to you all."

"Oh, sure, Hoyt. Please go ahead," Sue says.

"Well, this is hard. I honestly don't view this as a good-bye, but I wrote down a few things that I wanted to say. So here goes," I say as I look down and start reading from my notebook.

> *Well, as I sit here in the day room and write this, it's 1 a.m. on Friday morning. I can honestly say I'll be leaving this place as scared as I came in. Now, of course, the reasons for my fears are different. I remember eight weeks ago and recall my intense fear of food, eating with these new strangers, and recovery in general. I remember wondering, how could I ever conquer this? Well, fast forward two months and I can honestly say that fear has been conquered to where I feel it's manageable and no longer controls my life. That came about because of all of you. Your support, guidance, encouragement and—most importantly—love have helped me to face my fear and start to move beyond it.*
>
> *Kyle, I remember when I first met you and thought to myself, "Lord, what have I gotten myself into? What could I possibly have in common with a fifteen-year-old kid?" Little did I know what was in store for me. The more appropriate question I ask myself now is, "How will he ever know how blessed I've been to have been in his presence on this journey?" I'll never forget Tetris, your smiley face wrist band, black hats, smoke breaks, the diet soda pyramid, Tainted Love, Lucky Charms, "Army of Darkness," Bulimia Pond—and of course, my personal favorite, twenty-minute bathroom breaks at the movies. I marvel at your strength, courage, and insight and have been all the better to be on the receiving end of your loving support. If you had to come back a second time, I'm thankful I could be here.*

J.R., I remember my first day here and before we met hearing all these wonderful compliments about you. I was thinking, yeah, right, this kid can't be this great. Now I think to myself everyone was just being modest. You're even more incredible than they said. I'll never forget journaling, Mozart, Blockbuster rewards card, the diet soda pyramid, "Army of Darkness," Bulimia Pond, Final Fantasy soundtracks, and Rummy 500. From my first day, I have been in awe of your honesty, integrity, and willingness to put yourself on the line in order to push us further along our recovery journey. I have to admit, I was pretty fucking (explicative inserted for Kyle's benefit) nervous about having a roommate. I can honestly say I don't think I could have made one any better than you.

And then there's Sue. Gosh, what can I say? You basically know everything about me, warts and all, and you haven't run screaming for the hills. So you're either on track for sainthood or the loony bin—probably a little bit of both. Honestly, though, I can say that the group and individual therapy sessions have been the most electrifying and fulfilling therapy and personal experiences I have ever had. All this is in part thanks to you. Thank you for making me feel like my words always fell on sympathetic, understanding, non-judgmental ears and for never once making me feel ashamed or weird for anything I told you. It has made a world of difference to me.

I have hope because I can look back on my time here at Rogers and see how I was able to confront my fear and win. So now, in this uncertain time regarding my health, I know I can confront this fear, because you all have shown me how wonderful life can be when you truly allow yourself to be supported. I know without a shadow of a doubt that, no matter where we all are, we will be supporting each other, and that all of us will continue in a forward direction down our recovery road. And if anyone gets turned around, feel free to give me a call and I will be more than happy to provide a swift kick in the ass to get you in the proper direction. Life is measured in love, and we have shown here we have plenty of it!

I exhale and close my notebook. I wrote those words and now I've just read them, but I'm not sure I feel them. Sheepishly looking up, I'm met with the penetrating gaze of three beautiful people. Sue gives me a coin that's given to everyone on their last day. On one side it says: "To Thine Own Self Be True." On the other side: "God grant me the serenity to accept the things I cannot change, courage to change the things I can, and wisdom to know the difference."

I smile and feel proud. *I earned this, damn it!* I drop the coin in my right pants pocket and rub my forefinger over it. It feels nice.

We stand and hold hands. As we say our mantra, I smile, trying to prevent my tears from making an encore appearance. We hug. I look over their heads as tears fill my eyes. We hug again and make promises to keep in touch. I shut down as soon as my mind tries to interject the harsh reality that I will probably never see these people again.

I slip my book bag on and begin to roll my large suitcase down the hall to the elevator. Fifty-eight days after my arrival, this time I enter the elevator with my mom. As the doors close, I say good-bye to the home where I started learning to live. I hope that it wasn't for nothing.

PART III

Recovery

41

Saturday, August 24, 2002

So last Saturday mom and I got up at 5:15 a.m. and left by 6 a.m. We didn't get home till fifteen hours later. We got to see Illinois, Indiana, Ohio, West Virginia, and North Carolina. Pretty crazy!

Now, a week later, I have a surgery date set for the day after Labor Day, September 3. I think my brain has gone back into survival mode. None of this seems real. My eating has been pretty decent. No active restriction until today, and that's because I ate a lot of chocolate cake someone brought over. Everyone has kept saying how wonderful I've been doing. Maybe I don't want to be such the good little boy! But it's also hard to short-change myself because I always hear the Rogers voices over my shoulder, asking if that would be good for me. Lord, they got under my skin.

I think I'm starting to get mad and very scared. I'm mad at what this tumor has done to my life. In one fell swoop, it blasted me out of treatment. I didn't get the normal good-bye and relapse-prevention counseling. I feel like my wonderful, safe treatment world was deflated and I was pushed into the big, bad, hard world of reality too soon.

I'm mad at how this further complicates what my next step will be. I may not have a choice about my job—I may just lose it. Then how the hell am I going to pay for my apartment? It looks more and more everyday like I will be leaving N.Y. without another formal good-bye. That really pisses me off. I'm also scared that I might not have the stamina and patience to live here with Mom and Dad again. They're great, but I still have issues, and plus it's just plain hard coming home again. Then again, maybe this is what I need to do to change my life in a more healthy way.

I'm scared. Just plain scared. Not scared about surgery or cancer but scared of what happens next. I can handle the big life traumas. It's everyday life that scares me. I just want to be happy!

I'm also mad because I have to write a good-bye letter to everyone in case I don't survive the surgery. What twenty-five –year-old should have to write something like that?

I guess the best way to sum up all of this is that it's freaking surreal. The mind has an incredible capacity to fool itself into thinking everything is okay and to keep functioning as normal. I think that may be good and healthy, because Lord knows we'd never get anything done or be able to live life if we were falling apart all the time. I honestly wouldn't change or trade any of this. My time at Rogers was wonderful, and years from now, I'll probably still be gleaning wisdom from that place. It was truly a godsend.

Thursday, August 29, 2002

Well, reality has set in more. Last weekend, I got into restricting some because the reality of everything was hitting me. It shocked me and scared me how easily my ED crept back in. I was like a duck in water. I'm now back on track. I guess it is true you can always go back to where you've been.

This week, I talked to J.R. and it was weird. I felt numb. It was great to talk to him, but I'm afraid I might be doing the "keep going forward and never look back" routine. It's easier to run from those awkward feelings than to face them—or so it seems.

I find myself in the mindset of not wanting anyone to visit me other than family after the surgery. And I know for a fact that's my way of shunning support and not wanting to open up and be vulnerable. Again, it's easier to run than to stop, feel, and process those feelings. On this front, I know I'll be pushed, because there are a lot of people saying that they are going to come visit.

I met with the dietician today and that went well. I feel pretty good about my weight because she said she's not going to let me go over 165 pounds. So that sounds doable to me—not great, but doable. So I really only have a little more than ten pounds to gain, then. It's scary right now because it's easy. I'm still not really in recovery. I just have to follow a plan. But once I hit that weight, the hard work starts. I'll have to maintain it. I'll really have to be listening to myself and monitoring for warning signs.

I've been trying a lot lately not to think about surgery. It's successful some of the time. At times, when I do think about it, I'm scared about what happens next. Part of me feels like I need it to be a malignant tumor. I feel bad saying that, but that's how I feel. I think I might need it to be cancer so that it really drills home the importance of life and helps me get in touch with some of those emotions. I know, though, that me wanting it to be cancer is an avoidance of the next step in my life and a desire to stay in this cocoon of support I've found myself in the last few weeks. This cocoon is safe because nothing is required of me. I'm taken care of, I'm given a lot of attention, and I don't have to think for myself or decide what I'm going to do. Everyone around me, including my-self, is in crisis mode, and it's easy. In crisis mode, you don't have to really deal with life. And that deep-seated, shameful desire of wanting—almost needing—attention is fed by being so sick right now. I'm getting all the attention I thought I ever wanted. And my ego is saying it was right, because the only way you can get that attention you feel you need is by being sick. You don't get a medal or reward for being healthy in our society. You get it for be being sick.

The fucked up part is that I don't feel better getting all this attention. Part of me, and it's probably the healthy part, wants this to stop. This isn't filling the void. It's only making it bigger. I know, somehow, that I have to be healthy and fill the void myself. No one and nothing can do that for me. And there's the rub—I have to step up and do it for myself, and shit if I know how to do that!

It's funny. I think my brain tumor has been the talk of the town. The phone rings off the hook. You would think it's a big deal or something. People treat you differently. They look at you funny and ask you stupid questions. It's almost like they expect you to be hunched over and twitching or something. I'm like I'm just fine—you can't tell by looking at me or talking to me. It's not like I'm a walking time bomb, even though I was afraid that's what I was.

It's horrifying if I allow myself to think about it. They are going to knock me out, tube me, and drill into my head and then take out a chunk of my skull. Afterwards, I'll be in ICU for a day. For all of this trouble, I feel like it had better be something big—like cancer—or else I'm going to be pissed. I guess my mind can't fully grasp it, so I run and shut down. I have noticed that, as I get closer to the date, I'm more anxious and uptight.

42

Wow, *I look different.* I lean forward over my bathroom counter and peer into the mirror. I'm trying to decide whether I like my hair. After the brain surgeon told me he was not going to shave my head for the surgery, I decided to get my hair dyed. If he had said he was going to shave my head, I was going to go platinum blond. But since I will be keeping all my hair, I went a more conservative route and had it dyed a darker blond, or honey, color. It definitely is different, but I'm not sure I'm really sold on it. At least it doesn't jump out at you.

Part of me really wishes my head was going to be shaved, because then I could have gone all out with some wild color. Whatever. I run my hands through my hair and style it the best I can. With my glasses on and my face still giving me trouble, I'm not able to focus very long.

I leave the bathroom and finish getting dressed. As I strap on my watch, I glance at the time. Seventeen hours. In seventeen hours, we will be driving to Duke University Hospital. And this time tomorrow, I will be in ICU, hopefully.

It's weird. This last day of freedom should feel different. I feel like I should be wanting to go paint the town red or, on the flip side, be curled up in the fetal position in bed. For some odd reason, though, it just feels like any other day. I don't feel all that different, but in a few hours, my whole life could change.

I choose not to dwell on my apathy. Instead, I walk down the hall. I can hear voices coming out of Jessica's bedroom. I step in, but no one is in there. Then I realize the voices are coming from her bathroom, so I peek in.

"Hey, what are ya'll doing?" I ask, standing in the doorway. Instantly, my heart skips a beat. The energy isn't what I was expecting. It's heavy. Even though the sun is brilliantly lighting the room and filling it with a warm glow, the mood in here is anything but sunny. Jessica is sitting in her chair slumped over, and Amy is sitting on the toilet with the lid down.

"Oh nothing, just sitting here talking," Jessica says not looking up at me. I can tell she is upset. *Damn, I can't very well just turn around and leave, though I would love to.* I don't really want to be in the middle of some emotional conversation right now.

"Yeah, Jessie and I were just talking about you," Amy says, squinting her eyes at me, almost as if she's ordering me to stay. Big sisters have a way of barking out orders without saying a word.

"Oh yeah?" I say as casually as I can, hoping these few words will not elicit much elaboration.

"Yeah, she's finally let down. She's scared," Amy says matter-of-factly.

"I'm fine," Jessica interjects, trying to get Amy to shut-up.

"What's wrong?" I ask. I know I need to be the nice big brother and fully engage in this conversation.

"I'm fine," Jessica says, sitting up straight and running her left hand through her hair.

"Yeah, right. We've been talking. She's scared about what's going to happen," Amy informs me.

"What are you scared about?" I ask, looking right at Jessica.

"Ugh, I'm just ... I don't know ... I'm just scared. It's scary not knowing what's going to happen. You know, if something bad happens," she says, briefly making eye contact with me.

"It's okay, you can say it. You're scared I won't make it," I say. I smile, trying to lighten the mood and address the one topic no one has dared broach with me. Now that I feel a bit more comfortable because I'm in control of the conversation, I walk into the bathroom and sit on the floor facing Jessica.

"Yeah, I guess," she replies, staring down at the floor.

"I know, I'm scared, too. It's messed up. But I know I have the best surgeon, and he feels like it's going to go well," I reassure her. I guess it's my fate today to play Positive Patty, even though it seems screwed up that the sick one—the one who may not live through this—has to be the strong one.

"Yeah, I know," Jessica says.

"I mean, think about it, Jess. I've been through 9/11 and an eating disorder all within the past year. If those things didn't get me, I doubt a little brain tumor will." I decide to play the logic card. It seems like a sound argument to me. The odds *should* be in my favor.

"Yeah, it has been a wild year," Jessica admits.

"You can say that again!" I laugh.

"Yeah, it's been all about Jeff all year long," Amy adds, grinning. She loves to tease me and Jessica about how much we got away with, but I know this little comment is shrouded in truth. I can only imagine the endless hours I've been the topic of conversation, and how many times Amy and Jessica have had to listen to Mom worry about me.

"Well, what can I say? I'm just an interesting guy." I shrug and smile right back at her.

"So, you think it's a brain tumor?" Jessica asks.

"Gosh, I don't know. I just keep saying that. The surgeon seemed to be leaning that way, but who knows? I guess this time tomorrow we'll find out." I turn to Amy and ask, "How are you doing?"

"Oh, I'm good. I know you'll be fine, and I'm looking forward to seeing what they do and how the ICU is," she says lightly. Leave it to my older sister to be practical. I know she's in nursing school and this is probably proving to be a great teaching moment for her.

"Oh, great. Well, you're not allowed to do anything to me. I know I have great veins, but stay away!" I laugh again, but I mean every word.

"Oh, come on!" Amy says laughing. I notice Jessica has perked up some and is smiling now.

"I'm just excited about the drugs," I say. "I better have some damned good dreams or an out-of-body experience."

"Yeah, that would be cool," Jessica comments.

"So, how have Mom and Dad been?" I ask.

"Oh, they're fine, I guess. Mom's pretty worried about you, and she's scared you're going to relapse and stop eating after the surgery. You are going to keep eating aren't you?" Amy asks, glaring at me.

"I know everyone is scared I'm going to relapse. But I'm going to keep eating. I'll be good. I met with the dietician and I'm on a plan. So it's all good," I say as convincingly as possible. I don't mention that being doped up on drugs will prevent me from gaining weight and might even cause me to lose.

"So what time are we leaving tomorrow?" Jessica asks.

"I think around five," I answer.

"5 a.m.?" Amy asks, shocked.

"Uh, yeah. I have to be there at six, I think," I reply.

"Damn, that's early," Amy says.

"I know, but at least there won't be any traffic on the road."

"Are we taking two cars?" Jessica asks.

"Yeah, I think. And I'm totally riding with ya'll." I love my parents, but after a fifteen- hour trip with Mom the other week, I've had my fill.

"Sounds good," Amy says.

"So ya'll didn't say anything about my hair today. You like it?" I ask, wanting some reassurance of my own.

"Oh yeah, it looks good!" Amy says enthusiastically.

"Yeah, I like it," Jessica says.

"Thanks. But I'm still wondering how I would have looked with platinum blond hair." "Oh yeah, you should have done that," Amy says.

"I was too scared to do it after I found out that the surgeon isn't going to shave my head."

"Really? He's not shaving your head?" Jessica asks.

"No. He said he wouldn't need to. He'll just shave a small line where he makes his incision."

"What side?" Amy asks.

"It's the left side. I think it's straight back behind my left eye."

"Oh, okay. So is it affecting your vision?" Amy asks.

"No, not at all. And I think my Bell's Palsy is getting better. At least the pressure on my face feels a bit lighter."

"That's good," Amy says.

"Yeah. I was bummed, though, because Mom called the woman who gives her massages to see if she could give me one before surgery, and she wouldn't do it. She was concerned that, since I was dealing with something in my brain, the increased blood flow from a massage could affect what's going on with me."

"Oh yeah, I could see that," Amy says.

"So, are you feeling better?" I ask Jessica.

"Yeah, thanks."

"Good. It's going to be okay," I add as I stand up and leave Jessica and Amy to finish getting ready.

The rest of the day goes by fast. Nothing really exciting happens. We have dinner at home and then spend a couple of hours sitting around the table talking about world issues. In a way, it feels nice to be talking about something other than me and what will be happening in the next few hours. In another way, it feels like no one is willing to talk about the pink elephant in the room. We all know that, within the next few hours, our family could be changed forever.

I feel bad that I'm the cause of all of this uncertainty and pain, but I also know I'm not up to the emotional task of talking about it right now. I feel too responsible and always feel the need to reassure everyone. And right now, I'm not up to that. I know my family must be hurting, but I don't want to have to make them feel better. Plus, I don't know that things will get better. It may get worse, and I'm scared for them about that. I know I have the easy job.

I'm the first one to excuse myself for the night. I'm exhausted and I need to write letters to everyone. I say good-night and go to my room. Sitting at my desk, I take out my journal first. I need to write down a few thoughts, just in case.

> *Monday, September 2, 2002*
> *Well, it's about 11 p.m. Monday night, and in a few hours I have to get up to drive to Duke for my surgery. I can honestly think of a few other things I'd rather do.*
> *Just now, we all were sitting at the dinner table debating world issues. It was good and we talked for a long time. I know everyone is struggling and I just hope they can get some sleep. I would take away all their worry and fear if I could.*
> *It's weird thinking this could be my last journal entry. Puts things in perspective. I don't know what to say. I'm more afraid of the lack of direction in my life than I am of not waking up—that would be easy—too easy, I guess.*
> *These last few weeks have been a wild ride, and I wouldn't change any of it. I've been pushed in areas I've needed to be pushed in for a long time. I've grown so much. I'm so thankful!*
> *So if this is my last earthly journal entry, or just an end of a chapter, I'd like to quote a song the Divine M sings in "Beaches" that I think pretty much sums it all up: "You've got to laugh a little, cry a little, and always have the blues a little. Because that's the story of, that's the glory of love."*

I close my journal and smile. The sound of muffled voices permeates my room. My bedroom is right above the kitchen, so it's never totally quiet. It's nice to know I'm not alone. After listening for a few moments, I take out the notebook I was using at Rogers. Opening to a clean page, I freeze. My heart starts to pound harder, my stomach feels heavy, and my breath quickens.

I know I need to do this. Sue even told me I needed to do this—but now I'm not sure I can. A letter. A good-bye letter to my family. How the hell do I write this? What do I say? This is just … fucked up! If they read this, then it means I'm dead. If that happens, I don't know that anything I say could ever ease that pain.

I take a deep breath and do what I always did as a kid when I was apprehensive about getting into a cold swimming pool. I shut off my mind and just jump in.

> *Dear Mom and Dad,*
>
> *Well, if you're reading this, then I guess it means I have transitioned on. The thoughts of having to sit here and write a letter to my parents in the event of my death, to let them know what I want to leave them with, is very overwhelming. In one regard, it seems unnatural—the child shouldn't be leaving this world before the parents. But in another regard, it does seem natural. You saw me safely in, and now you get to see me safely out. That brings me peace and comfort.*
>
> *In regards to what I want to say to you, I think the most sincere and direct thing is thank you! I have never wanted for anything in my life. You two were wonderful providers and gave me a solid foundation to experience life. I don't think I could find more supportive parents. I never once felt anything I needed or wanted to do was either unattainable or an unworthy pursuit in your eyes. I have to say, for every curve ball I've been throwing since I was two, you both seem to handle them with grace and composure—no matter how hard I tried to catch you off-guard. For all of this- and of course the love, I thank you!*
>
> *I guess it's that time in the conversation that I'm supposed to end with some words of wisdom or advice. Now me giving advice to my parents—I think I could get used to this. I guess if I could say one thing, it is to keep pushing yourselves emotionally, to learn and to live life. We are put here to learn and to grow emotionally through our interactions with people. We*

don't do that by sticking to the same old boring routine and coming home every night and doing the same thing. Get out there and learn—interact with people. Experience life.

We learn in the hard times and good times. And right now I'm sure is a really bad time. Push yourself. Better yourself. Don't run from emotional things. Deal with it—face it head on. Allow it to mold you so you become stronger and smarter. When we run and try to exert too much control, that's when we really lose ourselves and never gain what we are seeking.

Please know I'm in a much better place. Never doubt that, even as clichéd as it sounds. You have the hard path to walk ahead of you. You can run from it and choose not to live life fully, or you can make the harder and more courageous choice and face it head on. Deal with it—feel the pain and then work through it and know in the end you'll be the better for it. I'm looking forward to our reunion. It will be sooner than you think.

It's been one hell of a ride, one I wouldn't trade for anything. I love you and I will see you soon. So again I say, thank you!

Love,

Jeff

I drop my pen on the page and rub my left hand. I did it again. Gripping that pen for dear life has cramped my hand. I just stare for a while at the blank wall in front of my desk. I don't really feel much of anything. That's not a very long letter, but I don't feel like I have anything else to say. Plus, writing exhausts me these days. With my face and head, it's hard to sit here and write. I know I can't say everything. I just need to trust that, if they read this, the spirit of it will somehow comfort them.

Okay, just one more left to do. I turn the page and start.

Dear Amy and Jessica,

Well, I won't say what all these letters open up with by saying that if you're reading this then I guess that it means I died. Oh well, I just did—sorry, I couldn't resist. Okay, I'll get serious now.

Honestly, having to write this letter really sucks. It seems too large a task to write in one letter what I feel about you two and want to leave you with. One thing is for certain: nothing I write could possibly express the love I feel for you two nor how much you two have given me over the years. The passion, love, and grace you two express have truly blown me away and made me so much better off to be on the receiving end of it. I have been honored and blessed just to be in your presence. The unwavering love and support you two always showed me never ceased to amaze me. So for making my life Technicolor, I thank you!

If I could leave you two with one thing, it would be to never lose your passion! You both are so passionate—that's what I loved about you all. You both definitely kept life interesting. I think the one reason you two were so spread out in age is, if you were closer and we all were under one roof longer, the passion would have killed us all (sorry, that last sentence may not have been appropriate given my state, but sometimes the truth isn't appropriate). So live life and stay passionate. I have no doubt you both will.

Amy, all the best with nursing. I know every patient will be better off for having you. You'll be great! Thank you to you and Craig both for letting me be a part of your sons' lives. They are great boys, and when I look at them I feel a sense of that intense love that would do anything. They truly are a gift. You and Craig are wonderful parents.

Jessica, never lose sight of your passion and go for it! I know you will make a great doctor. Go out there and show them how it's done! I also can't wait to meet your children some day and your husband of course—that is, if you have one. Not that you have to have one or anything—there's nothing wrong with being single.

I know it's going to be hard for a while, but know I'm with you every step. It takes a whole lot more courage and strength to face life and deal with it than to run. Feel it, experience it, work through it, learn from it, and live life. You take the good with the bad (I'll stop there before I break out into the "Facts of Life" song, but when you think about it, it really says it all).

Thank you again for all the love, support, laughter, and tears, and for just being my sisters. I think we planned it pretty damn well!

I love you and will see you soon.

Love,

Jeff

Done! Exhaling, I drop my pen. Thankfully, my hand doesn't hurt as much this time.

I can't read these letters. I probably should proof them, but I just can't. I don't want to think about my family really reading these. I feel exhaustion trying to take over my body, so I close the notebook and take a sticky note from the desk drawer. I scribble "Read This" on the top. I place the note inside the notebook at the spot of the letters I just wrote. The note sticks out the top just enough so you can read what I wrote on it.

I put the notebook in the middle drawer and softly close it, hoping no one will find this unless I do actually die. Fear grabs me at the thought that maybe it will never be found. My parents, in their grief, may not think to open this drawer. *Ugh, now I don't know what to do.*

I definitely want them to read this if I do die, but I don't want to leave it lying out in plain sight, either. I don't think it would be helpful for them to read this if everything goes well. After debating the merits of my hiding place, I decide to leave it put. I can't control everything. I just have to trust that, in the event of my death, these letters will find the light of day.

As if in a trance, I undress and climb into bed. The sound of voices below provides enough comfort to allow me to drift off into sleep.

43

*D*amn, *it's cold in here. This is just more of the same.* I feel like I've "been here done this before." But not really. I can't say I've ever had major surgery. I guess there's a first for everything.

In front of me on the small bench is the plastic bag the nurse gave me to put all my clothes into. *I can do this.* All I have to do is get undressed, put on this lovely gown and socks and just walk back out into the hallway and say good-bye.

I take a deep breath and try not to think about that last part. I don't want to think about my family standing just outside the door, waiting for me. I know I have the easy part today. I get knocked out. For me, everything will go fast. They have to wait. Waiting is something I don't do well.

I slide off my shoes and take off my pants, then my shirt. The gown goes on easily this time, and I successfully tie it shut on the first try. I slip off my socks and put on the socks with the rubber grips on the bottom of them. They feel nice. With my gown fully draped around me, I slide off my underwear. *Yep, it is cold in here.* I don't know why hospitals have to be so cold. It doesn't make sense. All the patients, the paying customers, are practically naked. You would think they could bump up the temperature a bit.

After shoving all my clothes and shoes into the bag, I just stand there. It's early and I'm tired, but I feel like every cell in my body is on high alert. I feel like all my senses are at full attention. Every light, every sound, every smell feels like it's penetrating my body at full speed. This place is intense. *Okay, I can do this.* I grab the bag, walk to the other side of the room, and swing open the door.

I take one step out of the door and turn to my right, and there they are. My mom notices me first. At this moment, I wish I didn't have my glasses on. I wish I couldn't really see everyone's face. My mom's face is kind. I always see kindness when I look at her. It's soft, too.

"Hey," my mom says.

"Hey, well, I'm all ready I guess," I say, not really looking at anyone.

"Nice gown," Amy says.

"Thanks. It actually stays closed," I say, grateful that I don't have to use my free hand to keep the gown from exposing my butt to the world.

"So, here's my stuff. I think they said you'll be able to bring it to my room tomorrow," I say as I hand the bag to my mom.

"I'll take that," my dad interjects. He takes the bag from me.

"So, I guess I've got to go back in there for them to get me ready," I say, somewhat hesitantly. I don't want to just run away, but right now that seems like a good option. Standing in the middle of this white, sterile, overly bright hallway, I feel numb—totally numb. This is just surreal. I feel like I'm in some dramatic, sappy movie. I hope my mom won't have to run around the nurses' station yelling for someone to give me pain meds, á la Shirley MacLaine in *Terms of Endearment*.

"Okay, well, we'll see you soon. We'll be here when you get done. I love you," Amy says as she walks toward me and gives me a big hug. I squeeze back, briefly. I don't want to really feel this. Then again, right now I'm not feeling much.

"Thanks, love you too," I reply. Amy lets go and it's Jessica's turn. We embrace, and then my mom is next in line.

"Love you. It's going to be okay. We'll be right here. We love you, Jeff," my mom says quietly into my right ear, repeating herself several times. Her reassurance is comforting. I wish I could say something back just as reassuring, but it's just not there. The best I can do right now is to just hug her back.

"I love you too. Thanks for everything," I say, exhaling to make more room for her tight embrace. The hug lingers. I pull back and freeze. My dad is standing right next to my mom. He's holding my bag full of clothes. I don't know what to do. Our usual thing is just to shake hands, but that doesn't seem appropriate at this moment. For all I know, this could be the last time I'll see my family. I don't know the last time I hugged my father.

Before I know what's happening, my dad leans in and his arms are around me.

"Good luck," he says. "We love you."

"Thanks," is all that comes out.

And just like that, it's over. The hug is done and I'm standing there just looking at them.

"Oh yeah, here, can you take these?" I say to my mom as I take off my glasses and hand them to her.

"Sure, I'll hold onto them."

"Thanks." It's no use. My lack of clear vision still doesn't dampen the intensity coursing through my body. I'm here, but I'm not. I don't feel anything right now, but I'm feeling everything—every emotion, every fear, every heartache that these four people are experiencing is pulsing through me. I can feel all of it and, because of that, my mind is doing its best to shut down. I can't go there.

"Okay, I'm gonna go now. Thanks for everything, and I will definitely see ya'll soon," I say. I smile and start to turn around. I push the door open and turn back around and look at everyone again—or in their direction, at least. I can't really make out their faces from here, but I can feel them. I love them more than they will ever know. And for a brief moment, that is enough. For a brief moment, the thought of not waking up is okay. Unexplained peace washes over me. For some reason, everything feels safe. *Maybe love is more powerful than I thought. Maybe just being loved, regardless of what happens, is enough.*

I push open the door and walk inside. The rest of this journey, I will have to walk alone. Though, unlike my time in the ER back in Wisconsin, I don't feel lonely this time.

"Hey, Hoyt, you ready?"

"Uh, yeah," I reply as I step forward. I can make out the shape of a nurse. I assume it's the nurse who checked me in earlier.

"Follow me. We're going in here," she says.

I follow her and am led into a very large, open room. From what I can tell, it's full of hospital beds. All of them are just lined up. It feels like a huge staging area. The nurse directs me to one of the beds and I climb on. By this time, my body has adjusted to the cold. Now I'm just nervous, and my nerves are keeping me warm. All my vitals are checked and an IV is started. Then the nurse asks me something very unsettling.

"So, what side are we operating on today?" she asks.

"My left," I reply without thinking as I point to the correct side. The nurse leans in and, with a black Sharpie marker, makes a dot on my left temple. *You've got to be joking. You're telling me you had to ask me, the patient, what side you're operating on today? Aren't you supposed to know that, honey?* This is not instilling confidence in me. Maybe I need to re-think this place.

Anxiety has now completely overtaken me. I do my best at breathing deeply while my mind is racing at what just happened. It's almost laughable. *I can't believe that just happened. They are cutting open my skull, and they asked me what side to cut on!*

I'm left alone. I lie on my back, staring up at the ceiling, and I just wait. People swirl around me. I listen to the woman in the bed next to me tell the nurse her story and who will be picking her up after surgery. I'm jealous that the woman gets to leave here today. The nurse didn't ask me who was picking me up after surgery. I try not to accommodate the thought that it might not matter for me.

After waiting for quite a while—too long, if you ask me—two men walk up to my bed.

HOYT J. PHILLIPS, III

"Mr. Phillips?"

"Yeah, that's me."

"Hello, I'm Doctor Azar. I'll be the anesthesiologist today. This is Dr. Petes."

"Hi," I reply. Dr. Azar seems to be older and is from India, if I had to guess. Dr. Petes seems awfully young. Maybe he's an intern.

"So we're going to take you to the OR now. Is there anything you need?" Dr. Azar asks.

"Uh, well, I actually really need to go to the bathroom," I reply. The last time I went to the bathroom was around 5 a.m. and it's probably past eight now. My bladder isn't too happy, and I'm sure my nerves aren't helping.

"We don't have time for that," Dr. Azar says briskly. "We'll get you in the OR and you'll be out and it won't matter."

I just lie there with a blank look on my face. *Thanks, doc. I'm the one paying for this fun today, and you won't even let me pee. Thanks a lot.*

"Sorry, I would have let you go," Dr. Petes says quietly as he leans down toward me. I like this guy.

Dr. Azar has unlocked the bed and I'm being wheeled out of the room. Less than two minutes later, I'm inside a very small operating room and have been placed on top of a bed in the middle of the room. Just like when I had the angiogram, two small table extensions have been pulled out from under the table and my arms are now strapped to them. I feel like I'm on a cross. It doesn't feel comforting. More IV's are inserted, and I'm feeling pretty good.

"Okay, Mr. Phillips we're going to put this mask over you, and I need you to start counting backwards from one hundred. Okay?"

"Okay," I reply, feeling scared and somewhat surprised that the movies got it right. The mask goes on and I start counting and counting and ...

"Hey, Jeff"

"Hey, how are you?"

Haze. All I see is haze. I open my eyes slowly and start to see two figures in front of me. Oh, it's ...

"Hey, I'm just waiting to go in for surgery." I say weakly.

Laughter. I hear two voices laughing at me.

"Don't laugh," I grumble, annoyed.

"You've had surgery. You're done."

"Oh." *I'm done. Oh yeah. My head.* My head is ... I slowly raise my left arm. My body seems to be positioned slightly on my right side. My arm is very heavy, and then it makes contact with ... what's this?

"Oh, you've got staples," Amy tells me. Both my sisters are standing at the foot of my bed.

"Staples?" I ask, somewhat confused. No one ever said anything about staples. My hand lightly touches what feels like a zipper protruding from the side of my head, a very large zipper. Feeling too tired, I drop my hand back down to my side.

"Oh yeah, you've got forty-five of them. Jessica counted," Amy informs me.

What? Forty-five staples in my head? "Oh," is all that comes out. *My mouth. What's wrong with my mouth? It's so so ... dry.* I can barely open my mouth. It feels like someone poured a bucket full of sand down my throat.

"My mouth," I mumble as I open my lips and try to unstick my tongue from the roof of my mouth.

"Oh yeah, that's normal. They gave you a drug to dry up your mouth," Amy says.

"Oh."

"Hey Jeff."

"Oh, hi Mom. Where's Amy and Jessica?" I'm confused, since my sisters were just here.

"Oh, they only let two of us in here at a time," she says. "How are you feeling?".

"I'm fine," I reply without thinking. *Yeah, I'm fine. I just feel weird.* My head doesn't really hurt, but I feel pressure up there. And damn, I feel out of it! I swear Amy and Jessica were just here a second ago.

"Hey Jeff."

"Hey Dad. So how are you two?"

"We're fine. The doctor said everything went really well," my mom says.

"Cool," I reply. *That's nice. It went well. I hadn't thought about that. I guess it's good I'm awake now. I woke up. Yeah, I woke up. That's cool.* "How long did it take?" In a moment of clarity, I realize I want to know how long I was under.

"About five hours," my dad says. *Wow, five hours. I was out for five hours.* Then it dawns on me. It didn't feel like five hours. One minute I was on the table, and the next I'm in here. And damn it, nothing. That's right—I didn't have any dreams and not one out-of-body experience. *Great, I was out for five hours and I've got nothing to show for it except these staples in my head. I bet I look like some Dr. Frankenstein experiment right now.*

"Hoyt, Hoyt." I open my eyes slowly. Some annoying voice is yelling at me.

"Yeah."

"Do you know where you are?"

"DUH."

"Hoyt, do you know where you are?"

"DUH." *Can't she hear?*

"Where are you, Hoyt?"

I guess this chick isn't getting it. "Duke University Hospital," I spit out the best I can with a tongue that feels like it's a piece of lead and a mouth that feels like it was wiped clean with a piece of sand paper. *D.U.H. lady. Don't you even know the acronym for where you work?*

"Great. Now Hoyt, can you open your mouth and stick out your tongue?" the nurse asks.

"Ahh." I do as requested, but I notice my jaw feels tight. Very tight, in fact. My tongue scrapes my teeth as I push it out.

"Good. Now, the doctor had to cut through the muscle that's on the side of your face. It's the muscle that controls your jaw. So it may become tight. You might have some trouble opening your mouth all the way in a few days. You'll just need to slowly work with it and re-stretch it out," the nurse tells me. *What? This is weird. My jaw is going to be tight?*

"Now Hoyt, we're going to take you to get an MRI, okay?"

"Okay," I reply, not caring what the hell she's going to do. I'm tired.

Whoa! Before I have time to comprehend what's going to happen, I'm being lifted into the air and placed on another bed. I get wheeled somewhere and then I hear another annoying voice.

"Hoyt, we're going to place you in the MRI machine now, okay? It's going to be loud, so we're putting these ear plugs in your ears, okay?"

"Okay," I mumble. Again, I'm lifted onto another bed. *Ughhh, damn, my … my dick! It hurts! It's being pulled. Oh God, someone stop!*

"Oh, his catheter," I hear a male voice say.

"Oh, sorry about that, Hoyt." And then it stops. *Thank God. Damn, that hurt.*

"Oh hey," I say as I notice mom and Amy in my room.

"Hey you," my mom replies. I can't get used to this. I thought I was getting an MRI, and now I'm back here in this room with my mom and Amy. This time lapse thing is starting to get annoying.

"How are you feeling?" Amy asks.

"I'm fine. I just feel so out of it. It's weird. One minute I feel somewhat normal and then the next I'm gone."

"Oh, that's probably the morphine they have you on," Amy says.

"So how do I look?" I'm dying to know.

"You look good," my mom replies. She's no help.

"It's cool," Amy says. "Your incision goes all the way from the front of your forehead over the top of your skull and then ends in front of your left ear. It forms a big horseshoe shape." Amy has walked closer to me.

"Oh really? I didn't know I was getting staples," I say, still not able to fully comprehend the metal protruding from my head.

"Yeah, it's supposed to give you less of a scar," Amy says.

"Wow," I reply, lifting my left hand up again. I can't help but wonder how they get these out.

"Hello Hoyt."

"Hi."

"I'm Joan. I'll be your nurse tonight."

"Okay."

"Here are some Jell-O squares. It's been awhile since you ate. You feel like trying to eat something?"

"Sure." I suddenly realize my stomach is totally empty.

"I can help with that," my mom says as she steps closer to my bed.

"Here you go. Just let me know when you're done and I'll come back." Joan hands my mom a small dish with a fork.

"You feel like eating?" my mom asks.

"Yeah, I'm getting hungry," I say.

Mom pierces a red Jell-O square and moves it toward my mouth. *Heaven.* My mouth sings with the sweetness flooding my taste buds. It tastes incredible. I inhale it and ask for another. I eat for several minutes and then drink some even better-tasting water.

"Oh wow, that was great. Thank you," I say to my mom.

"You're welcome. It's good to see you eat." She smiles. Oddly, even though I don't have my glasses on, my eyes have adjusted amazingly well. I can't see great, but I can make out a lot more than I thought I could.

I relax back into the bed and then my mind snaps into lucidity. I'm taken back to a few years earlier when I had outpatient surgery on my foot. I remember lying awake in the post-op area and hearing and seeing everyone around me come out of anesthesia. It wasn't pretty. In fact, several of the people were puking when they woke up. *Great, is that going to happen to me now? I've now got something in my stomach.* My body tenses. I try not to think about it. I turn my attention to Amy and Mom.

"So what time is it?" I ask.

"Oh, it's almost six," Amy says, looking at her watch. *Six? Wow, I've been here twelve hours. It doesn't feel nearly that long.* We make small talk for a few more minutes, and then my self-fulfilling prophecy emerges.

"Uh, I don't feel so well," I moan as my stomach rumbles and my throat starts to open up. "I'm nauseous," I moan again as I shift in the bed.

"It's okay. Let me get something," Amy says as she walks to the other side of my bed and picks up a small tray.

"Oh God!" I exclaim.

"It's okay. Here, just let it go in here," Amy instructs me as she holds the small tray in front of me. Behind Amy, I notice my mom slowly take several steps backwards. She's barely in the room now.

"Oh … here it comes … ugggh." My stomach lurches upwards and my throat is now wide open. I lift my head slightly as I heave. Nothing. I heave again. Nothing. I heave a third time and pale pink liquid shoots out.

My head is starting to get annoyed. Pressure. The pressure in my head is screaming for my stomach to chill out. I heave several more times and a small stream of liquid fills the tray. Then it's over. My stomach calms down and I flop back into the bed. My forehead is hot. Amy grabs a small, wet washcloth and pats me. It feels nice. Well, at least this time the heaving was productive.

"There, you feel better?" Amy asks in a motherly tone.

"Yeah, thanks."

"Mom, it's okay, you can come back in. I'm done," I call to her.

My mom hesitantly takes a couple steps back into the room. "You okay?" she asks.

"Yeah, I'm fine," I say, smiling.

"What, the puking doesn't agree with you?" Amy asks my mom, laughing.

"Uh, well, you know. I just have a weak stomach," Mom says, grimacing.

"Yeah, I know. It was funny seeing you dart out of here so fast," I say. I'm trying not to laugh too hard. My head doesn't like that.

"I didn't dart. I just stepped back a bit," Mom says, somewhat defensively.

I decide to drop the subject. I don't think she's up to being teased right now, though it is pretty damn funny—my own mother fleeing the room when I got sick.

"Hoyt, just let me know if you need anything during the night, okay? You're right here in front of the nurse's station, so if it gets too loud, just let me know," Joan says. She's leaning over me, right in front of my face. *You're nice, Joan, but you don't have to be leaning so close to my face. I can hear you just fine.*

"Yeah, okay," I reply.

"Code ... get the cart over here ... okay, clear ... clear ... clear ... you got it? He's gone ... call it ..." There are no walls to these rooms. We're only separated by curtains, so I can somewhat follow what just happened. A guy just died. *Wow, that's ... not what I thought it would be like.* There were no alarms going off, no one yelling. It was fairly quiet and controlled. He just died. They tried to revive him and then nothing. It's now quiet again. There's a dead body just a few feet from me. I don't know how that makes me feel.

I have no idea what time it is. It's late, I guess. I'm tired and have now been given oral pain meds as well as the ones through my IV. *Oh no, not again ... my dick. Ahhh, it hurts! Damn it, that damned catheter is pulling. Shit, this doesn't feel good.* I shift more to my right side, trying to give the tubing that protrudes from my crotch more room. It doesn't work. It's still pulling. *Great.*

"Hoyt, how you doing?" Joan asks.

"Oh fine, but my, um, catheter feels weird," I reply, weakly trying to wake-up.

"Oh yeah, it's kinked up. You should have said something. Here you go," Joan says as she untangles the tubing on the side of my bed. Instantly, the pressure subsides. I exhale in relief. If this thing didn't hurt, I could get used to just lying in bed and peeing. It's nice not having to get up.

"So Hoyt, before we move you up to the ward, I'm going to take out your catheter and then we're going to change your bed linens," Betty informs me. She's the day nurse on duty.

"Okay," I reply, not liking the first part of her statement. I'm not sure I want my catheter taken out. I was lucky that I was knocked out when they inserted it, but I'm not so sure it's going to feel good coming out.

"Well, I need to lift up your gown, okay?" she says.

"Okay," I reply as she lifts up my gown and places it over to my right side. *Here I am. Full Monty, just for Betty. Again, this is such a turn-off.* Looking down, I notice the plastic tubing coming out of my penis. *If I had one of these on long trips, it would be so convenient.*

"Now I'm going to deflate the ball inside your bladder," Betty says as she takes a syringe-looking thing and inserts it inside this offshoot coming off the plastic tubing. She pulls back on the syringe.

"Now it's just a small tug," she says as she places a few fingers on my penis to hold it in place and ... *Whoaaa, Betty! Pain, sharp pain and ... it's out.* I exhale a sigh of relief and just look straight ahead. *Okay, that was somewhat awkward and embarrassing.* What do I say now? This woman has had her hands on my junk. I feel somewhat violated, even though I'm sure she's done this a thousand times.

"Okay, all done. Now Berta here is going to help you bathe and change your linens," Betty says as a very large woman walks-in. Berta looks nice, though she has no expression on her face. *Did Betty say bathe? Lord, please, I don't want a sponge bath by this woman. I'm sure she is nice, but I just don't want a sponge bath, by anyone. That's just too much.*

Berta educates me on what's going to happen. I feel a sliver of relief. I'm not in for a sponge bath, but I am in for some cleaning. She takes some powder and scrubs my legs. It feels odd but somewhat soothing at the same time. I haven't been out of bed in more than twenty-four hours, and I know my legs are tired. Berta hands me the scrub and a wet wash cloth and gives me privacy as I clean my crotch. At least I'm afforded that dignity. She comes back and, amazingly, changes the sheets beneath me while I'm still in the bed. It happens so fast I'm not sure exactly how she does it. Before long, I'm wheeled upstairs to a private room that actually has four walls.

"Hey Jeff."

"Oh, hey guys," I reply as my mom and Amy enter the room.

"How are you doing today?" my mom asks.

"I'm good. It's nice to be out of ICU. But my jaw feels weird. I don't think I can open my mouth all the way," I reply as I demonstrate for her. I swear it's not opening as wide as it used to.

"Yeah, the doctor told us about that. It will take some time, but that muscle will stretch back out," my mom says.

"And what did they actually do in the surgery?" I ask. I wish I could actually see a video of it.

"Well, they took out a small tumor that was causing the seizures," my mom explains. "They had to put three small metal plates in your head to fit the skull piece back in place. The doctor said the metal will fuse with the bone."

"Wow, that's wild. It's weird not having any more zapping. I kinda got use to it," I say, somewhat surprised at the fact that I now have metal in my head for the rest of my life.

"Yeah, you'll be like Cousin Eddie now. You can't get too close to a microwave or else you'll piss your pants and forget who you are," Amy chimes in, laughing, with a reference from our favorite holiday movie.

"Oh, thanks," I say, trying to stifle a laugh so I won't upset my head.

"Amy, that's horrible!" my mom says in protest.

"Oh mom, he knows I'm only kidding," Amy replies.

"Yeah, it's cool," I reassure my mom.

"So how was your night?" Amy asks.

"It was fine. Went by fast, though it was weird. A guy died last night," I say, feeling bad.

"Oh, that's sad," Amy says.

"Yeah, I know, it was weird."

"Jeff, I talked to the surgeon, and he said everything looks good. He thinks everything is fine and that it was a benign tumor. He sent it to pathology and it will take a few days to get the official report, but it looks good," my mom says proudly. I can tell she is relieved. It seems the worst is now finally behind us.

"Thanks, Mom."

"Oh, and he scheduled your follow-up appointment to take out the staples for the eleventh," she says, stopping suddenly. She just looks at me.

"Okay."

"Did you hear what I said? The eleventh. That's okay with you?" she asks, somewhat surprised.

Oh. September 11th. Wow, I get to go get staples taken out of my head on September 11th. What the hell, it's not like I have anything else to do.

"Yeah, it's fine," I say, choosing not to over think it.

"Okay, I'll let him know."

"So what time is it?" I ask. I still have no frame of reference for time around here.

"It's almost one," Amy says.

"Damn, it's weird I have no concept of time," I say, somewhat annoyed. I don't like being cooped up in here. I feel shut off from the rest of the world.

Amy and my mom hang around for a while. We talk. I sleep some and then an occupational therapist comes in and makes me walk down the hallway and back again. I do it. It feels weird, but I'm thankful I can walk. I'm also thankful it seems I don't have any side effects from the surgery, except for this jaw thing. It would have been nice if the surgeon had told me beforehand about the jaw.

I spend another full day in the hospital. It goes by fast with all the pain meds being pumped into my body. On Friday morning, I get another round of antibiotics that burns my veins so much that, when the IV is taken out, it looks like someone has been shoving nails up my arm.

By Friday, I'm shocked at how my body has decided to finally react to the surgery. I can see my lower left eyelid without looking down. It's so swollen, it looks like someone inserted a baseball beneath my eye. And when I look in the mirror, I'm shocked to see that the entire left side of my face and upper neck is a sickening, greenish purple. And the staples encasing the left side of my head are lightly coated in dried blood. Every time I talk, I feel them move slightly. I look like I lost a fight with Mike Tyson.

I'm discharged on Friday afternoon and am able to convince my parents to let me go to the Cher concert in town that night. I'm a huge fan, and not even brain surgery can keep me away. Plus, it's practically mandatory; I don't want my gay card to get revoked for not attending.

My mom agrees to escort me, since I'm in no position to drive. My dad, kindly, goes to the mall and finds a stylish skull cap for me to wear. I don't want to scare all the queens at the concert with my new Frankenstein head ornamentation. I look more appropriate for a Metallica concert than Cher, but holding onto my mom's arm for balance, I manage to enjoy myself. Cher's performance and costumes are even more spectacular when experienced through the haze of pain meds.

The next few days go by in a blur. Before I'm ready, September 11th comes. I go through the motions that are required of me that day. My post-op visit goes well and, to my surprise, the staples in my head are actually removed with a staple remover.

Everyone is nice and no one really talks about the anniversary. I'm given a lot of room. I get the feeling that everyone is afraid that

I'm going to fall apart any minute. The funny thing is, that couldn't be further from the truth. I don't think my mind can fully comprehend what I've been through this past year. And I'm good with that. Before bed, I sit down to capture a few thoughts.

Wednesday, September 11, 2002

Been home about a week now. I get a fair amount of pain and swelling. I take a lot of pills and sleep a lot.

Today I got the forty-five staples removed from my head. It didn't hurt that bad, which was nice.

So on the 11th I've dodged terrorists and had metal removed from my head. I think next year I'm in store for something happy!

The depression is setting in. It's hard not to get overwhelmed and be like, okay, what now? What do I want to do with my life? I just need to get to feeling better, I guess.

Everyone has been so nice and I've gotten a lot of flowers. The kitchen and living room look nice.

The eating has been hard. I don't feel great. I don't feel hungry and am not regular, so it's tough. But I try to muddle through it somehow.

It's hard to believe all that's happened this year. I still think I'm in la la land with it all.

Today it was nice to get out and see the doctor so I didn't have to obsess about the anniversary. It does help, I think, that I'm still doped up. I'm not totally lucid. I think I was running some today. It's hard to face all this, especially when the future seems just as chaotic and scary. I just hope and pray for direction, peace, and passion for my life.

And so it's been 365 days since the sun stood still, and yet life goes on ...

Six weeks later, fully recovered from the surgery and Bell's Palsy, I went back to New York and resigned from my job. Before I moved to Greensboro, I visited Ground Zero by myself. It was the first time I had been back there, and I cried the entire time. I haven't been back since.

44

J ournal Entry:

November 11, 2016

*My editor asked me the other day about the "2016 Hoyt."
She liked the memoir but felt it ended too abruptly and left too
many questions in the reader's mind. I hate to admit, but she
was right. I knew after writing the "last" chapter that there were
many unanswered questions— but I didn't want to go there.*

*My first thoughts about the Hoyt of 2016 are about the
people in my life. My family has been amazing and continues
to support me in ways that, at times, I don't feel worthy of.*

*Amy went on to graduate from nursing school and even-
tually earned a masters degree. She now works as an oncology
and hospice nurse practitioner in Florida. I once asked her
how she deals with death all the time and her answer was
beautiful: "We celebrate life coming into this world. It seems
only natural we should celebrate life transitioning from this
world."*

*Kellen is now in his first year in college and Brooks is
in 11th grade. A younger sister has been added into the mix,
Avery, who is ten going on thirty. She has both her brothers
and father wrapped around her little finger. Both boys know*

that I am gay and thought it was hilarious when Avery, as a younger kid, would get confused and call me Aunt Jeff. The older the kids get, the more love I seem to have for them. I never knew that I could love in such an unconditional way. Their energy, honesty, and compassion astounds me. I'm grateful every day that Amy and Craig allow me to be such an active part of their kids' lives.

Jessica went on to graduate from my alma mater, The University of North Carolina at Asheville, with a degree in psychology. She got married to a great guy in 2013 and works full-time as a cardiac care nurse. She has an adorable two-year old, Lleyton and just gave birth to Leo, who based on his 10 pound weight is primed to follow his father into sports. Jessica's dedication and work ethic to helping others is truly inspiring.

Unfortunately, as feared, I lost touch with everyone I met at Rogers. When I stop to take the time, I can still hear Kyle's laugh and J.R.'s kind words, and I can see the compassion in Sue's face. I pray that all of them are experiencing a life worthy of how wonderful they are.

Sabrina and Mike are the only friends from my time in New York that I am still in contact with. Sabrina lives in Texas and Mike and his partner live in Chicago. Even though distance separates all of us, there is a love that I feel will keep us in each other's lives for a long time.

My parents are still in Greensboro, N.C. and just celebrated their forty-seventh wedding anniversary in 2016. I can never thank them enough for what they have done for me, but in some small way, this memoir is an attempt to do that. Much of what I've written in my memoir, I never told them. I will never fully understand the hell they went through during that year, but I hope that by reading my words they can take comfort in knowing just how strong and healthy I truly am. I know that my strength is from their love and support. I never would have survived any of the crap I went through if it weren't for them.

Damn, I'm out of people to talk about. I'm stalling and I just need to answer the question of who is the 2016 Hoyt? When my editor first posed this question, I got really scared. I didn't sleep well that night. I knew that the answer to that question would be the end of my memoir. I now realize I was scared of not being good enough. The little boy deep inside —the one that I thought was healed —was scared to death. I worried that, after reading this book, someone might judge me for not being perfect today.

This fear surprised me. I thought I had dealt with all this shit back in 2002. It's amazing how the Universe will keep presenting things to you until you truly learn the lesson. I know that the notion of perfection is just the ego's attempt to control the heart.

I can see that, starting on 9/11/2001, I was placed on a path of moving out of my head and into my heart. Living entirely in my head and letting my ego run the show had disastrous consequences. Surrendering to my heart and accepting myself unconditionally, though at times challenging, has proven to be more rewarding than I could have ever imagined. The memories from that day in September don't haunt me anymore, but my thoughts and prayers will forever be with everyone affected by the attacks.

I've been sober from alcohol since 2002. I delight in eating at least three meals every day, and my relationship with food continues to deepen. I practice yoga several times a week, which has developed within me a newfound love and appreciation for my body.

I surround myself with friends and family who are dedicated to being healthy. I do volunteer work that I'm passionate about. My spiritual life has grown immensely over the last few years through the exploration of traditions such as Hinduism,

Buddhism, and Native American Shamanism. I meditate every morning, and I still keep a journal. I'm proud to be an active participant in making my life what I want it to be.

My weight, now stable for more than a decade, is in the low 140s, which puts my BMI in the average range. I don't own a scale anymore, but I do check my weight several times a year to hold myself accountable.

I no longer see a therapist or take any prescription mental health medications. I made the decisions to stop therapy and medication in consultation with my doctors. I'm aware that therapy and medication are valuable tools and if I ever need to use them again, I will.

After years of therapy, I now view myself as an addict who at one time abused booze and food in an attempt to escape life. I know having an eating disorder is a serious mental illness, but focusing on the addiction aspect of my personality encourages me to take responsibility for the choices that I make. I'm not naive enough to think that I can't go back to where I've come from or that I can't develop some other addiction or obsession. The difference now is that I work at being healthy every day.

I don't consider myself recovered or healed. To me, life isn't that black and white. I'm grateful that I no longer obsess about food or my body, nor do I beat myself up for not looking like a model. Are there things about myself that I would like to change? Of course! I'm human.

My desire to self-destruct is almost gone and my desire to make choices that honor my life is growing stronger every day. Most days, I hit the mark, and in the times that I fall short, I make an effort to embrace grace in every thought and action.

Today I can honestly say that I am more self-aware and happier than at any other time in my life. There is a peace within my spirit that I never experienced when I was engaged in my disorder. Basically, in 2016, I'm not living in

*perfection; I'm living in reality, elated with the knowledge that
I'm a work in progress.*

Writing this memoir has proven to be, next to being at
Rogers, the most challenging and gut-wrenching undertaking
I have ever attempted. I cried more during this process than I
have in years. It was cathartic, exhausting, horrifying, and
exhilarating— all at the same time. This was the first time in
my life that I had taken the time to sit down and truly examine that year. I knew what I had gone through, but in many
ways, it felt like it had happened to someone else.

During the writing process, I got to relive every moment,
thought, fear, obsession, failure, and triumph from those three
hundred and sixty-five days. The result of all of this was that
I fell in love with myself. It feels weird saying that, but it's true.
I've walked away from this experience with a new respect for
who I am as a person and what I have to contribute to the
world. I discovered a strength that has always been there but
was just waiting for me to acknowledge it.

In 2004, the National Conference for Community and
Justice of the Piedmont Triad (NCCJ) asked me to be on staff
of ANYTOWN, their summer leadership camp for teenagers.
This camp explores issues such as power and privilege, race,
religion, gender, faith, family, sexual orientation, and those
who are differently-abled with the goal of inspiring young people to be the change they wish to see in the world. Specifically,
I was asked to facilitate the sexual orientation workshop and
to come out to more than seventy adolescents.

I said yes, but I had no idea what I was going to speak
about. My mom strongly suggested that I talk not only about
being gay, but also about being at Ground Zero on 9/11, my
eating disorder, and my brain tumor. I shot her idea down,
thinking that that year in my life had nothing to do with
my sexuality. When I finally sat down to write my talk, the
words just flowed onto the page. The speech I wrote ended up

encompassing everything my mother had suggested. She was right, and I was wrong.

Since then, I've done ANYTOWN nine times and counting. Every time I give my talk, at ANYTOWN or to some other group, I'm in awe of how the audience not only listens to what I have to say but how many of them confide in me their own similar struggles. The journey of self-acceptance that underlies my talk resonates with more people, gay or straight, than I ever thought possible.

For a few years I did consulting work for NCCJ, facilitating programs and helping to educate young people about broader social justice and bullying issues. It was a joy to be part of an organization that is striving to end bias, bigotry, and racism. I earned a Master of Arts in Teaching degree in 2014 and taught 5th grade reading and social studies for a couple of years before transitioning into a role at Teaching Tolerance where I get to help support teachers who strive to make their classrooms more equitable and inclusive for all students.

My life is extraordinary, and I'm doing my best to continue to evolve, learn, and grow. The person I am today isn't the person I will be tomorrow—and that prospect excites me.

Rosalind Russell says it best in the movie Auntie Mame *when she exhorts, "Yes! Live! Life's a banquet and most poor suckers are starving to death!" These days I'm taking her advice. Namasté.*

EATING DISORDER RESOURCES

Rogers Memorial Hospital: www.RogersHospital.org or 1-800-767-4411
Rogers Memorial Hospital is a nationally recognized, not-for-profit, behavioral health care provider for children, teens, and adults. Rogers Memorial provides inpatient or acute care, partial hospitalization or day treatment, and specialized residential treatment for: eating disorders, chemical dependency, obsessive-compulsive disorder and other anxiety disorders, and child and adolescent mental health concerns.

Overeaters Anonymous: www.oa.org
OA offers a program of recovery from compulsive eating using the Twelve Steps and Twelve Traditions of OA. Worldwide meetings and other tools provide a fellowship of experience, strength, and hope where members respect one another's anonymity.

National Eating Disorders Association: www.NationalEatingDisorders.org or 1-800-931-2237
NEDA supports individuals and families affected by eating disorders and serves as a catalyst for prevention, cures, and access to quality care.

LGBTQ RESOURCES

GLBT National Help Center: www.GLBTNationalHelpCenter.org
Free and confidential phone and email peer-counseling, information, and local resources for the GLBT community

GLBT National Hotline: 1-888-843-4564
Mon- Fri: 4 pm – Midnight EST & Sat: Noon – 5 pm

GLBT National Youth TalkLine: 1-800-246-PRIDE (7743)
Mon – Fri: 8 pm – Midnight EST

Trevor Hotline: www.TheTrevorProject.org or 1-866-4-U-TREVOR (488-7386)
Crisis intervention helpline for LGBTQ youth, staffed 24/7

Parents, Families, and Friends of Lesbians & Gays: www.pflag.org
National organization that promotes health and well-being of LGBTQ community and their friends and family. Local chapters around the country hold monthly meetings.

Human Rights Campaign: www.hrc.org
National civil rights organization striving to achieve equality for LGBTQ Americans.

Gay, Lesbian and Straight Education Network: www.glsen.org
National education organization focused on ensuring safe schools for ALL students. Resources for students and educators.

Spirit Journeys: www.SpiritJourneys.com
Spiritual retreats and workshops for the LGBTQ community. Facilitators use a wide variety of tools, teachings, and practices to aid in the exploration of your Self. Spirit Journeys does not preach one dogma, but instead draws upon traditions, practices, and philosophies from throughout the world.

ACKNOWLEDGMENTS

I wouldn't have been able to write this without the support of my family. My parents have been wonderful examples of integrity and support. I know I wouldn't be alive if it weren't for them.

Amy, my older sister, was the first person I told about my adventure in writing and it was her kind words after reading the first few chapters that encouraged me forward. Jessica, my younger sister, was right behind Amy cheering me on.

The title of this memoir actually came from an ex-boyfriend, Chris. I owe him a huge amount of thanks for his kindness and encouragement. Plus I think he came up with a pretty kick-ass title.

I'd like to thank Pamela Guerrieri and Kimberley Jace, two wonderfully talented editors who helped fine-tune and guide this book. This was my first endeavor in attempting to write anything of this magnitude, and Pamela and Kimberley were amazing to work with.

Finally I'd like to thank everyone I had to privilege of knowing while I was at Rogers Memorial Hospital. Though I've lost touch with everyone there, they are still in my heart and thoughts and I'm forever grateful for the impact they have had on my life.

ABOUT

Hoyt currently lives in Montgomery, AL where he works for Teaching Tolerance helping support K-12 educators across the nation create more equitable and inclusive classrooms for all students. He loves being an uncle to his four nephews and one niece and tries to spend as much time as possible at the beach.

Made in the USA
Lexington, KY
23 September 2017